Fourth Edition

DISTANT MIRRORS
America as a Foreign Culture

edited by

Philip R. DeVita

WAVELAND

PRESS, INC.

Long Grove, Illinois

For information about this book, contact:
Waveland Press, Inc.
4180 IL Route 83, Suite 101
Long Grove, IL 60047-9580
(847) 634-0081
info@waveland.com
www.waveland.com

Of all the authors that he has encouraged and
nurtured through the publication process,
I hope I might be the first to dedicate
a volume to Tom Curtin.
Unending thanks for friendship and fond memories.

Contents

v

Emeritus Professor **Philip R. DeVita** was, before becoming a cultural anthropologist, Captain Phil DeVita, a blue water sailing skipper who spent a major part of his first thirty-four years sailing to and living in foreign places. Even at eleven years of age, he made three brief voyages to Cuba aboard his uncle's charter fishing vessel. From his mid-twenties there were lengthy voyages to the Caribbean, Mexico, Latin and South America, and the South Pacific—as far west as Australia. Whether living in Mexico off and on for a three-year period or during extended periods in Polynesia or the Galapagos Islands, he would return to the United States having been strongly influenced by the valuable, poignant, and often confounding foreign experiences. The values and customs of friends made in Melville's Taipi Vae, Gauguin's Atuanna and Papeete, Darwin's Encatadas, and even Australia of the 1960s, contributed to early critical questioning of the implicit and explicit rules of thinking and behavior to which he had unquestionably marched growing up in the projects of New York's affluent Westchester County (there was niche where blacks and poor Italians and Irish lived).

In August of 1966, Captain DeVita was seriously injured outside the Panama Canal after lightning struck him when he was delivering a motor vessel from Florida to California. He was physically incapable of returning to sea. During a two-year recuperation he completed his university education, graduating with a BA in Philosophy as a member of UC Irvine's first graduating class. As his health improved, he decided to earn a graduate degree in Anthropology in the hopes that the career would provide another avenue for him to spend time in foreign places. Influenced by his friend and mentor, Ed Cook, he developed ideas relating to ethnographic problems of understanding other people. This resulted in two publications on personalized fieldwork experiences, which were later compiled into a single volume, *Stumbling Toward Truth: Anthropologists at Work* (2000, Waveland Press).

The idea for the initial volume of *Distant Mirrors* derived from Professor DeVita's earlier times spent outside the United States: How can we learn to better understand ourselves from the perceptions of what others believe about us? So often, living in other cultures, he himself felt doubly the outsider, not only on Pacific Islands, but also when returning to his own country.

Understanding Ourselves

PHIL DEVITA

Historically, Americans have been known to prefer newness and bigness. This feature of American culture was recognized by Alexis de Tocqueville in his groundbreaking and largely accurate observations first published in 1835 as *Democracy in America*. In this light it appears inevitable and traditionally very American for me to expand on the first three editions of *Distant Mirrors*, volumes edited with Dr. James Armstrong, about American culture. For this edition, my friend and colleague was too busy with administrative and teaching duties to work on the project. Even though twenty-four years have passed since the publication of the first edition, based upon the suggestions of colleagues and reviewers I have made very few changes. The subject remains the same and the orientation is identical to earlier versions. The search has been for the startling or subtle features of "outsiders'" perspectives of various aspects of American culture to enable us to better understand ourselves. In these twenty-one essays, seven of which are new, I believe that the goal has been well achieved.

As with every edition the intent has been not only to explicitly orient the undergraduate reader to the breadth of issues relating to questioning and understanding from within but also to consider the contributions of others to our everyday activities. *One Hundred Percent American* and *Body Ritual Among the Nacirema,* as well as *Professor Widjojo Goes to a Koktel Parti* serve extremely well as enjoyable and stimulating pedagogical introductions (whether tongue-in-cheek or analytically astute) addressed to how truly strange we "Usans" might appear to outside observers. The remaining contributions are essays written by anthropologists and other scholars. Two new additions, an insightful and contemporary critique of select aspects of American culture by Professor Serena Nanda and the foreign-student-centered analyses of American university student culture by Professors George and Sharon Gmelch, succinctly address the complex habits and beliefs of America's multicultural arena. The seven new contributions are, like those that have been retained, engaging, personalized essays that unveil ethnographic perspectives of American culture. The authors have situated themselves in their essays so the reader can identify with their experiences as they teach us about the background and context affecting their experiences.

Cultural anthropology has a lengthy history of concern with the "other," the contrastive differences, the oftentimes strange. The focus on others and their cultures gives cultural anthropology a comparative perspective that provides a reflective lens for understanding ourselves—the beliefs, values, and behavior implicit in our own world. However, the ethnographic arenas of today differ immensely from the ones traditionally inhabited by peoples seemingly untouched by Western influence. The global village is a fact and the romantic vision of ethnographic adventure in remote places among pristine peoples is an enterprise of the past. We are, therefore, compelled to look closer to home for the strangeness and the similarity that arouse the ethnographic experience.

It certainly appears difficult for young students of American culture to fully appreciate the strangeness and wonder of their own cultural lives. The cultural assumptions we grow up with are most compelling. As insiders, speaking a common language, following the accepted patterns of behavior embedded in a particular way of life, it is easy to take most aspects of our own social action for granted. Generally, we speak and behave in a most appropriate manner and are seldom challenged to analyze what we say or do prior to speaking or acting. We are wonderfully successful performers on the complex and often confounding sociocultural stage. Furthermore, when others around us are similarly embedded in a particular way of life, we are less likely to question their actions or perceive the underlying assumptions therein. We accept our own routine behavior as essentially uninteresting or natural. As Americans, we often interpret our behavior as the product of our own individual choice rather than as a product of a tradition of similar choices. We don't think about, or feel no need to ask the questions that reveal, the implicit meanings underlying our beliefs and values. In essence, when looking at ourselves, our own mirrors may be clouded.

With this new edition of *Distant Mirrors* the intention again is to throw American culture into sharper relief. The collection offers other mirrors, other reflections. Outsiders, having grown up in other cultures, will not take as much for granted about our behavior as we do. They will not necessarily share our assumptions about what is appropriate or acceptable. They will attend to different things and ask different questions than we would. They will interpret our routine behavior in other ways and establish significance in what for us might seem meaningless. They will provide other ways for understanding how American behavior is culturally constructed. Their lack of emotional involvement and embeddedness in the contexts they encounter, and hence, the freshness of their viewpoints, will provide us with understandings different from those we gain by ourselves.

This is not to say that insiders, studying themselves, do not have advantages. Certainly our self-knowledge and self-awareness give us a head start in studying ourselves. Many American scholars from various disciplines have written insightful interpretations and critiques of American culture, our institutions, and the events, rituals, processes, places, and people that give Americans meaning. Yet, cultural insiders studying their own culture, especially those employing the ethnographic method of experiencing life firsthand, are required to manufacture distance from the subject they seek to understand in order to discover the most significant questions. Cultural outsiders, by virtue of their otherness, do not have to manufacture distance. It is already there. Thus, they may be more keenly aware of what warrants questioning and understanding. In making sense out of what appears strange or simply different, outsiders might more easily read between the cultural lines and contextualize our behavior in a broader comparative perspective. Therefore, what they might miss through lack of awareness is more than compensated for by their relative lack of familiarity and their personal access to explicit comparison.

From the first edition to this fourth, anthropologists and scholars from many areas of the world were solicited to write essays about their own experiences and interpretations of American culture. It was suggested that the essays be personalized and literate. There were no holds barred. Articles could be humorous, caustic, critical but not in the style of the formal academic presentation. During the editing of the first volume, it readily became evident that the commentary by the majority of foreign authors lacked any hint of criticism of the negative aspects of American culture. I was indeed expecting critical comparison on issues such as poverty, social injustice, ethnic prejudice, militarism, and the crime rate.

After publication I had the pleasure of spending time with Dr. Ramos in Évora, Portugal. He provided the first hint that was later confirmed by other authors as to why there was such an obvious lack of criticism. The scholars had been guests in our country, and overall, it simply would not have been polite to criticize. For all of us, another lesson learned.

In the effort to compose a new volume so many years after the first, given the nature of the dynamic geopolitical changes over more than twenty years, I earnestly solicited contributions from Middle Eastern scholars. In this, for unknown reasons, I was unsuccessful and I will always feel that an important gap remains in this current collection.

References

Deutsch, Richard. 1994. Review of *Distant Mirrors: America as a Foreign Culture. American Anthropologist* 96: 1009–1010.

Miner, Horace. 1956. Body Ritual among the Nacirema. *American Anthropologist* 58: 503–507.

Tocqueville, Alexis de. 1966. *Democracy in America*. New York. Harper & Row.

1

One Hundred Percent American

RALPH LINTON

How much of the values and material aspects of our "American Way" do we take for granted? This very brief article by Ralph Linton, written in 1937, directs us to question our concepts of international superiority and ethnocentrism. Historically, we owe so much of our heritage to the ideas and inventions of people and cultures from distant lands. What does this article, as significant today as it was eighty years ago, instruct us as to the issue of cultural relativism?

Ralph Linton (1892–1953) received his BA from Swarthmore College, and he earned his PhD at Harvard in 1925. He taught at University of Wisconsin, Columbia University, and Yale University. Linton began his training as an archaeologist but, during his 1920 to 1922 research in the Marquesas Islands, developed an interest in living peoples and switched to cultural anthropology. From his broad-reaching studies in the South Pacific, Americas, Africa, and Madagascar, Linton developed insights into the process of acculturation and complex cultural-psychiatric relationships. He was the first to formally introduce the concepts of status and role to anthropological analyses. Among his most important works are *The Study of Man* (1936), *The Cultural Background of Personality* (1945), *The Science of Man in the World Crisis* (1945), and *The Tree of Culture* (1955).

There can be no question about the average American's Americanism or his desire to preserve this precious heritage at all costs. Nevertheless, some insidious foreign ideas have already wormed their way into his civilization without

1

his realizing what was going on. Thus dawn finds the unsuspecting patriot garbed in pajamas, a garment of East Indian origin; and lying in a bed built on a pattern which originated in either Persia or Asia Minor. He is muffled to the ears in un-American materials: cotton, first domesticated in India; linen, domesticated in the Near East; wool from an animal native to Asia Minor; or silk whose uses were first discovered by the Chinese. All these substances have been transformed into cloth by methods invented in Southwestern Asia. If the weather is cold enough he may even be sleeping under an eiderdown quilt invented in Scandinavia.

On awakening he glances at the clock, a medieval European invention; uses one potent Latin word in abbreviated form, rises in haste, and goes to the bathroom. Here, if he stops to think about it, he must feel himself in the presence of a great American institution; he will have heard stories of both the quality and frequency of foreign plumbing and will know that in no other country does the average man perform his ablutions in the midst of such splendor. But the insidious foreign influence pursues him even here. Glass was invented by the ancient Egyptians, the use of glazed tiles for floors and walls in the Near East, porcelain in China, and the art of enameling on metal by Mediterranean artisans of the Bronze Age. Even his bathtub and toilet are but slightly modified copies of Roman originals. The only purely American contribution to the ensemble is the steam radiator, against which our patriot very briefly and unintentionally places his posterior.

In this bathroom the American washes with soap invented by the ancient Gauls. Next he cleans his teeth, a subversive European practice which did not invade America until the latter part of the eighteenth century. He then shaves, a masochistic rite first developed by the heathen priests of ancient Egypt and Sumer. The process is made less of a penance by the fact that his razor is of steel, an iron-carbon alloy discovered in either India or Turkestan. Lastly, he dries himself on a Turkish towel.

Returning to the bedroom, the unconscious victim of un-American practices removes his clothes from a chair, invented in the Near East, and proceeds to dress. He puts on close-fitting tailored garments whose form derives from the skin clothing of the ancient nomads of the Asiatic steppes and fastens them with buttons whose prototypes appeared in Europe at the close of the Stone Age. This costume is appropriate enough for outdoor exercise in a cold climate, but is quite unsuited to American summers, steam-heated houses, and Pullmans. Nevertheless, foreign ideas and habits hold the unfortunate man in thrall even when common sense tells him that the authentically American costume of gee string and moccasins would be far more comfortable. He puts on his feet stiff coverings made from hide prepared by a process invented in ancient Egypt and cut to a pattern which can be traced back to ancient Greece, and makes sure that they are properly polished, also a Greek idea. Lastly, he ties about his neck a strip of bright-colored cloth which is a vestigial survival of the shoulder shawls worn by seventeenth century Croats. He gives himself a final appraisal in the mirror, an old Mediterranean invention, and goes downstairs to breakfast.

Here a whole new series of foreign things confronts him. His food and drink are placed before him in pottery vessels, the proper name of which—china—is sufficient evidence of their origin. His fork is a medieval Italian invention and his spoon a copy of a Roman original. He will usually begin the meal with coffee, an Abyssinian plant first discovered by the Arabs. The American is quite likely to need it to dispel the morning-after effects of over-indulgence in fermented drinks, invented in the Near East; or distilled ones, invented by the alchemists of medieval Europe. Whereas the Arabs took their coffee straight, he will probably sweeten it with sugar, discovered in India; and dilute it with cream, both the domestication of cattle and the technique of milking having originated in Asia Minor.

If our patriot is old-fashioned enough to adhere to the so-called American breakfast, his coffee will be accompanied by an orange, domesticated in the Mediterranean region, a cantaloupe domesticated in Persia, or grapes domesticated in Asia Minor. He will follow this with a bowl of cereal made from grain domesticated in the Near East and prepared by methods also invented there. From this he will go on to waffles, a Scandinavian invention, with plenty of butter, originally a Near Eastern cosmetic. As a side dish he may have the egg of a bird domesticated in Southeastern Asia or strips of the flesh of an animal domesticated in the same region, which has been salted and smoked by a process invented in Northern Europe.

Breakfast over, he places upon his head a molded piece of felt, invented by the nomads of Eastern Asia, and, if it looks like rain, puts on outer shoes of rubber, discovered by the ancient Mexicans, and takes an umbrella, invented in India. He then sprints for his train—the train, not sprinting, being an English invention. At the station he pauses for a moment to buy a newspaper, paying for it with coins invented in ancient Lydia. Once on board he settles back to inhale the fumes of a cigarette invented in Mexico, or a cigar invented in Brazil. Meanwhile, he reads the news of the day, imprinted in characters invented by the ancient Semites by a process invented in Germany upon a material invented in China. As he scans the latest editorial pointing out the dire results to our institutions of accepting foreign ideas, he will not fail to thank a Hebrew God in an Indo-European language that he is a one hundred percent (decimal system invented by the Greeks) American (from Americus Vespucci, Italian geographer).

Study Question

1. Provide five examples of how, in your daily life, you employ something that had its historical origin in a culture that was not invented in the United States. Do not use examples provided in the article.

Note

Ralph Linton, "One Hundred Per-Cent American," *The American Mercury* 40 (1937): pp. 427–29. Reprinted with permission of *The American Mercury*, Box 1306, Torrance, California.

2

Reflections on American Culture

JOHN JAY COLLEGE OF CRIMINAL JUSTICE

*An essential aspect of cultural anthropology is to develop an understanding
of others, and these understandings lead us to reflect more deeply on our
own culture. American culture is, like other cultures, diverse—and even
contradictory; yet, at the same time there is a widespread consensus on
many aspects of American culture, from the seemingly trivial to the essential. The things people notice about American culture derive from contrasts
between America and one's culture of origin, just as our perceptions of others' cultures are derived from our own. The concept of "distant mirrors"
perfectly exemplifies this relationship and is central to my "Reflections."*

Serena Nanda, Professor Emeritus of Cultural Anthropology at John Jay
College, City University of New York, has carried out extensive fieldwork in India. Her publications include *Culture Counts*, an introductory
textbook, *American Cultural Pluralism and Law*, *Gender Diversity: Cross-
cultural Variations*, and most recently, two culturally based mysteries,
The Gift of a Bride and *Assisted Dying*.

> *Oh, that God the wisdom gie us, To See ourselves as others see us.*
> Robert Burns

The theme of distant mirrors and my recent celebration of America's most
patriotic holiday, the Fourth of July, lead me to reflect once again, on the concept of American culture, and especially how it is perceived by outsiders. The
term "outsiders" has a double meaning: to me it refers to people who live in

other cultures around the world and also to some Americans who, by virtue of their race, religion, or ethnicity, feel themselves to be marginal in American society.

A central goal of cultural anthropology is to look at other cultures from the inside and to look at our own culture from the outside. This dual perspective hopefully leads to a more objective view of what culture, and specifically American culture, is all about. Anthropologist Clyde Kluckhohn noted the importance of this cultural self-reflection in his prizewinning book, *Mirror for Man*, written more than 65 years ago, in which he included a chapter, "An Anthropologist Looks at the United States" (1944). Much of what Kluckhohn wrote about American culture remains relevant today, although American culture, like all others, contains many ambiguities, paradoxes, and contradictions and also changes over time. Perhaps because of our culture's emphasis on individualism, Americans often deny the influence of culture on their behavior and values, believing these to be solely a matter of individual choice. Indeed, the importance of individualism leads many Americans to deny that there even is an American culture (Cerroni-Long 2016).

Outsiders see it differently. While recognizing the great multicultural diversity of the United States, there is a widespread consensus by foreigners on many aspects of American culture. What outsiders notice about American culture derives partly from its contrasts with their own cultures, but there is a surprising consensus, on Internet sites, for example, about what foreign tourists, businesspeople, or exchange students must learn about American culture if they are to "fit in" and succeed.

Equality and Liberty

The most commonly recognized aspects of American culture, and the most commonly praised, both by foreigners and Americans, are equality, liberty, and independence, enshrined in our founding document, the Declaration of Independence. The Declaration opens with the statement, "We hold these truths to be self-evident, that all men are created equal, that they are endowed by their Creator with certain unalienable Rights, that among these are Life, Liberty and the pursuit of Happiness—That to secure these rights, Governments are instituted among Men, deriving their just powers from the consent of the governed. . . ." From this stirring statement derives the right to dissent from government policy, to protest in public places, to speak freely on all issues of importance, to resist peacefully but loudly when an individual or a group does not feel it is being heard. Given the brutal oppression of so many military dictatorships against those who contest their governments, the right to dissent is probably one of the most cherished values of both Americans and immigrants. Unlike violent government responses to events in places like Syria, Ukraine, Tiananmen Square in China, Tahir Square in Cairo, just to name a few, millions of Americans take to the streets to protest what they see as unjust government policies in the United States, protests that Americans and much of the world see as the essence of our democracy.

But what do these words of our Declaration of Independence actually mean and how have they been acted upon in our history? This continues to be a subject of much debate (Allen 2015). One question that immediately arises is the relationship between equality and liberty. Are all Americans equal in their right to liberty? In 1937, the black singer Marion Anderson was invited to sing in Washington DC, but the Daughters of the American Revolution refused to let her perform in Constitution Hall. This led to a strong protest initiated by A. Philip Randolph, a black union activist, and soon reached the ears of Eleanor Roosevelt, President Franklin Roosevelt's wife. She arranged for Ms. Anderson to sing on the steps of the Lincoln Memorial, a performance that attracted a crowd of 75,000 people, with millions more listening on the radio. Ms. Anderson began her concert with the opening lines from an American patriotic hymn: "My country 'tis of thee, Sweet land of liberty, Of thee I sing." In spite of the unequal treatment she had received as a black person, this expression of her love for her country is an inspiring testimony to the optimism that America inspires.

Ideally, equality means equal treatment under the law and in civil society: as one immigrant from West Africa expressed it, "The rule of law . . . it's amazing . . . where I'm from if you have an issue with somebody, and this person knows the right people, they'll get away with it. . . . But here, I've seen that no matter how rich you are, the same law will be applied to you. You cannot use your wealth . . . to crush other people. I know many countries pledge this, but here in America, you actually see it" (Wu and Huang 2015). Hmm . . . maybe. Police killings of unarmed blacks, among them Eric Garner of Staten Island, New York, Michael Brown of Ferguson, Missouri, and Tamar Rice of Cleveland, Ohio, suggest that the rule of law does not apply evenly to all Americans.

In fact, historically, the claims of equality and liberty have often pulled in opposite directions, and the claims of individual liberty have dominated those of equality. And like equality, liberty also means different things to different people. For many Americans liberty means independence; it means that as individuals we all have the right to make our own decisions and resist control either by social networks, such as a kin group, or by structures of authority, such as the government. When it became public knowledge that a public service lawyer sued the Kraft Corporation for including unhealthy transfats in Oreo cookies marketed to children, one of the many emails he received in return said, "We live in America, land of the free, where we can eat whatever the hell we want!!! If you don't like it, move to Afghanistan, you damn terrorist" (Richtel 2015). Alexis de Tocqueville, a French visitor to our shores in the 19th century, wrote in his famous book, *Democracy in America* (1835/2004), that independence and its corollaries, personal responsibility and self-reliance, were central to American culture and were reflected in many American cultural institutions. American courts, for example, generally have rejected the cultural defense in excusing an individual's criminal actions: "culture made me do it" is not part of American culture.

Self-reliance as an American cultural pattern is often praised by people from other societies where the middle class and the elites have servants to do all their "dirty work." In *The Ugly American* (Lederer and Burdick 1958/1999), an American diplomat in Asia asks a Chinese man at an embassy party why he is not dancing. The Chinese diplomat answers, "Why should I dance when I have someone to do it for me?"

And perhaps the more things change, the more they remain the same. This American value of self-reliance spurred an international incident when Gary Locke, the newly appointed American ambassador to China, was photographed carrying his own backpack and luggage while checking in at the airline counter for his flight to his new post; he also carried his own luggage at the Beijing airport. Ambassador Locke's actions surprised—and pleased—many ordinary Chinese people, but were considered a grave insult by the political elites who, in China, often live secret and very privileged lives that despite their Communist ideology depend on the services of others (Wong 2011; Lafraniere 2011).

Another element in America's self-reliant society is a fast-food culture, most widely symbolized today, but by no means limited to, the McDonald's fast-food restaurant chain, which has spread throughout the world. By the mid-20th century, fast, do-it-yourself food service had reached a pinnacle in the Horn and Hardart cafeterias, a New York City cultural icon, where people could choose their own meals piece by piece from glass cases. Horn and Hardart was replaced by "take-out" or home delivery service, which, however, most often depends on immigrant labor to deliver the food to the door. Home food delivery undercuts the American ideal of self-reliance, a cultural contradiction not often consciously recognized by those who use it. When a friend of mine got married, her husband said, "I don't want you to cook," and gave her over 100 take out menus from their new neighborhood. Eating hot, fresh food is central to many cultures, and foreigners are often surprised that Americans eat a cold lunch, frequently a sandwich that they buy from a fast-food outlet and then eat quickly when they get back to work.

Two Views of Government

In American ideology, self-reliance is intrinsically related to liberty and to the freedoms of thought, speech, action, and expression, which are admired both here and abroad. And although American self-reliance has been compromised by globalization, for many Americans it is most strongly undermined by government regulation and social safety nets that they see as a threat to our democracy. America is polarized regarding the legitimate role of government: on the one hand Americans pride themselves on their independence and self-reliance, but on the other hand, much of the success and social mobility in our society was—and is—fostered by government support. For example, the expansion of the American middle class from the 1940s to the 1970s was to a large extent based on the growth of the labor unions, but also by government programs including the G. I. Bill, Social Security, Medicare, unemployment insurance, a progressive income tax, and federal mortgage assistance programs. These government programs were—and are—based on the view that government should attempt to improve the economic security and opportunities of its citizens, a view much more widely held in Europe. Supporters of this view emphasize that a government safety net is not only a moral obligation, but it has economic benefits: putting more money in the hands of consumers will lead to an increased demand for goods, a growing economy, and a more just and equitable distribution of wealth. Then, as people experience improvement in their economic lives, they will become more invested in the core values of our democratic society and more willing to participate to keep these values alive.

Ideologically competing with this view is the view that the best government is the least government. Sometimes called the "gospel of wealth," a phrase coined by late 19th-century capitalist Andrew Carnegie, this view holds that government regulations stifle entrepreneurial initiative, that progressive taxation and minimum wage laws undermine investment in the economy by small businesses and large corporations, and that government entitlement programs such as social security, welfare, and health care leads to the demise of individual responsibility. In 2012, Mitt Romney, the Republican candidate for president, was caught on video appearing to contemptuously dismiss 47% of Americans as lazy freeloaders, "dependent on government, who believe that they are victims, who believe the government has a responsibility to take care of them, who believe they are entitled to health care, to food, you-name-it." He added that "I'll never convince them that they should take personal responsibility for their lives." Many political pundits perceived Romney's words as an expression of contempt for almost half of the American population and as an important factor in Romney's electoral defeat. On the other hand, many Americans obviously agreed and voted for him!

Proponents of the quintessentially American "gospel of wealth" hold that policies that increase corporate profits lead to higher rates of economic growth and will "trickle down" in the society, providing opportunities and jobs that will ultimately benefit most people. They hold that privatization, whether in the form of individual savings accounts as a replacement for Social Security, privately insured health care as a replacement for Medicare and Obamacare, or school vouchers as a replacement for publically funded education is sound economic doctrine and will force people to take responsibility for their actions and their future. Perhaps this is what Clyde Kluckhohn meant when he said America is a culture of business. Kluckhohn noted that the United States is the only country in the world in which so large a part of the population "clings to laissez-faire principles in economics and government, a belief that he calls an 'unrealistic, phantasm [fantasy] of our past'" (Nader 2014). Kluckhohn's perception is right on target. Americans committed to the "gospel of wealth" strongly object to government support programs—even though they themselves benefit from them. This cultural bias was highlighted in a 2012 Republican political rally in Florida where an elderly man yelled "get the government out of my Medicare."

This culture of liberty and its corollary of self-reliance are embedded in American history: our country began in a revolutionary war to free ourselves from the control of England. It fostered an attitude that as independent individuals we don't want government to tell us what to do and to raise our taxes in order to do it. It is no accident that today's strongest proponents of the gospel of wealth call themselves the Tea Party, a direct throwback to the revolutionary protest against the English tax on tea. On a recent trip to Paris I noticed that Parisian dog walkers leave their dogs' turds on the sidewalks. When I asked a French friend why France doesn't have a "pooper scooper" law, like America, where you get fined if you don't clean up after your dog, she reminded me that Americans would rather not pay taxes but do such things themselves, in contrast to Europeans, who are willing to pay high taxes for a wide range of government services.

Individual Freedom

The commitment of Americans to self-reliance and individual decision making is often a source of amazement to people from other cultures. For Asian visitors, the independence of even American toddlers is an eye opener. An anthropologist from the Philippines was awestruck that American children choose their own food when the family goes out to eat in a restaurant (Ojeda 2016). A Portuguese anthropologist expressed shock at the independence of American youth: "Is it true," he asked, "that the great ambition of an 18-year-old youngster is to leave his parents' house?" Jay Sokolofsky, an American ethnographer working in a Mexican village, reports that his respondents were both puzzled and repelled by the American custom they had heard about, of young children having their own room, with a door they can close! A Nigerian immigrant who worked as a nanny was appalled at the many choices American parents give their children, from choosing cereal at the supermarket to choosing the toys they want for their holiday presents (Adichie 2013).

One Russian "expert" on America says that this American emphasis on freedom and autonomy "destroys families" and that Americans lack the "close . . . relationships that surround a Russian from birth." Unlike in Russia, he emphasized, "instead of spending their 50s and 60s [caring for their grandchildren] American women are busy with their own lives" (Barry 2012). It is true that even very elderly Americans value their independence greatly, often preferring to live alone or in a residential institution, without children or other relatives nearby, something unheard of in many cultures. This leads to a situation in which the American custom of the teenage babysitter might be culturally shocking: according to this same Russian, "an average Russian mother would no sooner entrust her children's upbringing to a local teenager than to a pack of wild dogs." And a first-generation American from Mexico, raised in Southern California, expressed his cultural shock when he visited his high school classmates at home: he was amazed that they eat before their father comes home and worse, they talk back to their parents! I remember well from my own fieldwork in India, an Indian matron who asked me, in a tone both surprised and critical, "I hear that in America you must make an appointment to see your parents!" Not that far off the mark, perhaps. An advertisement in the New York City subway by the culturally perceptive Manhattan Mini-Storage company says, "If you store your stuff with your parents, you have to visit them." When I asked my students, most of whom were immigrants, what they thought of this ad, they were either puzzled as to what it meant, or thought it was a joke—who wouldn't want to visit their parents! And for the many cultures where arranged marriage, which always involves parents or other relatives, is the norm, the American cultural pattern of marriage based on romantic love between two individuals is viewed negatively, both for the individuals and for their families (Nanda 2016; Nanda and Gregg 2009).

As the examples above suggest and as many anthropologists have noted, the American sense of themselves as unique, autonomous, self-motivated, and self-made individuals contrasts with the perception of people in most other cultures, who predominantly think of themselves as interwoven with other people, interdependent not independent (Luhrmann 2014). The goal in most societies is to fit in and adjust to others, not to stand out: an individual's identity is imagined primarily as part of a larger whole. Americans say the squeaky wheel gets the oil, but the Japanese say that the nail that stands up gets hammered down. Chinese students notice these cultural differences in their classes; as one student put it, Chinese culture "teaches us to be good listeners, American values teach us to be a good speaker" (Levin 2010). And a Nigerian immigrant resented "class participation" being included in her final grade: "It merely made students talk and talk . . . class time wasted on obvious . . . hollow, sometimes meaningless words" (Adichie 2013). Adichie's comment reminded me of one of my own foreign students who once asked me, "Why do you always want to hear what we have to say?" And I am not alone in this very American value. At my university one of the most important points on which students are required to evaluate faculty is "to what extent the instructor encouraged students to inquire, to problem-solve, to question their assumptions, and to think critically." American schools are a hotbed of American culture!

The American Dream

For both foreigners and Americans, self-reliance is central to the concept of the American Dream. In the American Dream the United States is viewed as a land of opportunity for all: no matter how low your social status at birth, if you work hard and are willing to sacrifice, you can move up the social ladder, achieve happiness, and lead a life of material abundance. The American Dream is built on other American cultural values: optimism, experimentation, especially in new technology, and a youth culture in which change is progress. In America our eye is on hopes for the future and as my dear friend Kojo from Ghana constantly reminded me, Americans, to their detriment, downplay past traditions and ignore the wisdom of the elders.

Belief in the American Dream means that even a person from the most humble beginnings can become president. As Ted Cruz, a 2016 Tea Party candidate for president said, "All a man need[s] is a horse, a gun and the open land, and he could conquer the world." Evidently, therefore, for many Americans equality does not mean that all people are alike or should be treated the same, but only that there is equality of opportunity for all people and it is up to individuals to make the most of their lives.

The belief in the American Dream is intrinsically associated with the widespread material affluence of the United States, which until recently, had the highest standard of living of any nation in the world. Many foreigners express awe at the material abundance of even ordinary Americans, and the desire to improve one's economic status is a main attraction for the many immigrants who come to America. As one Mexican migrant explains to her son, "I am going to the United States because you can make lots of money there." An El Salvadorian agrees, "If you work hard [in the United States], you can have anything you want." And a child from Sudan joining his father in the United States was amazed that "he has glass in his windows, a refrigerator, a telephone, running water and I sleep in a bed" (Chong 2012).

Some foreigners see a downside to this material abundance, claiming that it results in a "mania" of consumerism, turning Americans into "permanent adolescents" concerned only about materialism and afraid of death and old age. Some Americans agree; as one writer put it, American culture "thrives on store-bought pleasures and disposable dreams"; another notes that "Spend, Spend, Spend [is] the American Way" (Schiller 2012). But for people from former Communist nations, with their inferior and scarce consumer goods, extreme consumerism is a positive aspect of American culture. One Albanian migrant considered that she had achieved the American Dream when she married a plastic surgeon and acquired her own credit cards. "It's not like Communism," she remarks, "the shopping is better. The sex is worse" (Prose 2011). And a student of mine from Russia told me, "Living in Russia was like a black and white film, living in America is Technicolor." Well, maybe not for everyone.

Social Class

The widespread belief in the American Dream leads many Americans to deny the relevance of social class—at most characterizing our society as "middle class." But Americans, like other peoples, consciously or unconsciously ignore what doesn't fit into their cultural imagination. And with growing economic inequality, things have changed. In 2001, most Americans considered themselves middle class; today one-third of Americans define themselves as lower class, including growing numbers of people under 30, Hispanics, and whites (Morin and Motel 2012.) The Occupy Wall Street movement raises important questions about the current concentration of wealth and power in the United States. The movement highlighted the huge and growing gap between the 99% of ordinary people and the 1% of the elite, a concept created by anthropologist David Graeber that has brought economic inequality to the center of political debate in America. One of Occupy's slogans is "They call it the American Dream because you have to be asleep to believe it."

Compared to race and ethnicity in explaining American culture, the role of social class is most often repressed, but it clearly exists if you know where to look. A recent Congolese migrant expressed amazement that "in America, people stay with their dogs in the house! In my country you cannot see this," he said. But he was even more amazed that "in the winter I see dogs putting on clothes!" Is there a culture of pets in America? Does it have deeper meanings? Some outsiders think so: South African President Jacob Zuma commented about Westerners, that "people who loved dogs more than people had a lack of humanity" and stated that (black) South African dog owners were trying to "emulate whiteness." The billions spent in America on pets and the dressing up of dogs in the New York Easter parade, among other things, seems to suggest that dog ownership may be, as Jacob Zuma suggests, a status symbol of upward social mobility. In addition to its relation to social mobility, the expansion of pet ownership may also have a psychological aspect: as more people are getting married later, or not marrying at all, or live alone away from their families, perhaps the emotional need for pets also expands; 41% of older Americans have pets, but so do a high percentage of younger people (Zane 2015).

The important but unconscious role of social class and upward mobility in American culture also shows up in our concepts of beauty and views of the body. When the leader of the Russian Moiseyev Folk Dance Company came to America in the late 1950s, Sol Hurok, the impresario, asked the troupe's leader, "What surprised you most on your American tour?" Moiseyev replied, "In America the workers are fat and the millionaires are thin" (Robinson 1994: 355). This relationship between social class and body size still largely holds true in the United States, in contrast not just to Russia, but to many other cultures; in India, for example, obesity is traditionally viewed as a sign of affluence. And as a Nigerian immigrant noticed, describing someone as fat in America is an insult and commenting to a Nigerian woman that she has lost weight is not the compliment it is to an American woman. When I lost weight in India, my Indian friends would tell me sadly, "Oh you have so pulled down since we last met."

Race and Ethnicity

Social class status is, of course, only one criterion of unequal treatment in the United States, and race, ethnicity, and gender feature more prominently in exclusion from American ideals. Our earliest history was one of slavery, indentured servitude, violence against Native Americans and Hispanics, denial of women's rights, and later on, with the increase in immigration, restrictions on ethnic minorities, from Asia, Africa, the Middle East, and some even from Europe. America is praised as a nation of immigrants, but the emphasis of American culture and its immigration policy always focused on the assimilation of foreigners to the dominant Anglo-Saxon culture of England and Northern Europe. In the 19th century, for example, American law outlawed many Native American rituals, relocated Native Americans on reservations where individual ownership of land replaced former ideas of collective ownership, and sent Native American children to far away boarding schools where they were not permitted to speak their native languages or follow their cultural traditions.

Thus, although America is made up of very diverse cultural, racial, regional, class and religious communities, America only began to embrace multiculturalism in the 1960s, with the emergence of the civil rights movement. America today is much more racially, ethnically, and religiously mixed than in earlier centuries, and the question of American identity is now more openly discussed in our society. But because America's diverse racial and cultural groups are not treated equally, many foreigners characterize America as a racist or racialist society. Is that true? The sense of not being accepted in America because of one's race or culture of origin is expressed by many immigrants, especially those from non-European societies.

Ping Chong, a Chinese American playwright, has constructed a widely praised theatre piece called "Undesirable Elements" in which contemporary immigrants tell the stories of the reception they received when they came to America (2012). The term "undesirable elements" was first used in the United States to apply to immigrants whom many Americans believed could never fit into American society because of the cultures from which they originated. Listening to our newest immigrants confronting American xenophobia requires us to more deeply reflect on the question of what it means to be an American and look at some of the undersides of American culture.

Many of these new immigrants are from nations such as Sudan, Somalia, El Salvador, Kurdistan, Vietnam, or Iraq, which are familiar to Americans only because of United States' political or military interventions. But in fact, most Americans have little knowledge of these cultures. Indeed, American indifference to and ignorance about many cultures are widely perceived as typical. In a recent episode, *This American Life*, a public radio and television show out of Chicago that aims to provide its audience with encounters with "ordinary Americans" introduces us to an Iraqi man traveling around the United States with a booth offering people the chance to speak with a real live Iraqi. He wants to find out more about why America invaded Iraq when so many Americans claim they were against it and know so little about it (Cavanagh 2011).

Unlike immigrants from the late 19th and early 20th centuries, many contemporary immigrants and refugees who have come to America are more likely to be found in rural Wisconsin or Georgia, in small cities in the southwest, or in the far reaches of Maine or Minneapolis than in ethnically and racially diverse urban centers. And what is it today's immigrants have to tell us? Like outsiders in all cultures, their reactions are shaped by the culture and history of their own societies.

A Bulgarian man rebels at his suburban Neighborhood Association's strict regulations regarding manicured front lawns, which reminds him of his early restricted life behind the Iron Curtain. A Kurdish girl tells of an incident at a bus stop where an African American woman told her, "You foreigners don't have the right to be here if you're not going to learn English. Why don't you go back to your own country?" The Kurdish girl continues, "Everybody on the American TV shows we watched at home was blond-haired and blue-eyed, but when we arrive in America, they are not. This is the REAL America."

Another Kurdish immigrant says, "I don't speak English. It's hard. Some kids think I'm weird because I'm quiet in class. I look different. I have black eyes and black hair and I am polite. One of the kids in my class when I point to Iraq on the map and tell him that is where I am from he says, 'you must be for Saddam Hussein.'"

A middle school girl from war-torn Sierra Leone, seeing kids playing outside is afraid for them, because "here [in America] neighbors don't know each other. I worry about people here. They aren't used to war, they don't know how to protect themselves." Another immigrant teenager, fleeing the violence accompanying the fall of the Shah in Iran, a strong American ally, couldn't understand the anti-Iranian bumper stickers that she saw on cars or the restaurant signs stating that Iranians would not be served. "I am very confused," she said, "I thought I was an American." Saul, a teenaged Mexican immigrant is shopping in a mall in Atlanta, Georgia. He notices that he is being closely followed by a white salesperson. Now, when Saul enters a shop he tells a salesperson, "yeah, I'm Mexican, but don't worry, I'm not going to steal anything; I have money."

In New Jersey, gangs of whites called "dotbusters" attacked Indian immigrants whom they identified by a red powder dot Indians often wear on their foreheads for religious or decorative purposes. Perhaps a most telling comment on American ethnicity comes from a migrant now applying for college: "I had to check a box: Caucasian, black, Hispanic, Asian, other. I don't know which one to check. The administrator tells me, you are from Venezuela, check Hispanic. I say, but Hispanic is someone from Spain. I'm half Lebanese, half Venezuelan, half Catholic, half Druze from the Middle East. People here talk about race and color, but that doesn't happen in Venezuela or Lebanon. What does it have to do with what people are?" A very good question indeed!

Friendliness and Informality

Yet, many foreigners also note the good hearts of Americans, the desire to help others less fortunate than themselves that is expressed in the many volunteer organizations to which Americans belong. Foreigners connect this charitable nature of Americans to the large-scale American aid abroad and the widespread practice of helping the poor in American society, such as in food kitchens for homeless people and shelters for victims of domestic violence. Indeed, Americans rank at the top of the countries in the world in their charitable giving. Much of this goes to religiously based organizations, which is not surprising as America is one of the most religious of the developed nations of the world.

Related to foreign perceptions of Americans as generous and good hearted is the frequently noted friendliness and informality of Americans, both abroad and in the United States, especially in American small towns. My husband, who is from India, still talks about how kind and friendly his professors were when he first arrived in this country, citing especially his frequent invitations to people's homes and the hospitality extended at the quintessential American holiday of Thanksgiving. A Polish anthropologist notes another dimension of the kindness and informality of Americans: "When I make new acquaintances, including the dental hygienist, everyone calls me by my first name" (Mucha

2016). This practice also surprised a Japanese immigrant who noted, "Only my mother calls me by my first name. In Japan, except for very close friends, you call people by their last name and add 'san,' a term of respect."

But this American friendliness and informality can be confusing to foreigners. Is it just a formality? It takes some immigrants time to realize that when they leave someone's house after a social visit, the typical farewell, "Now you all come back to see us," is not really meant to be answered. The foreigner's response "when should I come?" leaves the American host nonplussed. Nor do all Americans have a positive view of American informality and the use of first names. One professor from a suburban Pennsylvania town writes that such informality is unwelcome, gender biased, and, in a business encounter just a pretense used as a marketing device (Norgren 1986). And many of my own students, both immigrants and Americans, found it difficult to adapt to my request that they call me by my first name, when few of their other professors would permit such informality. And the big American smile that goes along with American informality—how sincere is that? The first tip from the world champion selling Girl Scout cookies says, "Smile: no one wants to buy from a person who is frowning." And American politicians who are now besieged by people with "selfies" are warned to look happy and smile, it's a great vote getter and if you frown or look serious it can be held against you.

American informality and friendliness seems allied to another American behavior pattern noted by many foreigners, that of complete strangers telling them the most intimate details of their lives. A Portuguese anthropologist finds it discomforting that American men at a urinal will chat with strangers, about the weather, football, or even politics (Ramos 2016). At the same time, many foreigners comment on the relatively wide physical space Americans put between themselves and others with whom they are interacting. For men, especially, there is no embracing "like brothers," no touching, and no kissing, as is common in many Latin American and European cultures. From a Russian perspective, any touch to an American is taken as a violation of his personal space, so as a rule, he notes, Americans do not take each other by the elbow and do not tap each other on the shoulder.

And in spite of the friendliness and even politeness for which Americans are known, some foreigners see Americans as arrogant, overly assertive, and even rude, and especially resent the American view of themselves as an exceptionalist society. "Americans are very patriotic," one visiting anthropologist noted, but they also have "a . . . blinding conviction that their ways are much better than the ways of other people . . . they do not [try] to understand the ways of other peoples" (Mucha 2016). Some foreigners see this American exceptionalism as the source of military invasions of other, smaller, poorer countries such as Iraq and Vietnam, and the largely ignored imperialism regarding the annexation of Hawaii and the commonwealth status of Puerto Rico (Norgren and Nanda 2006). Other cultures are also ethnocentric, but they do not have the power to impose their views on others.

Violence in America

Indeed, the American cultural pattern of friendliness and informality by no means excludes the use of military force or the widespread use of lethal violence. This seeming contradiction in American culture has been noted by many Europeans. For example, one English visitor wrote that in contrast to his own culture, the first thing he ever heard about Americans was that they all carried guns but that when he actually had direct contact with this "ferocious sounding tribe" he found out they were quite friendly (Dyer 2010). In fact, both are true: Compared to the polite reserve widespread in English culture, Americans are friendly, but they are also a "ferocious tribe": American gun ownership is 20% higher than in any other advanced nation in the world. For many foreigners—and Americans—our "gun culture" and the deadly violence it engenders is a dominant pattern of American society. My Spanish friend Jose, a policeman who frequently visits America and follows American news tells me, "I am now watching the disturbances in the streets because of the white teenager who shot dead the people in the Southern black church [in South Carolina]. In my opinion, like here in Spain, the people shouldn't have guns. But I know the American people love guns and it's a great problem for Obama. Big problems, big solutions. No one should have a gun except for policemen and hunters with a license."

The many mass shootings in the United States—Columbine high school, the school shooting in Newtown, Connecticut, the mass shooting in a Colorado movie theatre, and the shooting of nine black people in a South Carolina church—are most often marketed as news in ways that fit into American cultural predispositions. As media anthropologist Andrew Arno notes in his aptly titled book, *Alarming Reports* (2009), news presentations focus on the audience's fears and are often inaccurate, contributing to the widespread American cultural pattern of denying reality, especially regarding extreme violence. Arno correctly points out that the dominant media commentary about the South Carolina murders used concepts like "lone wolves, conspiracies, and senseless hate crimes" none of which provided a full context for the murders. The crime was not senseless to its perpetrator, who one politician described as "a whacked out kid"; in fact, the percentage of mass murders in America committed by mentally disturbed people is less than 1%. Rather, the perpetrator of the murders, encouraged by white supremacist websites, "explains" himself as reacting to the "black takeover of America," an expressed motivation that reflects the long American history of white violence against blacks. As President Obama noted, white violence against blacks, beginning with slavery, is in the DNA of American culture.

The issue of the easy availability of guns as a factor in this murder (and previous mass murders) only came later in news presentations: it is a cultural issue that journalists—and politicians—are reluctant to take on, partly because the National Rifle Association is such a powerful political lobby. And beyond the easy availability of guns, it may be, as one more thoughtful commentator suggested, that Americans are "addicted to violence," giving the example of the wide appeal of football as our national sport: more Americans watch Sunday football than go to church, and the 2015 Super Bowl was the most-watched television program in American history (Rich 2015). Given this American culture pattern, it is no coincidence, Arno notes, that "alarming news" dominates all our media.

American culture, like all cultures, is complicated. In the 1950s, the Swiss photographer Robert Frank, published a widely acclaimed book of photographs called *The Americans* (1959/2008); one of its most iconic photographs is that of a Fourth of July celebration in a small American town, which features a huge American flag, with two small white girls beside it. But if you look carefully, the bottom of the flag is torn. And so, Frank, like many other artists, writers, anthropologists, and visitors, demonstrates the importance of reflecting on America through a distant mirror.

Study Questions

1. What are three main characteristics of American culture, as described in this article? Describe any other aspects of behavior or values that you would include in a description of American culture.

2. America is often described, by insiders and outsiders, as a multicultural society. Do you think this is an accurate description? Give your reasons, using specific examples from the article or from other sources.

3. Culture is in the details: what detailed evidence would you list as a demonstration that violence is a core aspect of American culture? Or do you disagree that America is a violent society? Discuss your evidence.

4. The American Dream is one of the most positive aspects of American culture for both insiders and immigrants. Do you believe the American Dream is still alive? Is the dream equally alive for different groups in American society such as women, racial groups, social classes, or ethnic groups? Defend your answer.

5. Discuss a personal experience you have had that exposed you to the idea that there is indeed an American culture. How did this experience change your consciousness or behavior?

Acknowledgments

Many thanks to the folks who made helpful suggestions: Jeni, Jill, Joan, Maggie, Phil, Rich, and Robin.

References

Adichie, Chimamanda Ngozi. 2013. *Americanah: A Novel*. New York: Anchor/Random House.

Allen, Danielle S. 2015. *Our Declaration*: A *Reading of the Declaration of Independence in Defense of Equality*. New York: Liveright Publishing.

Arno, Andrew. 2009. *Alarming Reports: Communicating Conflict in the Daily News*. New York: Berghahn Books.

Barry, Ellen. 2012. A Hunger for Tales of Life in the American Cul-de-Sac. *New York Times*, December 11, p. A12.

Cavanagh, Kimberly. 2011. This American Life. Television Series Review. *American Anthropologist* 113(4): 659–660.

Cerroni-Long, E. L. 2016. Life and Cultures: The Test of Real Participant Observation." In Philip DeVita (ed.), *Distant Mirrors: America as a Foreign Culture* (4th ed., pp. 89–106). Long Grove, IL: Waveland Press.

Chong, Ping. 2012. *Undesirable Elements: Real People, Real Lives, Real Theatre*. New York: Theatre Communications Group.

Dyer, Geoff. 2010. "Letter from London: My American Friends." *New York Times*, January 3, p. 23.

Frank, Robert. 1959/2008. *The Americans*. Göttingen, Germany: Steidl, Gerhard Druckerei und Verlag. (Originally published in 1959.)

Kluckhohn, Clyde. 1944. *A Mirror for Man*. New York: Fawcett.

LaFraniere, Sharon. 2011. Chinese Flock to U.S. Envoy, but Leaders Are Ruffled. *New York Times*, November 12, p. A5.

Lederer, William J., and Eugene Burdick. 1958/1999. *The Ugly American*. New York: W. W. Norton.

Levin, Dan. 2010. The China Boom. *New York Times*, November 7, p. 16.

Luhrmann, T. M. 2014. Wheat People vs. Rice People. *New York Times*, December 4, Op-Ed.

Morin, Rich, and Seth Motel. 2012. A Third of Americans Now Say They Are in the Lower Classes. *Pew Social and Demographic Trends.* Available at www.pewsocialtrends.org/2012/09/10.

Mucha, Janusz, L. 2016. An Outsider's View of American Culture. In Philip DeVita (ed.), *Distant Mirrors: America as a Foreign Culture* (4th ed., pp. 136–144). Long Grove, IL: Waveland Press.

Nader, Laura. 2014, February 21. An Anthropologist Looks at the United States. *Huff-Post, The Blog,* http://www.huffingtonpost.com/american-anthropological-association/an-anthropologist-looks-a_b_4831434.html.

Nanda, Serena. 2016. Arranging a Marriage in India. In Philip DeVita (ed.), *Distant Mirrors: America as a Foreign Culture* (4th ed., pp. 124–135). Long Grove, IL: Waveland Press.

Nanda, Serena, and Joan Gregg. 2009. *The Gift of a Bride: A Tale of Anthropology, Matrimony, and Murder.* Lanham, MD: Rowman/Altamira.

Norgren, Jill. 1986. Please Stop Using My First Name. *New York Times,* April 5, OP-Ed.

Norgren, Jill and Serena Nanda. 2006. *American Cultural Pluralism and Law* (3rd ed.). Westport, CT: Praeger.

Ojeda, Amparo B. 2016. Growing Up American: Doing the Right Thing. In Philip DeVita (ed.), *Distant Mirrors: America as a Foreign Culture* (4th ed., pp. 145–151). Long Grove, IL: Waveland Press.

Prose, Francine. 2011. *My New American Life.* New York: HarperCollins.

Ramos, Francisco Martins. 2016. My American Glasses. In Philip DeVita (ed.), *Distant Mirrors: America as a Foreign Culture* (4th ed., pp. 152–162). Long Grove, IL: Waveland Press.

Rich, Nathaniel. 2015. The Super Bowl: The Horror the Glory. *New York Review of Books,* March 3, p. 54.

Richtel, Matt. 2015. When This Man Is Irked, He Might Just File a Suit. *New York Times,* July 12, B3.

Robinson, Harlow. 1994. *The Last Impressario: The Life, Times, and Legacy of Sol Hurok.* New York: Viking.

Shiller, Robert J. 2012. Spend, Spend, Spend. It's the American Way. *New York Times,* January 14, p. BU3.

Tocqueville, Alexis de. 2004. *Democracy in America.* Trans. Arthur Goldman. New York: Library of America. (de Tocqueville's original book was published in 1835.)

Wong, Edward. 2011. Photo Turns U.S. Envoy into a Lesson for Chinese. *New York Times,* August 18, p. A14.

Wu, Annie, and Julia Huang. 2015. New Americans on Why They Love America. *Epoch Weekend,* July 3–9, p. W7.

Zane, J. Peder. 2015 Retirement. *Honolulu Advertiser,* May 31, p. D3.

3

Body Ritual among the Nacirema

HORACE MINER

Professor Horace Miner discovers a culture bound by many strange beliefs and habits. Where else in the world do we find a culture, believing that the human body is ugly, totally devoted to shrines and rituals to overcome this predominant configuration? The conduct of these peoples' exotic behaviors, in many ways both sadistic and masochistic, is investigated by a highly respected anthropologist. The findings were published in the prestigious American Anthropologist.

Horace Miner (1912–1993) received his AB from the University of Kentucky and his PhD from the University of Chicago in 1939. Miner began his training as an archaeologist, but shifted to cultural anthropology during his graduate training. He began his teaching career at Wayne University in 1939. His academic career was interrupted by the Second World War, in which he served with distinction. In 1946 he became an assistant professor of sociology at the University of Michigan. Subsequently, he received an appointment at the Museum of Anthropology at Michigan. Miner is best known for his work in Africa, but also did significant research in Canada and Iowa. Among his best known publications are *St. Denis: A French Canadian Parish* (1939), *Culture and Agriculture* (1949), *The Primitive City of Timbuktu* (1953), and *Oasis and Casbah: Algerian Culture and Personality and Change* (1960). Although he made notable contributions to applied and psychological anthropology, he is probably best known for the article included in this collection.

The anthropologist has become so familiar with the diversity of ways in which different peoples behave in similar situations that he is not apt to be surprised by even the most exotic customs. In fact, if all of the logically possible combinations of behavior have not been found somewhere in the world, he is apt to suspect that they must be present in some yet undescribed tribe. This point has, in fact, been expressed with respect to clan organization by Murdock (1949: 71). In this light, the magical beliefs and practices of the Nacirema present such unusual aspects that it seems desirable to describe them as an example of the extremes to which human behavior can go.

Professor Linton first brought the ritual of the Nacirema to the attention of anthropologists twenty years ago (1936: 326), but the culture of this people is still very poorly understood. They are a North American group living in the territory between the Canadian Cree, the Yaqui and Tarahumare of Mexico, and the Carib and Arawak of the Antilles. Little is known of their origin, though tradition states that they came from the east. According to Nacirema mythology, their nation was originated by a culture hero, Notgnishaw, who is otherwise known for two great feats of strength—the throwing of a piece of wampum across the river Pa-To-Mac and the chopping down of a cherry tree in which the Spirit of Truth resided.

Nacirema culture is characterized by a highly developed market economy which has evolved in a rich natural habitat. While much of the people's time is devoted to economic pursuits, a large part of the fruits of these labors and a considerable portion of the day are spent in ritual activity. The focus of this activity is the human body, the appearance and health of which loom as a dominant concern in the ethos of the people. While such a concern is certainly not unusual, its ceremonial aspects and associated philosophy are unique.

The fundamental belief underlying the whole system appears to be that the human body is ugly and that its natural tendency is to debility and disease. Incarcerated in such a body, man's only hope is to avert these characteristics through the use of the powerful influences of ritual and ceremony. Every household has one or more shrines devoted to this purpose. The more powerful individuals in the society have several shrines in their houses and, in fact, the opulence of a house is often referred to in terms of the number of such ritual centers it possesses. Most houses are of wattle and daub construction, but the shrine rooms of the more wealthy are walled with stone. Poorer families imitate the rich by applying pottery plaques to their shrine walls.

While each family has at least one such shrine, the rituals associated with it are not family ceremonies but are private and secret. The rites are normally only discussed with children, and then only during the period when they are being initiated into these mysteries. I was able, however, to establish sufficient rapport with the natives to examine these shrines and to have the rituals described to me.

The focal point of the shrine is a box or chest which is built into the wall. In this chest are kept the many charms and magical potions without which no native believes he could live. These preparations are secured from a variety of specialized practitioners. The most powerful of these are the medicine men, whose assistance must be rewarded with substantial gifts. However, the medicine men do not provide the curative potions for their clients, but decide what the ingredients should be and then write them down in an ancient and secret language. This writing is understood only by the medicine men and by the herbalists who, for another gift, provide the required charm.

The charm is not disposed of after it has served its purpose, but is placed in the charm-box of the household shrine. As these magical materials are specific for certain ills, and the real or imagined maladies of the people are many, the charm-box is usually full to overflowing. The magical packets are so numerous that people forget what their purposes were and fear to use them again. While the natives are very vague on this point, we can only assume that the idea in retaining all the old magical materials is that their presence in the charm-box, before which the body rituals are conducted, will in some way protect the worshipper.

Beneath the charm-box is a small font. Each day every member of the family, in succession, enters the shrine room, bows his head before the charm-box, mingles different sorts of holy water in the font, and proceeds with a brief rite of ablution. The holy waters are secured from the Water Temple of the community, where the priests conduct elaborate ceremonies to make the liquid ritually pure.

In the hierarchy of magical practitioners, and below the medicine men in prestige, are specialists whose designation is best translated "holy-mouth-men." The Nacirema have an almost pathological horror and fascination with the mouth, the condition of which is believed to have a supernatural influence on all social relationships. Were it not for the rituals of the mouth, they believe that their teeth would fall out, their gums bleed, their jaws shrink, their friends desert them, and their lovers reject them. (They also believe that a strong relationship exists between oral and moral characteristics. For example, there is a ritual ablution of the mouth for children which is supposed to improve their moral fiber.)

The daily body ritual performed by everyone includes a mouth-rite. Despite the fact that these people are so punctilious about care of the mouth, this rite involves a practice which strikes the uninitiated stranger as revolting. It was reported to me that the ritual consists of inserting a small bundle of hog hairs into the mouth, along with certain magical powders, and then moving the bundle in a highly formalized series of gestures.

In addition to the private mouth-rite, the people seek out a holy-mouth-man once or twice a year. These practitioners have an impressive set of paraphernalia, consisting of a variety of augers, awls, probes, and prods. The use of these objects in the exorcism of the evils of the mouth involves almost unbelievable ritual torture of the client. The holy-mouth-man opens the client's mouth and, using the above mentioned tools, enlarges any holes which decay may have created in the teeth. Magical materials are put into these holes. If there are no naturally occurring holes in the teeth, large sections of one or more teeth are gouged out so that the supernatural substance can be applied. In the client's view, the purpose of these ministrations is to arrest decay and to draw friends. The extremely sacred and traditional character of the rite is evident in the fact that the natives return to the holy-mouth-men year after year, despite the fact that their teeth continue to decay.

It is to be hoped that, when a thorough study of the Nacirema is made, there will be a careful inquiry into the personality structure of these people. One has but to watch the gleam in the eye of a holy-mouth-man, as he jabs an awl into an exposed nerve, to suspect that a certain amount of sadism is involved. If this can be established, a very interesting pattern emerges, for most of the population shows definite masochistic tendencies. It was to these that Professor Linton referred in discussing a distinctive part of the daily body ritual which is performed only by men. This part of the rite involves scraping and lacerating the surface of the face with a sharp instrument. Special women's rites are performed only four times during each lunar month, but what they lack in frequency is made up in barbarity. As part of this ceremony, women bake their heads in small ovens for about an hour. The theoretically interesting point is that what seems to be a preponderantly masochistic people have developed sadistic specialists.

The medicine men have an imposing temple, or *latipso*, in every community of any size. The more elaborate ceremonies required to treat very sick patients can only be performed at this temple. These ceremonies involve not only the thaumaturge but a permanent group of vestal maidens who move sedately about the temple chambers in distinctive costume and headdress.

The *latipso* ceremonies are so harsh that it is phenomenal that a fair proportion of the really sick natives who enter the temple ever recover. Small children whose indoctrination is still incomplete have been known to resist attempts to take them to the temple because "that is where you go to die." Despite this fact, sick adults are not only willing but eager to undergo the protracted ritual purification, if they can afford to do so. No matter how ill the supplicant or how grave the emergency, the guardians of many temples will not admit a client if he cannot give a rich gift to the custodian. Even after one has gained admission and survived the ceremonies, the guardians will not permit the neophyte to leave until he makes still another gift.

The supplicant entering the temple is first stripped of all his or her clothes. In every-day life the Nacirema avoids exposure of his body and its natural functions. Bathing and excretory acts are performed only in the secrecy of the household shrine, where they are ritualized as part of the body-rites. Psychological shock results from the fact that body secrecy is suddenly lost upon entry into the *latipso*. A man, whose own wife has never seen him in an excretory act, suddenly finds himself naked and assisted by a vestal maiden while he performs his natural functions into a sacred vessel. This sort of ceremonial treatment is necessitated by the fact that the excreta are used by a diviner to ascertain the course and nature of the client's sickness. Female clients, on the other hand, find their naked bodies are subjected to the scrutiny, manipulation and prodding of the medicine men.

Few supplicants in the temple are well enough to do anything but lie on their hard beds. The daily ceremonies, like the rites of the holy-mouth-men, involve discomfort and torture. With ritual precision, the vestals awaken their miserable charges each dawn and roll them about on their beds of pain while performing ablutions, in the formal movements of which the maidens are highly trained. At other times they insert magic wands in the supplicant's mouth or force him to eat substances which are supposed to be healing. From time to time the medicine men come to their clients and jab magically treated needles into their flesh. The fact that these temple ceremonies may not cure, and may even kill the neophyte, in no way decreases the people's faith in the medicine men.

There remains one other kind of practitioner, known as a "listener." This witch-doctor has the power to exorcise the devils that lodge in the heads of people who have been bewitched. The Nacirema believe that parents bewitch their own children. Mothers are particularly suspected of putting a curse on children while teaching them the secret body rituals. The counter-magic of the witch-doctor is unusual in its lack of ritual. The patient simply tells the "listener" all his troubles and fears, beginning with the earliest difficulties he can remember. The memory displayed by the Nacirema in these exorcism sessions is truly remarkable. It is not uncommon for the patient to bemoan the rejection he felt upon being weaned as a babe, and a few individuals even see their troubles going back to the traumatic effects of their own birth.

In conclusion, mention must be made of certain practices which have their base in native esthetics but which depend upon the pervasive aversion to the natural body and its functions. There are ritual fasts to make fat people thin and ceremonial feasts to make thin people fat. Still other rites are used to make women's breasts large if they are small, and smaller if they are large. General dissatisfaction with breast shape is symbolized in the fact that the ideal form is virtually outside the range of human variation. A few women afflicted with almost inhuman hypermammary development are so idolized that they make a handsome living by simply going from village to village and permitting the natives to stare at them for a fee.

Reference has already been made to the fact that excretory functions are ritualized, routinized, and relegated to secrecy. Natural reproductive functions are similarly distorted. Intercourse is taboo as a topic and scheduled as an act. Efforts are made to avoid pregnancy by the use of magical materials or by limiting intercourse to certain phases of the moon. Conception is actually very infrequent. When pregnant, women dress so as to hide their condition. Parturition takes place in secret, without friends or relatives to assist, and the majority of women do not nurse their infants.

Our review of the ritual life of the Nacirema has certainly shown them to be a magic-ridden people. It is hard to understand how they have managed to exist so long under the burdens which they have imposed upon themselves. But even such exotic customs as these take on real meaning when they are viewed with the insight provided by Malinowski when he wrote (1948: 70):

> Looking from far and above, from our high places of safety in the developed civilization, it is easy to see all the crudity and irrelevance of magic. But without its power and guidance early man could not have mastered his practical difficulties as he has done, nor could man have advanced to the higher stages of civilization.

Study Questions

1. What is the precise geographical location of this strange tribe, the Nacirema?

2. What are the private and secret shrines of the Nacirema?

3. Who are the Nacirema's holy-mouth-men?

4. What is the *latipso* used by Nacireman medicine men?

5. Who is the witch-doctor "listener" who is able to cure bewitched people?

6. Is Miner's interpretation of Nacirema body rituals ethnocentric? Why or why not?

References

Linton, Ralph. 1936. *The Study of Man*. New York: D. Appleton-Century Co.

Malinowski, Bronislaw. 1948. *Magic, Science, and Religion*. Glencoe: The Free Press. (Reissued by Waveland Press, 1992.)

Murdock, George P. 1949. *Social Structure*. New York: The Macmillan Co.

———— 4 ————

Professor Widjojo Goes to a Koktel Parti

WESTON LABARRE

An eminent African anthropologist analyzes the apparently strange customs at American rituals that he has an opportunity to directly observe. Of course, his only reference points are those from his own cultural background. In observing others, we tend to contrast their behavior to our own value systems. Thus, the visiting scholar's efforts at understanding the rituals of the American "drinking season" may be lacking in culturally relativistic clarity. One would wonder how the visitor to America would view other customs or perhaps interpret the drinking habits of Usan college students and dating rituals.

Weston LaBarre (1911–1996) received his AB from Princeton and his PhD from Yale in 1937. LaBarre taught at Rutgers University and at Duke University where he was the James B. Duke Professor of Anthropology for many years. He was a prolific writer and had exceptionally broad interests and research experiences. He considered himself to be a psychiatrically oriented anthropologist, but is equally well-known for his work on religion. LaBarre's major publications are *The Peyote Cult* (1938), *The Aymara Indians of Lake Titicaca Plateau, Bolivia* (1948), *The Human Animal* (1954), *They Shall Take Up Serpents* (1962), *The Ghost Dance: Origins of Religion* (1970), *Muelos: A Stone Age Superstition about Sexuality* (1984), and *Shadow of Childhood: Neoteny and the Biology of Religion* (1991).

"Of course," mused Professor Widjojo, the eminent anthropologist of the University of Nyabonga, "the natives of the U.S.A. have many strange and outlandish customs; but I must say the drinking rituals of the Usans impressed me the most. These rituals occur yearly during an extended period in the calendrical round, beginning at the time of the harvest rites of Thanks-for-Blessings and ending largely at the drinking bouts at the New Year. This is called The Season, after which those who can afford it usually leave their homes entirely and flee southward into retirement for recuperation."

"Rather like our Nyabongan puberty ordeals?" asked a brilliantly dark matron dressed in a handsome apron of tiki feathers and little else.

"Well, no, not exactly," said Professor Widjojo, fingering his nosestick politely before replying. "Perhaps I could describe it best by telling you of the Usan *koktel parti*, as they call it. You know, of course, that the Usan women, despite their rigid tribal clothing taboos, in general take off more clothes at their gatherings, depending upon the time of day. The neckline drops more and more, both in front and in back, as the *parti* is held later and later in the evening. They are entirely covered in the daytime, but this night-time disrobing is considered to be more formal. At the same time the length of the skirt increases, until it reaches the ground or even drags on it.

"On the other hand, men put on more and more clothes as the formality of the occasion increases. The interesting point, however, is that the men, at *koktel partis*, do not ordinarily wear the beetle coats and white cloth neck-chokers of their most formal rituals, but dress rather more moderately as for church; furthermore, the women keep their hats on at *koktel partis*, thus clearly establishing the ritual significance of the *koktel partis*.

"Social status is indicated by the number of *partis* that a couple is invited to attend—and, of course, wealth, since a woman cannot wear the same dress and hat to more than one *parti*. People complain bitterly at the number they have to go to—sometimes even during the *parti* they are attending—but it is nevertheless plain that they are proud of their ability to sustain many ordeals, and this is a form of polite boasting. This point comes out most clearly in the *aignawg partis* when they are heard to boast, after they have stayed long enough at one to save face, that they must 'get on' to a number of other New Year *partis* before midnight. They always say they 'hate to go' though it is plain that they would really hate to stay.

"Not that these other rituals are any different, or that they provide escape from the ordeal," continued Professor Widjojo, "for at all of them the natives receive the same ritualized drink called *aignawg*. Everybody hates it, and freely says so in private, but they must drink some of it so as not to offend their hostess. Despite the superficial phonetic resemblance, *aignawg* has no connection whatever with eggs. It is really skimmed milk, made commercially and thickened with seaweed jelly; and the cream, if any, is whipped and placed on top of the handled cup they must drink it in.

"The ordeal aspect of the ritual is indicated in the fact that the hostess presses more and more cups upon her guests, who must pretend to praise the virtues of the drink—but even more so in the fact that they sprinkle *nutmaig* powder on top which, in larger quantities, of course is a violent poison inducing fainting, convulsions and death. But this *aignawg* has only enough *nutmaig* on it to make the people ill for several days. The Usan natives pride themselves on 'holding their liquor' so that this ceremony is plainly a contest between a hostess and her guests.

"But I am getting ahead of my chronology. Really, the drinking season of the Usans begins in the fall of the year, after a wholesome summer vacation, at the time of the *futbol* games. The purpose of the Usan colleges is to collect young men by competitive subsidies to engage in these mock battles, during which they rush ferociously at one another wearing padded armor and ritually kill one another. It seems to be some sort of contest over a sacred pigskin, and everyone gets up alive after each act in the ceremony. Rarely is a young man killed. However, the warriors are often 'punch-drunk' (an odd phrase because they are not allowed to drink, in contrast with spectators) and they may suffer broken legs, or faces mutilated by the nailed shoes of their opponents.

"Colleges seem once to have been trade schools where tribal lore was taught, but this was long ago and is now hardly remembered. The importance of a college nowadays is rated by the number of *futbol* games its team wins, and this in turn attracts further desirable young warriors to that college. The watchers urge on the warriors with blood-curdling chants, and between acts there are military maneuvers of a more rigorous form than in the battle itself. Afterward, they either celebrate their victory or 'drown their sorrows' in mourning if the warriors have sustained too many broken bones to win.

"These *futbol* ceremonies seem to be totemistic celebrations mainly, for each side has an animal totem—such as a bulldog, a tiger or a goat—which symbolizes the mystical unity of each side in their oddly named *alma mater,* or 'protective mother,' probably so called because she is the patron mother goddess of the young warriors frequently invoked in the battle hymns at these war games. Strangely, however, these totems do not govern marriage rules either inside or outside the *alma mater* group. I collected figures on this critical matter and found it is about as common to marry outside one's totem as within. In fact, *futbol* games are a recognized way to meet young people belonging to another totem."

"Are there totems governing marriage in the *koktel* gatherings you mentioned earlier?" asked a young girl just past her puberty ceremonial.

"No, I would think not," replied Professor Widjojo, thoughtfully. "On the contrary, the *koktel partis* more resemble a primitive orgy, with no reference to marriage bonds whatever. You see, as a point of etiquette husbands and wives do not remain near one another at *koktel partis,* but circulate around making conquests. After a few drinks, the males display their 'lines,' which are ritualized ways of approaching the brightly decorated and painted females—a strange custom, incidentally, since it is the males naturally who ought to be painted, as among us Nyabongans.

"The sexual nature of these ceremonies is shown in the magic plants called *mislto* which they hang up at these winter rituals in particular. These are parasitic plants with white berries that grow on oak trees—both of which have symbolical significance—but they are by no means necessary as a sanction or encouragement for pawing and kissing, especially at a New Year's *koktel parti* in full swing. The idea seems to be to crowd as many people together as possible, to increase inescapable physical contacts. Many times people moving restlessly about in search of new partners spill drinks on one another's fine clothes, and then the person who does this is allowed to rub the other ritually with a pocket-cloth, pretending to be much distressed at the accident."

"Are these *koktel partis* always orgies?" inquired a plump, middle-aged Nyabongan man.

"Not entirely, perhaps," replied Professor Widjojo. "There is one which is called a *literari koktel,* the ostensible reason for which is to celebrate the birth of a new book. Naturally, no one ever discusses the book being celebrated, since no one has read it, although everybody expresses a readiness to analyze it critically. Mostly, the people talk about their own books, past, projected or purely conjectural. They allude meaningfully to the amount of their royalties, complain about editors and publishers, mention their translation into Japanese and other languages, including the Scandinavian, and make the most they can of some tenuous dickering for movie rights or 'coming out in paperbacks.' *Literari koktel partis* are mainly an opportunity to advertise books other than the one by the publisher giving the *parti.* At these there is much *karakter-as-asination,* or verbal witchcraft, designed to decrease the sales of rival authors and to increase one's own reputation for cleverness of expression and literary insight."

"Do the same people always go to one another's *partis?*" asked the tiki-attired matron.

"Well, this is largely the case," said the distinguished Nyabongan anthropologist. "However, hostesses complain proudly of the number of 'people we hardly know' whom they invite to their *partis*. The reason for this is probably owing to the fact that both host and hostess are too busy seeing that drinks are replenished to have more than a few words with any one person. But it is a matter of prestige, as guests, to meet the same people briefly at two successive rituals on one evening, and in this manner they can gather more people they hardly know for their own next gathering.

"Hostesses also compete with one another in exotic foodstuffs. Smoked oysters, fish pastes, rare fish eggs, sea-spider and shrimp purées are commonplaces, as are foreign cheeses; the successful hostess is one who uses something like *kashu-nut* butter on new and unfamiliar wafers before these in turn become commonplace. Some like to present new drink mixtures with names like Rag-Pickers' Toddy or Purple Nose or Longshoreman Slugger, but mostly *koktels* are of the same few types, like Manhattans (named after an island off the Usan mainland to the east), poured into an inverted conical or hemispherical stemmed glass—quite unlike the *aignawg* cup—with an onion or a stuffed olive or a cherry, which of course no one is required to eat, this being a sign of naiveté. Sometimes there are 'tall ones,' so called because of the long glass cylinders they are served in. But all these drinks contain some sort of drug that makes the people fatuous, foolish, talkative, tearful or amorous."

"Where does this word *koktel* come from?" another interested Nyabongan listener inquired.

"Well, literally, the word means the hind feathers of a male chicken or cock," replied the professor. "But, though Usan natives readily admit this derivation upon questioning, no one seems to know why they are called this. They claim that *koktels* began only as late as the Nineteen Twenties when they were forbidden and had to be obtained in secret ritual underground chambers called *speekeezies* or from *butlaigers*."

"But don't the Usans get exhausted running from one *koktel parti* to another, especially in this restricted season?"

"Oh, yes, and they frequently say as much," answered the Nyabongan savant. "There is another institution, though, that is protectively exploited in these circumstances. This is the *baybisitter*. The Usans do not have the extended family that we Nyabongans do, but live in one-family units called houses or apartments. For this reason they have to hire a *baybisitter* to take care of the children in their absence; of course, they couldn't bring the children to these ceremonies, because they would be trampled underfoot in their crowded ritual chambers.

"The word does not mean, despite its form, that they hire a *baybi* infant to sit, for these persons are often someone else's grandmother. It seems, rather, that they hire someone to sit on the *baybi*, to prevent its destroying the furniture while they are gone. *Koktel*-goers are able to invent the most fantastic and transparent excuses involving these *baybisitters* which require the imminent presence of the parents back home. Other parents at the *parti* commiserate, though disbelieving these excuses, and the couple is allowed to leave without losing face."

"Strange people, these Usan natives," said the fat, middle-aged Nyabongan. "That they are, that they are!" echoed Professor Widjojo, touching his nosestick thoughtfully.

Study Question

1. What other Usan rituals in which you participate would a foreign visitor interpret as Professor Widjojo did?

5

...ng in the Mirror
International Student Views on American Culture

GEORGE GMELCH & SHARON BOHN GMELCH
UNIVERSITY OF SAN FRANCISCO / UNION COLLEGE

What do international students make of American culture? What do they find different or unusual about their American classmates? Based on interviews with internationals on two college campuses, this wide-ranging chapter touches on everything from friendship to drinking behavior, from individualism to classroom behavior, and from greetings to sex. The comments made by international students not only reflect their own values but provide a critical lens through which to explore what it means to be American. The essay concludes with the American students' reactions to what the international students had to say.

George Gmelch teaches anthropology at the University of San Francisco and Union College. Trained at Stanford and UCSB, and the author of a dozen books, he has done fieldwork among Irish Travellers, English Gypsies, Alaska natives, Caribbean villagers, Newfoundland mariners and oil workers, and professional baseball players in the US.

Anthropologist Sharon Bohn Gmelch also teaches at the University of San Francisco and Union College. She has conducted field research in many places and on a variety of topics, and has run anthropology field schools in Barbados, Tasmania (Australia), Ireland, and Tanzania. She is the author of nine books and the co-producer of an ethnographic film.

*"Despite all the surface friendliness, I think it takes a long time
to get to know American people."*
Giovanna, Brazilian female student

Beginning in the early 1990s, we began asking the students in our Introduction to Cultural Anthropology classes at Union College and at the University of San Francisco (USF)[1] to each interview an international student. Initially, our aim was to give them hands-on experience "doing" anthropology using an essential fieldwork tool—the interview. They had to develop a list of questions or "interview guide," arrange and conduct an audio-recorded interview with an international student, and then use the data to write a 10-page narrative of that student's impressions of and adjustments to American culture and campus life. It wasn't long, however, before we realized that one of the real benefits of the assignment was the insights international students gave American students about their own culture and lives. What follows are the observations international students attending Union and USF most frequently made about Americans and campus life, and how their American-raised interviewers reacted to them.[2]

Both Union and the University of San Francisco are expensive private liberal arts colleges, but with a difference. Union is the oldest nondenominational college in the US (founded in 1795) and has an undergraduate student body of 2,200, while USF is a Jesuit university (founded in 1855) with about 6,200 undergraduates and 2,100 graduate students.[3] Union is located in the small, largely working-class city of Schenectady in upstate New York, while USF is situated in the middle of a large, affluent and vibrant city in California. Eight percent of Union's student body comes from abroad, while at USF the figure is 18 percent, which is among the highest of any US college.

The international students come to both schools from nearly all parts of the world (44 countries for Union and 81 for USF), with the largest contingent on both campuses coming from Asia, particularly the People's Republic of China, which in 2015 accounted for 38 percent of Union's internationals and 61 percent at USF.[4] At Union, Asia was followed by Europe in numbers; at USF, by Europe and the Middle East. Most internationals come from major cities, such as Beijing, Prague, Mumbai, Karachi, and Rio de Janeiro. Many come from affluent families who pay full college tuition. [5] Some are from countries like Brazil, South Korea, and Saudi Arabia that offer national scholarships to their students to study abroad; a few are recruited on sports scholarships.

Some students from well-off families in countries where labor costs are low, grew up with a live-in maid and cook—and sometimes a chauffeur and gardener as well—and consequently had never made their own beds or washed their own clothes before arriving in the US. Needless to say, learning this came as a shock to their American student interviewers. Most internationals' parents are successful professionals or work in, if not own, businesses and have encouraged their sons and daughters to choose "practical majors" like business, accounting, economics, or engineering that they believe will result in better job prospects and higher salaries or allow them to take over the family firm. Many Asian and South Asian students explained that their parents consider making a lot of money to be the true mark of success and the key to happiness. Many had traveled widely and had seen more of the world than their American-born interviewers. Nearly half had attended international schools at home and therefore spoke English and were familiar with an American-style curriculum.[6] Most were fluent in at least two languages, although quite a few Chinese students struggled with English.

Because so many of the foreign students on both campuses are from Asian countries, the following account in some respects represents their experiences more than those of students from other parts of the world. It is also important to keep in mind that the interview sample was an *opportunistic* one, not randomly selected. Nevertheless, what has surprised each of us over the years is the degree of agreement in what international students find striking about American culture and campus life despite the diversity in their own cultural backgrounds and the differences in the two American colleges they attend. What follows are the views and interpretations of our students.

What Did the International Students Expect to Find?

Before arriving, most international students expected Americans to be "friendly." They also considered them to be fairly "ignorant," especially about events beyond their borders. Their impressions of America as a *society*, as opposed to Americans as *individuals*, was that it was "wealthy," despite having lots of poor people, and a place where people could get ahead if they worked hard. Some used the well-worn phrase "promised land," either ignoring or unaware of the limited opportunities for social mobility that exists in the US today (near bottom in the industrialized world). America was also seen as a "violent" place with lots of guns, and its cities as "dangerous." Outside urban areas, internationals anticipated finding lots of open space. They also expected the scale of everything, from cars and buildings to body size, to be large. Their impressions of America—both the place and the people—came mainly from Hollywood movies and television programs.

Why Come to America?

Given such mixed views, why do so many international students choose to come to the United States rather than go to another country? "The reason that I, like most international students, came to the US," explained a student from Pakistan, "can be summarized in one word: Education!" American universities are known in many parts of the world for the rigor of their curricula, rich resources, and quality of teaching. Many students had been encouraged by their parents to apply to American schools. Internationals also mentioned the prestige that comes with a degree from an American institution and the opportunity it would give them to improve their English, both of which would serve them well in the job market. So, what did they find when they got here?

Friendliness and Friendship

One of the first hurdles most international students face is making sense of Americans' overt friendliness. "In China strangers don't look at strangers," remarked one student, "and people don't hold the door open for one another like everyone does here." Many reported being confused when a passing American student greeted them with, "How are you?" or "What's up?" Most took these questions literally and attempted to answer, only to find that the American student might not even slow down enough to hear their response. "At home," explained an Indian student, "when someone asks you how you are doing, you must tell them. But then in India to say 'Hi' to random people, like here in the US, would be seen as weird and kind of creepy." "It was a while," recalled a student from Nepal," before I realized that it was just their way of saying hi, and nothing more. They didn't really want to know how I was. Nobody wants a real response." In many parts of the world, it is still impolite not to take the time to stop for some small talk. The gradual realization that most American students' initial friendliness is merely a ritualized greeting and not a real friendship overture causes many internationals to conclude that Americans are superficial and insincere. A male student from Haiti, largely for this reason, had concluded that students at USF are "cold" and "unfriendly" in contrast to people back home.

Many international students talked about how different the concept of "friendship" seems to be in the US. While American students are friendly and claim to have many friends, from the perspective of international students their friendships are not as deep as those they have at home. A few internationals expressed amazement at the number of Facebook "friends" American students collect and are proud of. "Some of my classmates have more than a thousand friends," proclaimed a skeptical Argentine. "American students are walking Facebook profiles," asserted a disgruntled male Nepalese. "Social media is so huge. They have an image of themselves and are concerned with how they look to other people. They're focused on themselves. On the outside, almost everybody is friendly here, but it's very difficult to find an actual, real friend."

A Chinese male described walking across Union's campus with an American classmate, watching him say "Hi" to many of the students they passed, and then asking him if all those people were "friends." "Yes," he replied, "but we might never hang out or go out together." To the Chinese student, this revealed a fundamental cultural difference. "In China, we don't have so many friends. But the ones we do have are close, lifelong friends who you feel deeply obligated to and who will do anything for you. We don't just collect friends the way you do." A Russian student who had also attended high school in the US claimed, "Friendships here never progress past what I would consider an 'intermediate friend.' Many of what Americans call friends, I think of as acquaintances." According to a student from Ecuador, "At home we have fewer friends but they are deeply obligated and you are friends for life." "At home, friendship is a lifetime sentence," explained a Palestinian. "It is a sacred duty."

Some international students speculated about the reasons behind the differences they observed in friendships. A student from Brazil believes, "People here are just more into their own business, their own affairs, and don't seem to have a lot of room for others." Similarly, other internationals explained that American students' daily schedules are so busy that they simply don't have much free time to "hang out." Some implicated the fast pace of American life and missed the slower, less stressful pace of life at home, which allows more time for human interactions. Others suggested that because American youth tend to be more self-reliant and independent than those at home, they are less dependent upon or in need of true friends and the friendships they do have involve fewer obligations. A male Chinese student, lamenting the difficulty of getting to know American students, put some of the blame on communication difficulties: "Becoming friends with Americans is not an easy task in my opinion. Sometimes American students can't understand the way we talk and we don't understand the jokes they make, so they think, 'This guy sucks.'"

The internationals recruited for athletics had the easiest time developing friendships with Americans, and fitting in generally. When they arrive on campus, they automatically become part of a social group—the team—whose members hang out together and bond through practices, travel, games, and shared objectives. This is especially the case at USF, which has Division I teams that heavily recruit overseas. At Union, men's ice hockey is the only Division I sport, and its foreign recruiting is mostly in Canada.

Parents: Peers or Authority Figures?

Another relationship that many international students found strikingly different was that between their American classmates and their parents. The Americans, from their perspective, showed their parents far less deference or respect than they or their friends at home would. They seemed instead to treat them as they treat each other, perhaps worse.[7] Some internationals reported being shocked while listening to American students arguing with their mothers or fathers on the phone or talking back to them when they visited campus. A student from China described to her interviewer being appalled at how her American dorm mate ordered her parents around when they dropped her off on campus. "Some of my American friends are rude [to their parents]," reported a female from Ghana. "I have heard them call their moms 'bitch' and even say 'fuck' and 'what the hell, Mom.' Never in a million years would I raise my voice at my mom or say those things. In Ghana you don't ever, ever swear at your mom."

Some internationals, especially those from Asia and South Asia, noted that American parents seem to have less influence and control over their kids than parents in their home countries who frequently tell their sons and daughters what they will major in and what profession to strive for. Not in America. "In China, people care more about parents' opinion," commented one student. A Taiwanese student explained why: "They [parents] know more about society and have experience in how it works, so it makes sense for them to tell me what I need to do." A Brazilian student compared her relationship to her family with those of her Union dorm mates: "I really don't think they are as close to their parents. Just look at how many of them want to go far away to college, to get away from their parents. That's not how Brazilians are. I am only here in the US, far away, because I can get a better education here."

Other international students suggested that the reason has a lot to do with the value Americans place on personal freedom and autonomy.

Drinking

The amount and the way American students drink came up frequently in the interviews. One student wrote in some detail about her Chinese interviewee's puzzlement over her American roommate's drinking behavior. "Zhang's roommate is a 'partyer.' Zhang wasn't used to living with someone who periodically comes home in the wee hours of the night. Most of Zhang's friends don't drink or party, so when she sees people who binge drink such as her roommate it makes her feel uncomfortable. The intense drinking and partying that goes on at Union was a huge culture shock for Zhang. She didn't understand how anyone could possibly stay out late at night, sleep all day and then hope to still do well in school. She said that this is one aspect of American way of life that is very different from her culture."

Rather than drinking moderately with dinner and over conversation, as many internationals are accustomed to at home, they watch Union and USF students consuming large quantities of alcohol with the intention of getting drunk. At campus parties, drinking is an important social lubricant. "It's very dirty in the [Union College] frats," observed a male student from the Dominican Republic, "and you see so many people doing all sorts of weird things. And you have to go over and offer the girls drinks, practically going crazy to get their attention. For me, talking to girls is kind of difficult because I'm not from this country and I don't look like most white people at Union. I feel kind of scared to talk to girls that aren't Hispanic or ethnic."

Other typical comments about drinking and the social scene follow:

> My roommates start getting drunk right after the class on Friday, and on Saturday even before breakfast. They remain drunk throughout the weekend and do nothing else. I have never seen them doing something, anything interesting rather than partying. Back home, it is more "chill." We do drink and dance, but we go around interesting places and talk. Drinking is not the same thing like it is here. (Indonesian male)

> At home there's never this idea of "let's get messed up tonight," which seems to be the common attitude here [Union]. (Nepalese male)

> In Brazil everyone drinks, but most students don't drink to get drunk. We don't get trashed and pass out. We drink to enjoy it, to get happy,

to hang out, and to talk. If you are drinking to get trashed you're not from Brazil. (Female from Rio de Janeiro)

I just don't understand why so many American kids are crazy obsessed over wanting to get as drunk as possible. I don't see how that's enjoyable or fun to make yourself sick and not remember the things that happened from the night before. (Afghan male)

At uni [university] at home, it's just not cool to talk about having been drunk. (Australian male)

While most internationals were shocked by and disliked the drinking scene on campus, to a few—like those from the UK and Australia—it was not altogether different from home.

Many of the international students interpreted American students' drinking behavior as a sign of "immaturity," which, in turn, they think may be a result of the US's legal drinking age of 21, which is three to five years older than the legal age in most of their home countries. Many internationals had learned to drink when they were still living at home, sometimes drinking at the same table with their parents and siblings. "I'm really amazed so many people here [USF] have never had a sip of alcohol with their parents," remarked a Haitian student. "[Because of that] they really don't know how to drink. In Haiti you drink and talk or have an adventure. Here people just drink and do nothing, just drink to lose control." "By the time we go off to college," explained a German student, "we have grown out of it. In Germany the drinking age is 18 and minors under 18 can legally drink alcohol with parents. By university, it's no longer the forbidden fruit. It doesn't have the same appeal that it does to American college kids." In the words of an Iranian student, "When they [authorities] say you can't do something, that's when you want to do it most. That's the problem with the American drinking age being 21."

While heavy drinking was mentioned frequently by internationals on both campuses, it was far more striking at Union. Union has many more fraternities and sororities than does USF, and the campus social scene is largely organized by Greeks. Union is also primarily a residential school, while over half of USF's students live off-campus. Also significant is Union's location in a small city with fewer, readily available entertainment options compared to USF, which is located in the middle of San Francisco with myriad alternatives to campus life. Hence, at Union social life revolves around fraternity parties and alcohol.

Drug use by American students was mentioned less often by international students, perhaps because it is less noticeable than binge drinking and drunkenness. The internationals who did comment on drugs came mainly from Asian nations and the global South where there are very severe penalties for drug use. Not surprisingly, they were shocked that drugs were used fairly openly on a college campus.

Hooking Up

"Hooking up" or casual sex between students who often barely know one another—what one Chinese student referred to as "one-night love"—is linked in the minds of both American and international students with excessive drinking. An Iranian student reported being aghast the first time he saw his American roommate openly having sex in their dorm room with a girl he had just picked up at a party. While alcohol and drugs can be found at parties in Tehran, there is no physical contact between men and women. The idea of students having sex at parties was totally foreign to him. "In China, if two people are having sex," noted a male student from Shanghai, "they are in a relationship. Here, it seems like sex comes before relationships. In China there is no such thing as 'one night stand.'" A young woman from China observed that "American boys really like to 'hook up'"; according to her interviewer, "She was apprehensive about even speaking the phrase."

"Most of the girls blame it on the guys," opined an Indian student, "but since they are participating in it too, that means it is their fault too. For example, one of my floor mates hooked up with one of my close friends. When I asked her about it—since I thought they are dating—she told me that there were no feelings; it was just nice to talk to him and one thing led to another and they hooked up. Nothing more." It was not only American students' casual attitudes toward sex that astonished many internationals; it was also their willingness to talk about it openly. In the words of a student from Burma, "At home it's not just that girls don't have sex before they get married; if they do, it brings great shame on their family. So no girl or boy would ever talk in the open about having sex like they do here."

Dress and Undress

The casual way American students dress on campus—sweatpants, shorts, tights or leggings, T-shirts, flip-flops, and baseball caps—was another area many foreign students, particularly those from Asia and the Middle East, found very different from home. It is also something some found liberating and began to adopt. "Coming to the US I couldn't imagine wearing a pair of leggings," said an Indian female. "I thought, 'why would a person wear leggings when it lets people see your whole bum?' But now I wear leggings all the time. But I won't do it when I go home."

But most surprising to many of the internationals were the revealing outfits—short shorts and skirts and low-cut tank tops—worn by female students on campus and to class. Most, initially at least, regarded this as inappropriate, and some described the extremes as "provocative," if not "slutty." "The girls here show a lot more skin than you'd ever see in my country," said one student. "Even in warm weather," explained a Chinese female, "we do not wear shorts or tank tops to class. When it is hot, we wear thinner materials, still covering up." "At home in Japan," said a female student from Tokyo, "girls want to appear cute and young. Here, they want to dress sexy and mature."

Seeing American classmates in "revealing" clothing confused some male international students. As one Thai student noted about a girl in his chemistry lab, "She dresses in a way that says she wants attention, but when I flirt with her, she shuts me down and goes back to her girlfriends and gossips about how rude and gross I am. I don't get it."

Ironically, wearing short skirts, low-cut or snug tops, and second-skin tights or leggings does not mean that American coeds are comfortable with nudity, as we have discovered when taking students on terms abroad to Europe. When they travelled to French beaches and Eastern European spas where women sunbathed topless or bathed publically in the nude, our American students were very reluctant to remove their clothing, and usually did not. One student expressed great surprise at seeing European women who "did not have great bodies," removing their clothes. Similarly, a Finnish student at USF reported that the American students in her dorm were shocked when she ran from her room wearing only a towel or exited the shower area in the nude.

Food

Getting accustomed to a different cuisine is a challenge for most people. When asked what they missed most about home, many international students, especially those from Asia and South Asia, immediately said food. "Junrui came to life and showed the most emotion when I brought up the topic of food," reported an American student in her final paper. "I simply asked, 'Do you enjoy the food here?' She wildly exclaimed, 'No, No, No!'

When I asked how it compared to home, she said, 'Capital No,' and went on to explain that at home the food is more tasteful, more flavorful, more colorful, and healthier." Describing the food served in Union College's campus center, a Chinese student said, "Although there are different foods every week, I still cannot endure it. I really miss Chinese food, and if I have chance to go out for Chinese food on weekend that would be my happiest thing that week." Broadly speaking, the complaints internationals have about American food is that too much of it is processed, fried (described as "greasy" and "oily"), and bland. "My culture emphasizes the freshness and healthiness of the meals we eat," explained a student from Vietnam, "and my family puts a lot of effort into serving food that is fresh. Here [USF cafeteria] they serve a lot of greasy food, which sometimes upsets my stomach." Even the rice, say Asian students, tastes different in the US. "The dining hall rarely serves the type of rice that I have spent my entire life consuming," lamented a student from Cambodia. "I like the kindness of American people," an Indian student remarked, "but I do not like their food—too much fast food, too much fat, too much pasta. American people always like cheese, chicken, and barbecue. Not enough vegetables." A female student from Ecuador claimed that the hormones in American chicken and meat had caused her skin to break out.

Although the dining services at both Union and USF offer healthy choices and fresh fruits and vegetables, most international students at both schools still do not find the food appealing. Even when international students go off campus to eat at an ethnic restaurant—much easier to do in San Francisco than in Schenectady—the dishes are usually Westernized and do not taste authentic. "They don't seem to have the same spices," said an Indian female about the Indian restaurant she patronized in San Francisco, but it was still better than eating on campus. Only a few interviewees from England and the West Indies had no complaints about dining hall food.

"It's quantity versus quality," said a Swiss student summarizing the difference between food in America and his homeland. Many international students agree. "Just look at this!" exclaimed a student from London pointing to the muffin he was eating during his interview. "It's double the size of any muffin at home. It's nearly the size of the average human stomach." When eating out, one Chinese student tries to order off the children's menu—not always successfully. With obvious hyperbole, a female from Nepal said, "In Kathmandu, when you order spareribs you get one rib; in America you get the whole side of the cow." "Everything here is one size larger than at home," said a female from Peru. "A large portion at home is only a medium here. And a lot of times food gets wasted." In the opinion of a French student, "The large meals here are revolting."

Some of the dissatisfaction with American food is undoubtedly due to it being different from their home country's cuisine, making it difficult to distinguish unfamiliarity from genuine dislike. American students who go abroad also complain about food, although much depends upon the country they go to. But the uniformity of international students' comments about American food suggests their complaints are based on more than mere unfamiliarity.

Some international students must also adjust to different meal times. "I am accustomed to having my lunch around two or three o'clock," explained an Indian student from Rajasthan, "and then afternoon tea and a snack around four or five o'clock, and then dinner—rice, rotis, curries, daals, subjis, raita—at nine or ten at night." Such a schedule obviously does not fit with campus dining hours which typically end at 8:00 P.M. Another student from India was surprised that Americans order for themselves at restaurants even though the portions are large. "Back home the food is ordered for the table," she explained, "and everyone shares from it so that they can taste different food. This is a shock that many of us experience." "Eating is more of an individual thing here in the US," remarked a student from Honduras. "At home, the food is in the middle and everyone grabs and shares."

"I Came for an Education"

By no means were all impressions of American culture and campus life negative. With few exceptions, the international students at Union and USF were very satisfied with the academic side of campus life, and with the many opportunities available to them—from large libraries, gyms, tennis courts, and swimming pools to intramural and intercollegiate sports, visiting speakers, bands and live music, free movies, field trips to local attractions, campus clubs, and more. A Chinese student expressed shock when he discovered that Union even had an equestrian club. In general, many more opportunities and activities are available at Union and USF than are available at the internationals' home universities. Intercollegiate sports, for example, are largely unknown on campuses outside the US and Canada. An Indian student was surprised by how "famous" US college sports are since they are often broadcast on regional, if not national, radio and television: "At home, people play because of sportsmanship or fun and that's it." And in much of the world, female students do not play many sports.

The international students also appreciated Union's and USF's open spaces and landscaped grounds, which can be found on many American campuses. Union's Joseph Ramee–designed campus, with its brook-side garden, is considered among the most beautiful in the United States. USF is perched on a hill overlooking San Francisco and Golden Gate Park; some of its dorm rooms have views of the Golden Gate Bridge. In contrast, overseas universities are often a collection of downtown buildings with no or little green space and without dorms, requiring most students to be commuters.

Since most international students came to the US to get a good university education, how do they feel about their schooling now that they are here? In general, very positively. Most valued the wide choices they have in selecting courses and majors. "At home," noted one student, "when you go to college you already know what you're going to major in and you only take courses in a few fields." Most found their classes far more intimate and interactive than at home. At both Union and USF, classes are small and participation is expected. "At home," said a student from Japan, "you have no discussion, only questions at the very end of the class. You can't just ask a question in the middle of a lecture." Not every international student appreciates this, especially when class participation is factored into their final grade. Those who are shy or grappling with English find speaking up intimidating, even if they like the idea of a discussion-based classroom.[8]

Overwhelmingly, these international students found their American professors to be more "approachable," "engaged," "professional," and "hardworking" than their professors at home. "At home, sometimes they don't even give you a syllabus," remarked a student from Colombia. "Professors never seem to plan much, and they often come late to class, and once class is over they are gone. It's hard to talk to them. Here [USF] you can email your professor anytime, and they usually get right back to you." A Chinese female described professors at her university in Beijing who read to the class out of the textbook, adding that she thought an American professor who did that would get fired. She complained that professors in China are distant and "put on a pedestal." "They don't pay teachers very much at home," noted a student from Honduras, "and they often go on strike, and we miss a lot of class. Our education is very deficient. There isn't any equipment and what there is, is very crappy."

Unaccustomed to the numerous assignments, papers, and quizzes typical of American university classes, some internationals complained about "busy work" that leaves little free time outside of class. "There is always some assignment to do," said a British male. "In the Czech Republic," said an exchange student from Prague, "we do our homework in class and there isn't much of it. Here, every night you have a reading or something to write, some assignment. The work is constant; it never lets up." Many international students explained that they were accustomed to only having a midterm and a final exam, or in some cases, as in the UK, only a year-end final exam for each course, which enables many students to coast during much of the school year and then cram the last month before the exam. "Compared to India," explained an international from New Delhi, "there's a big emphasis on assignments. And unlike here, writing is not very important in Indian education. Also, attendance is not required, so very few students will go to class." The latter is true of university education in many, perhaps most, countries. Some internationals said they missed the freedom to skip classes without penalty. Finally, many of the internationals expressed dismay over the high cost of tuition in the US, in sharp contrast to their home countries where a university education is often free.

Individualism?

Many of the internationals noted the "individualism" of Union and USF students. While individualism is usually thought to mean being independent and self-reliant, the international students also connected it to a variety of other American attitudes and behaviors, both positive and negative. One quality of Union and USF campus life that many praised was each school's openness to and tolerance of diversity. A Rwandan male was shocked, for example, to learn of the existence of an LGBT theme house on Union's campus and, because Americans were so "individualistic," that no one on campus was bothered by it. On the negative side, some internationals noted that American students' individualism sometimes translates into actions that can be selfish or inconvenience others. Common examples included being loud in the dorms or on the street at night, and not flushing the toilet or cleaning the shared shower. One Chinese student described scenes in her dorm in which American girls indulgently yelled and slammed doors over minor upsets. A student from India described how "inconsiderate" it was of her friend's American roommate to kick him out of their shared bedroom whenever he had his girlfriend over, forcing him to sleep on their common-room couch. "I think students here [USF]," said a Japanese male, "try too hard to achieve own identity . . . and don't think about community, don't place value on what's good for the collective. In Japan, people usually make decision based on group interest and sometimes will sacrifice their own individual value to achieve group interest. I don't see much of that here."

Other internationals questioned whether American students really are as individualistic and independent as they like to think. "People here [Union] have so much pride in their individualism," said an Indian female, "but if you really look at them, you see that everyone dresses the same, eats the same, and listens to the same music. Before coming here, I thought how American society is based on the individualism; now it feels more like it's just outward appearances." A few commented on what they regarded as a contradiction between American students' cherished individualism and their lack of well-defined personal beliefs about religion or politics. "Back home [Karachi] everyone is aware of events going on across the globe," remarked one student about her college classmates in Pakistan. "Everyone has a strong opinion on politics, religion, environment, sports. Students here are not as much interested in the world affairs. Their knowledge about the current world events starts and ends with football, with sports. Most of the students I met at the ISIS discussion were there only for [free] food. The only opinions that they had were what others were saying and they agreed on everything. They were not aware of the situation of Syria. . . . My [American] roommate cannot even have a conversation with me about the US politics."

A student from Nepal talked about the concern of American students over their image and their tendency to play it safe. "They have a burning desire to have an acceptable image, and don't hold opinions or beliefs that will shake it. College-age Americans are shells of people with regard to openness about their character. If you asked someone in Nepal about their beliefs, they'd probably make you a cup of tea and talk to you for hours. Most of my American friends don't have any strong beliefs. Many don't even know about what's going on in their own government. And they don't have strong opinions about religion either. The people I know [here] are much more interested in sports. You can have a good argument with them about sports, but don't talk about religion or politics because they don't know much."

American Students' Reactions

How do American students react to these perceptions of them, especially the criticisms? During the last week of the term, after reading all our students' papers, we try to arrive at some generalizations from the patterns that emerge from their papers, which we then discuss in class. Afterward, we ask students to write a short paper reacting to the collective findings and class discussion. A student from Boston responded to the international students' confusion over greetings this way: "When I first heard this, I found it amusing. 'Well of course you don't actually talk about how you are! Everybody knows that.' But when I really thought about it, I realized the absurdity of it. Why would someone ask a question and expect no response? This is an aspect of American culture that I had never thought twice about before. I can now see how this would make Americans seem rude and standoffish."

How about the criticisms of American friendship? Most of our American students were surprised; many were defensive. "I think personally none of my friendships with people at school are superficial," wrote a Union student. "I think that foreign exchange students believe this because Americans are extremely friendly people. It's part of our culture to always say hello to everyone. I think foreign exchange students simply mistake this friendliness and willingness to talk to anyone with our having superficial friendships." But some students could see some truth in the internationals' criticism: "I didn't really expect the comments the internationals made about American friendship, but after reflecting on it I now feel that our culture places more emphasis on appearances than on being genuine. We want to appear friendly and as though we have a lot of friends, whereas other cultures seem to value having a few very deep friendships . . . they don't feel the need to collect tons of friends and to seem incredibly friendly all the time."

The internationals' assessments that American students are not as close to their parents as they are to theirs and are sometimes disrespectful came as a surprise to our students. Some challenged the characterization: "I find it hard to believe that they [internationals] have closer ties with their families. I am very close to my parents and I have many friends who are very close with their families. I can agree with the comments that American parents have less control over us, but I really think we are just as close." But other students could see truth in the internationals' observations. "I assumed that comfortable and intimate families were universal, based on my own experiences with my parents, and based on television shows like *Gilmore Girls* or *Modern Family*," wrote a Union student. "But I can now see how the international students feel that American children are too comfortable with their parents—that we interact with them in the same way we interact with friends. I think this 'disrespect' connects with American individualism." Other students elaborated on this latter point: "I think American students are just less inclined to listen to their parents because we were taught to be independent at a young age, which then leads us to wanting to make our own decisions and not necessarily follow what their parents think is best."

How about the internationals' criticism of binge drinking and drunkenness on campus, which perhaps more than any other behavior diminishes the respect internationals have for American students. In fact, two female internationals said they were not interested in dating American guys because they were "turned off" by the way they behave when they drink. Most of our students accepted the accuracy of the internationals' descriptions of campus drinking. Only a few resisted by pointing out that some internationals also binge drink, and one Union student retorted broadly, "I think it's very easy for them [internationals] to pick on Americans, because we don't know a lot and most of us only speak English." Some American students were surprised to learn that students in other cultures don't drink the way they do. They had assumed that college students everywhere in the world—at least the Western world—were like them.

Those students who attempted to explain or excuse excessive drinking usually blamed it on the stress and pressures of their academic work. "The comments about all the drinking and drugs," reflected a first-year anthropology major, "really made me think about the Union culture. I knew that drinking and drugs would be prevalent on campus and it became clear to me within a few days of being here, but I never really thought about what caused it. I really think a lot of it has to do with the stress levels that students are under. I have had more papers this year than I have ever had in my life, and there have been times where I was so stressed out that I broke down. The possibility of escaping through drinking or drugs draws some people in." A male classmate agreed, "I'm so tense that I have to go out and just blow it off [get drunk] to get rid of all the stress that builds up here." Others attributed it to the social pressures of campus life. "I think many students participate in binge drinking because they feel pressure from their peers," explained a student from Los Angeles, "not because they enjoy the behavior." "For the first time I realized how stupid we act by trying to get as inebriated as possible," wrote a Union College football player, "and a lot of it just to 'open up' and be able to converse with others. Jamaal [Afghan interviewee] made me realize that if American college students could switch our social life to focus more on conversation and less on binge drinking how much better that would be."

None of our students refuted or discussed the hookup scene in any depth. As with drinking and drugs, some related it to the need to relieve the stress created by what they regard as a heavy academic workload. "Study hard and play hard," said a fraternity member. But the remarks of some of the international students they interviewed made others really look at campus parties for the first time. "Paco's opinions on the party scene surprised me because I didn't even realize how crazy American students act," acknowledged his interviewer, "like the dances where you jump up and down and push against one another in a crowd. I now recognize all the ridiculous things kids do when we are out."

The internationals' comments reinforced the views of some American-born students, particularly women, who find the hookup scene demeaning and believe that it contributes to sexual harassment and date rape. A first-year Asian American who had made the decision to leave Union and transfer to a liberal arts college without a strong fraternity scene said, "I lost a lot of hope when I saw how crazy and obnoxious some students act in college. Before my freshman year, I expected a mature student body, with the dating scene where students wanted serious relationships. But instead I have found nothing but disappointment, especially with the whole hookup scene. I knew some guys like casual sex, but it brings on a great level of disrespect, which girls experience on a daily basis. Any girl who wants commitment has a hard time fitting in here." Her reaction, as an Asian American, raises an important, as yet undiscussed issue, namely, the diversity of American society. Whose culture are we talking about when we use the phrase "American culture"? Students born and raised in the US but whose parents are immigrants or who maintain strong traditions from their home countries, like the Asian American student just cited, sometimes found themselves identifying with the international students' criticisms, while at the same time reacting defensively to them as Americans.

When it came to the internationals' characterizations of American food, few students put up any defense. "One insight I got from [the interviews]," said a student from Connecticut, "was just how unhealthy Americans eat compared to many other places. Much of the food we eat is processed with copious amounts of fake ingredients that end up killing our bodies over time."

American students were pleased to hear how favorably most internationals rated the education they were receiving at Union and USF. "I never really knew how our education compared to other countries," said a student from New Hampshire, "so I was very glad to hear her [Argentine interviewee] comments about classes at Union. She went as far as to use the word 'inspired' in describing them. It made me feel fortunate enough to be taught by people [professors] who really care about their jobs as educators, who sincerely care about their students, which I guess is not the case in many of the countries the internationals come from."

What did the international students think about being interviewed? Almost without exception, they enjoyed it.[9] For many, it was the first time they'd had an extended conversation with an American student. Some explained that was the reason they had agreed to be interviewed in the first place, pointing out that American students rarely showed any interest in them. Several international students opined that the interview assignment should be required of every American student—as one put it, "to push them to learn something about the international students they live among and learn to feel more comfortable with people from other cultures."

Final Thoughts

One of the rewards of this assignment is that it makes American students take notice of the international students in their midst and learn something about their experiences, and it makes those interviewed feel good about the attention and interest they receive—as minimal as one assignment is. It also gives American students a better understanding of their own culture and of how similar yet different their experiences and perceptions can be from those of their age-mates in other countries. In the course of doing so, they become more aware of their own ethnocentrism. The assignment also makes some American students feel a deeper commitment to their own education. "The interview really forced me to take a look at how I live my life," commented one male student. "Afterward, I felt so guilty about the way I had been experiencing Union College, never appreciating all the opportunities and the resources around me. Nor did I realize how much information could be learned outside the classroom, from a single interview."

No two campuses are exactly alike. To a greater or lesser extent, every college has its own student culture. Union and USF are quite different from one another as are the cities in which they are located. We have noted a few of the differences that would most affect the experiences of international students—such as the dominance of fraternities in Union College's social life versus USF's students' use of the city of San Francisco for entertainment. (Readers of this essay may want to think about how their own campus and its culture and location affects the experiences of its international students.) As instructors and anthropologists, we believe the value of these interviews is not only what they reveal about how international students view American culture and college life, but also the questions they raise about ourselves and who "we" really are.

Study Questions

1. What are the challenges of trying to generalize and draw conclusions from the international student interviews?

2. What surprised you most about the opinions the international students expressed about American culture?

3. Did this chapter change your view of American culture in any way? Or, your opinions of international students?

4. Do you think that the anthropologists and authors of this chapter have let their own biases about American culture influence their account? If so, how?

5. Anthropological descriptions can sometimes give the impression that everyone in a particular culture holds the same or very similar set of cultural beliefs. In this account, how do the authors attempt to show the variation or diversity in opinion and beliefs of the international students interviewed?

6. How do the opinions of the international students compare with your own understanding and assessment of American culture and American students?

Notes

[1] We thank Howard DeNike, Richard Felson, Jerome Handler, David and Shannon Jaeger, Rabia Kamal, Genevieve Leung, Stephen Leavitt, Michelle Pawlowski, Stephanie Vandrick, and the students in USF's 2015 summer Culture and the Environment anthropology course in Alaska for their comments on this paper.

[2] The papers the students write must include some poignant or revealing quotations from the transcript to give the interviewee "voice," and give the reader a feeling for the individual; the narrative must also contain an analysis of one aspect or attribute of the international student's adjustment and a reflexive account of the research.

[3] All statistics and student quotes used in this paper pertain to the 2014–15 academic year.

[4] These figures pertain to the 2014–15 academic year. Nationally, 31% of international students at American colleges and universities come from China.

[5] Tuition, room and board, and mandatory fees for Union College in 2015 were $62,274; for USF, $56,285.

[6] Union does not offer an ESOL (English for Speakers of Other Languages) program (other than informal ESL [English as a Second Language] classes that students can sign up for voluntarily), and as a result, it requires a minimum TOEFL (Test of English as a Foreign Language) score of 90 for admission to meet the government requirement and its own educational objectives—that its international students have the English proficiency needed to succeed. USF requires a minimum TOEFL score of 80 for full admission and a minimum of 65 for conditional admission, which requires that students take formal ESL courses.

[7] In the same vein, some internationals, particularly Asians, commented that Americans don't seem to show much respect for the elderly, noting that families are quick to put grandparents in institutions instead of taking care of them at home.

[8] Some American students noted, however, that not all international students take full advantage of the education they are being offered. USF students, in particular, pointed to some of the Chinese students in their classes who "slack off," "don't pay attention," "pass exams around," "sit in the back and talk on the phone," and who they claim have "paid people to take their English exam for them" in order to be admitted." While true of some, such behavior too easily is generalized to all and becomes a stereotype. Some Chinese students feel victimized by this stereotype and others, including that their parents are wealthy and they're just in the US to have a good time and get a paper degree.

[9] Our knowledge of the international students' reactions to the assignment also comes from having informally asked many of them their opinions over the years.

6

An American in Kenya
Experiences at an African University

SIBEL KUSIMBA
AMERICAN UNIVERSITY

Any understanding of a culture is built up from an uncountable number of observations and impressions and ideas of what the rules are. Anthropologists have created something called culture, using it to label social formations both large and small. Certainly all of those formations encompass a lot of diversity, but any set of ideas, behaviors, rules and practices that might be shared by a larger group, no matter how diverse, could be called a culture. This is how an admittedly vast and diverse place called America can be thought of as having a culture. It is often when one is away from a culture and has attained a bird's eye view of it that one has enough perspective to call it a culture—to see the commonalities that a diverse group can share. A trip away from one's homeland can give one the perspective and the distance that a visitor has. And one can start trying to define that culture.

Sibel Kusimba is an anthropologist in residence at American University, Washington DC. She has conducted ethnographic research in East Africa since 1990. Her research interests include economic anthropology, mobile money, social inequality, and urbanism in Africa. Kusimba is also interested in social network analysis, which she has used to examine the role of money and cellular phone technologies in the socioeconomic practices of transnational families in Kenya and in the West. She is the author of a forthcoming book entitled *Mobile Economies: A New Digital Currency in Kenya*.

Being with someone who is a visitor and seeing the world through his or her lens is a way of getting the perspective and distance of a person outside your own culture. If you're married to that person or you are the child of that person, you almost automatically learn to position and reposition yourself as an insider and as an outsider, as events or your own analytical mind force you to consider and reconsider experiences from your own insider perspective or from an outsider's perspective. After a lifetime of this you actually start to wonder when you're an outsider and when you're an insider. It can get pretty confusing! In any case, a long-term stay in a country outside of America will still throw an American off balance. That clearer sense of observing America from afar can emerge. Things you take for granted suddenly get called into question.

As a first-generation American married to an immigrant, I've spent pretty much my entire life moving from insider to outsider, or perhaps better put, even occupying both stances simultaneously. My experiences abroad have given me the clearest view of American culture thanks to that removal and distance, insofar as that is possible given the common experience of the Internet so readily available just about anywhere these days.

While writing this essay, I am spending ten months teaching at a Kenyan university as a Fulbright scholar. This experience teaching for an academic year in a foreign country has given me a tremendous opportunity and perspective on the university setting as a culture. In this essay I will try to reflect on the American university as a culture from my vantage point as an American visiting an African university.

The first thing to be said is that any educational system is a place where culture is produced and reproduced. Any educational system is the crux of how learned behavior is transmitted to the next generation. The content of courses, the bases of knowledge that are inculcated in students, are perhaps the more functional level of this university "culture." Another more diffuse and pervasive aspect of this university "culture" is the social interaction, rules and the lived experience of the university. When you become a teacher or professor, you have the advantage of taking a job that has been modeled in front of you, both well and poorly, for many years and beginning in childhood (although that belies how difficult one's first years teaching are!). You also fit into a work environment and a set of social roles and interactions that you have absorbed and come to understand since childhood. As a college professor, I have spent many years on the American college campus as both teacher and student. As such, an African university is a fascinating look at how universities reflect and refract their wider culture.

At the time of its independence from Britain in 1963, Kenya had 30,000 high school students in 151 secondary schools. In 1991, it had 600,000 in 3,000 secondary schools, and in 2008 it had more than one million high school students. Because of its rapid population growth Kenya has devoted a very large share of its government budget to education and especially university education. In 1968 the University of Nairobi was established, followed by Kenyatta University, and in 1987, Egerton University near the town of Njoro, where I was based as a Fulbright lecturer. Since 1987, Kenya has chartered seven public universities and 12 private universities, which are springing up like mushrooms in different regions of the country. The public universities are supported by an annual budget of 12 billion Kenyan shillings, about 158 million US dollars.

Egerton University is blessed with a rural setting on land donated by Lord Maurice Egerton of Tatton, a British settler and one of five British Lords to settle in the Kenya Colony. His vast estate included a farm school he founded, which became Egerton Teachers' College in 1950. In 1986, the college was established as a constituent college of Nairobi University. In 1987, Egerton was fully established as a university through an act of the Kenyan Parliament. Lord Egerton's home, "The Castle," was only in 2001 opened to the public as a museum to bring revenue to the college. The castle, built in imitation of the lord's family home in Tatton, and the campus' many colonial-era buildings, sport hipped roofs of red ceramic tile and bands of wide windows and are surrounded by landscaping of abundant euphorbia, bottle-brushes, and poinsettias.

Some strong, concrete buildings, constructed in the 1970s, have jagged geometric lines, including an auditorium and housing for senior staff and families built by the US Government. A newer set of flats, with flimsy concrete walls through which every noise and pin drop could be heard, included my campus flat. These flats were also plagued with long interruptions in water service that lasted weeks. The student buildings are simple, narrow-storied square blocks; on weekends music blares and their washing dries on lines that crisscross the dorm compounds next to outdoor taps for household water.

There is much that is familiar about Egerton's students, and there is surely much that is universal about being in one's early 20s; here, as in the United States, it is a time of increasing independence from parents and family. Overall the youth and energy of college-age students is a universal human trait. When classes end here, large numbers of boisterous, sociable students leave classes in groups.

A walk around the campus would find students laughing and congregating in groups between classes, rushing en masse to a lecture, or holding hands as they walk (people of the same gender often hold hands here without romantic implication). There has been a growth in the prevalence of Western dress and middle-class tastes and habits more generally.

The wearing of braided hair extensions has become almost ubiquitous among Kenyan women. Only schoolgirls, housekeepers and nannies, and rural women wear their hair naturally. Among the college students on this campus rarely do you see a woman wearing her hair naturally short or pulled into a low, short ponytail or clip. While you might assume hair extensions is an "African" hairstyle, in fact it tends to mimic the Western aesthetic of long female hair. It is often sectioned, ponytailed, or banded similar to the long hair of Europeans. Red highlights or tints are also very common. Leaving aside the politics of African and African American hair, it still seems to me that the long braided hair is largely an imitation of Western hairstyles. As in American universities, too, the men tend to wear sportswear or jeans, while the women students are noticeably more put together, more attention being paid to their clothing, hair, nails, and shoes. Perhaps only makeup is more rare here than in the states.

Television and the Internet are regarded as the engines of globalization of images and standards of beauty. My informal discussions with my students established that TV and the Internet are luxuries they are occasionally exposed to and would like to see more of. Internet-connected computer labs on campus existed but were fairly rare; most professors are still placing readings on reserve at the library for student checkout. A US government–funded building for the study of agriculture, Utafiti House, sported a generator and one of the best computer labs on campus—an example of the problematic consequences of uneven aid opportunities on African campuses. My students preferred NTV network on television, which touts itself in advertisements as the channel for "young, affluent and urban" Kenyans and broadcasts a large number of American television shows from *Oprah* to *Ugly Betty*, to *Entourage*. This and other stations also show nightly wrestling or a televangelist displaying a supposedly five thousand-year-old fossil rock juxtaposed with a human and a dinosaur footprint, the dinosaur footprint looking like it's straight out of the *Flintstones*. I often wondered if my students would understand the ironic humor or references to sadomasochism in a typical episode of *Ugly Betty*. It is not the best example of American culture.

From a functional perspective, too, the place seems familiar to me as I also teach at a public university that relies on public funds. There seems to be a fairly well-understood universal model here based on an administrative block and several divisions and departments. The main administration building here faces a courtyard and a podium decorated with the national colors, clearly marking it as a public university. The division I am in, Faculty of Arts and Social Sciences (FASS), would be a recognizable category, the liberal arts here being somewhat smaller than in Kenya's other universities, largely because the school is historically an applied college for agriculture and education.

In spite of these similarities, the African culture comes through loud and clear. Unlike in our compulsively individualistic and democratic society, age and status are reinforced here. Prior to the colonial period, most Kenyan societies were organized as villages and other small-scale groupings, and decision making was usually based on the deliberation of a council of elders. Age sets organized the life cycle through a series of stages, marked by the transition to adulthood through a coming-of-age ceremony, and the passage into elderhood with the adulthood of one's youngest child. In such a system there was a kind of tension between the generations, especially adjacent ones, which were often characterized by an avoidance relationship. The rewards of elderhood included traditional beer and the leisure time to enjoy it.

The Senior Common Room provides a space where the senior faculty can have lunch or tea without students. After classes the social lubricant might be beer. In Britain, particularly at the collegiate universities, the common rooms were social bodies and meeting spaces—the Senior Common Room being for the faculty and doctorates, as opposed to the Junior and Middle Common Rooms, designated for undergraduates and postgraduates respectively. In East Africa only the Senior Common Room exists, and it has been transformed into a uniquely East African space. At Egerton's FASS there is a spacious Senior Common Room at the back of the cafeteria, actually twice the size of the student/staff area's. Senior staff (full-time faculty) can sit at tables and be served here, while those who use the cafeteria need to queue for their food at a counter. A separate structure with a patio close to the heart of campus is another Senior Common Room that serves lunch and dinner and boasts a satellite TV and plush velour sofas. These spaces for the senior staff are a very important demonstration of status. Women are the minority in these spaces. The academic and social life here includes vivid storytelling over *mandazis* (Kenyan doughnuts) at tea time (Atieno-Odhiambo 2002:38). The Senior Common Room is an important part of the African university and establishes it as hierarchical and not egalitarian. Age-related status makes its way into department offices; an emeritus neighbor of mine, often called "father" by other faculty members, occasionally invited me for tea in his office, catered in by the staff from the cafeteria in an adjacent building.

At the other end of the age-based hierarchy are the students. They can be very deferential at times. Students often help when seeing lecturers carrying books or unloading a car; in class whenever I rhetorically asked for confirmation of a particular point with an offhand "Right?" the students responded dutifully with a roar of "Yes, Madam,"—which took some getting used to after your average sullen class of American students. But just below the surface there is also harassment, particularly of female faculty; I was once deliberately tripped by a male student in a hallway to the smirks of his friends. Students here also feel that they need to make public the university's attempts to keep a lid on the ever-present prospect of student protests; on some campuses students have been known to riot over issues like fees, admission standards, tuition and loan repayment, and even the costs of a *matatu* (minibus) fare from campus to the main road. During my stay, Moi University was closed when students rioted and were killed turning over a vehicle, and a few months earlier, Kenyatta University had been closed over admissions policies and fees. My colleagues told me that students riot out of boredom and to avoid exams.

At Egerton, students and administrators locked horns over cooking facilities. Students are allowed to cook at some centrally located kitchenette structures that include outdoor patios for dining; most scorn the low quality of the meals served in the cafeteria, although a meal of beans and *ugali* (maize porridge) only costs 12 shillings (about $0.16) and helps many students push through to the end of the semester. Kitchenettes were constructed after passionate student lobbying when told they could not cook in their rooms—the issue of cooking was still a hot one during my stay, as the student government pushed for more kitchenettes. Most students seemed to prefer cooking for themselves or eating their friends' cooking, and several made money on the side serving cooked food to others.

Most students in Kenya take a national exam, and based on that score they gain entry into the university system. Because of a huge backlog of students, however, they have to wait two years to gain entry into the university. In a country with so many young people, it has become politically popular to support education and create university campuses. New universities are being created to absorb the huge numbers of young people resulting from one of the world's highest birth rates in the 1980s. Once students have been admitted, schools often have trouble with overenrollment. Students are also expected to pick a degree program in a particular subject and stick to it.

Kenya has enjoyed economic growth reaching 6% over the past five years. Most of the students seem to be under very similar kinds of economic insecurities and pressures. During my first week here, a particularly attentive student who always sits in the front row came to my office. She had been thinking of switching from history, where I was teaching, to community development, but had not been allowed by the school to do so. Because of the overenrollment problem, degree switching had been stopped. Over 100 students were enrolled in the community development program, as compared to 15 in history, one of the more traditional and less applied majors. She expressed concern about being a history major and about her employment prospects after graduation. I realized I was having the same kind of conversation that professors in liberal arts departments all over the world probably have, defending the kind of broad perspective and critical thinking that a history major would give her and that could prepare her for so many different careers, versus the narrower but ostensibly more practical field of "community development." I didn't have the heart to tell her of the dire straits that liberal arts programs find themselves in and the general crisis of relevance they face all over the world.

There is tremendous concern with the usefulness and marketability of a university education here. A newspaper letter to the editor criticized the universities for being ivory towers that have little to do with improving people's lives. Majors like "conflict management" and "community development" attract hundreds of majors per year, while the History Department struggles to retain students. My Prehistory of Kenya class started out with 20 students during a year of very high enrollment. Getting to know the class, I learned that only two of my students really wanted to do history; the rest were shut out of their favored majors like community development and education by high enrollments. After two weeks, interfaculty transfers were approved, and only four students were left in my class. One genuinely expressed admiration for history as "the reason why my world is the way it is," and the rest admitted to not having high enough scores on the national entrance test to transfer.

This has now created a fascinating debate on the role of university education in Kenya. Universities in Africa have been caught up in the struggle and debate over how the universities can contribute to "nation-building"—how can the university-trained students, destined for the elite, benefit their countries and not just themselves? At Masinde Muliro University of Science and Technology (MMUST—one of the newer universities), Vice-Chancellor Otieno says:

> In response to the current trend on the Kenyan market, MMUST has tailored courses to meet the development needs of the country. The unique courses include Ethics and Corruption Studies, Conflict Reso-

lution and Disaster Management, among others. The main objective
is to train and produce qualified personnel ready to contribute
towards capacity building for effective management of infrastructure
against disaster and sustainable development of society. (http://
www.mmust.ac.ke/index.php/welcome-message.html)

A *Daily Nation* editorial (Onyango-Obbo 2009) made fun of the new trend
toward "useful" majors, saying that degrees in political corruption would also
be advisable and "trainable" skills. (Almost in answer to the editorial,
Musinde Muliro University actually *does* offer a degree in corruption studies!)

The obvious and unavoidable problem of the Kenyan university is the
problem of ethnicity, which I found myself comparing to issues of race and
identity that often play out on American university campuses. Over the past
several decades, Kenya has shifted to a more open political system, which has
unfortunately led to ethnic and tribal violence based on colonial-era land
conflicts, engendered by political competition and let loose by hate speech
during campaigns (Osamba 2001). Twenty months before my stay more than
1,300 people were killed by interethnic violence. Egerton's presence in the Rift
Valley, the province where killings, rapes, riots, and burning villages led to
hundreds of deaths, contributes to the contentious atmosphere here. Just
beneath the relatively quiet campus atmosphere the tribal issue leaves the faculty and administration with many questions on how to approach and deal
with the problem of ethnicity on campus.

In the first few weeks of the semester and in response to student council
elections, trees and fence posts were covered with announcements of meetings, which called people from various districts, often by using tribal names,
to attend. The fliers often included messages of welcoming in tribal languages
(the use of which is actually illegal on campus). Several groups would compete for space on a single tree, announcing "urgent meeting!" Only rarely did
fliers on the official billboards in hallways and throughways advertise a club
for students with similar academic or leisure interests. I found only a handful
of these fliers—one for an economics club and one for a meeting about "negative ethnicity"—and I wondered why student activities could not be encouraged more on campus. After a couple of weeks, the tribal fliers were removed
and replaced by prominent messages from the administration reiterating that
only Kiswahili and English, Kenya's two official languages, were allowed on
campus fliers. After 24 hours someone had scrawled, "What about Gotab?"
on this official message, referencing the word for meeting among one particular ethnic group, the Kalenjin.

At a faculty meeting a discussion of writing a proposal about ethnicity led to questions about the flyers. Some wondered if the district meetings should be allowed. A few weeks later the student body held elections for about 20 officers and elected representatives for student government. Nothing could prepare me for the zeal and enthusiasm the students showed for the political process. Flyers and T-shirts were everywhere, and huge lorries plastered with candidate posters and blasting popular music moved through campus. Students told me privately that a strong tribal element shaped student voting patterns, and the groups among whom the greatest tensions existed were highly influenced by tribe in voting. The administration was considering what kind of response to take to such blatant expressions of political ethnicity. One flyer announced, "Luo! Come to vote for your preferred candidate" (Luo is one of the main ethnic groups of Kenya). After this poster was mentioned at the faculty meeting, it was removed later the same day. In its place was an administrative letter reminding students that postings were only permitted in Kiswahili or English. One faculty member commented that ethnic thinking and behavior was not learned at university but from family and community. So what was the role and responsibility of the university, especially given Kenya's history of political violence?

The problem is found at many Kenyan universities. Siringi (2009) writes that senior staff positions at many Kenyan universities are being taken almost exclusively by individuals from the dominant ethnic groups in the local areas, and that the Kenyan Union of Academic Staff has formally asked the minister of higher education to stop the trend of tribalizing universities. "We quickly fear running universities according to international standards as politicians and chancellors resort to the narrow thinking that universities should serve local communities," said Mr. Edebe, who is the Universities Academic Staff Union organizing secretary.

Certainly at American universities we have expressions of ethnicity. Minority groups in particular have student associations, and most of us believe such associations provide needed solidarity and support. So what has made ethnicity such a different discussion in the United States? On one level the difference is developmental. We already went through hundreds of years of racial hatred and violence, and Kenya is a new democracy, and the state is just beginning to define itself. Another difference might go back to the inherent individualism of American culture. The civil rights movement had as its goal the claim of individual rights regardless of color. Here in Kenya, political ethnicity is driven by a claim to superiority or entitlement on the part of groups. Political behavior here seems to be based on the collectivity and one's sense of belonging to it.

Study Questions

1. Do you think there is a university "culture" that might be found in different settings or places? What is a university culture characterized by?

2. In what ways does a university reflect the culture it is a part of, and in what ways might it challenge that culture? Or can the university experience be seen as a liminal phase, as betwixt and between, and a part of the rite of passage from childhood to adulthood?

3. What similarities exist between the Kenyan university in this chapter and your own university?

4. In what ways does the Kenyan university incubate a sense of identity based on tribe? What similar forms of social or political identity are nurtured on American campuses?

References

Atieno-Odhiambo, E. S. 2002. Historicising the Deep Past in Western Kenya. In W. R. Ochieng (ed.), *Historical Studies and Social Change in Western Kenya: Essays in Memory of Professor Gideon S. Were*. Nairobi, Kenya: East African Educational Publishers.

Buchere, D. 2009. Kenya: Loan Defaulters to Be Blacklisted. *University World News* Africa Edition, April 19, 2009. http://www.universityworldnews.com/article.php?story=20090419085039739 (Accessed Oct. 10, 2009).

Kigotho, Wachira. 2009. Is Kenya Ready for World-Class Universities? *The Standard*, Nairobi Kenya, July 1, 2009.

Onyango-Obbo, Charles. 2009. Our Varsities Need Courses on Beer, Potholes and Graft. *The Nation*, Nairobi, Kenya, September 23, 2009.

Osamba, J. O. 2001. Violence and the Dynamics of Transition: State, Ethnicity and Governance in Kenya. *Africa Development* 27: 37–54.

Siringi, S. 2009, March 21. Public Varsities Sink into the Muck of Tribalism. *African Platform—The Opinion Center*. https://groups.yahoo.com/neo/groups/africa-oped/conversations/messages/37538.

7

A Russian Teacher in America

ANDREI TOOM

This article contrasts Russian and American systems of higher education, focusing on the teaching of mathematics and the attitudes of students. Toom reveals for us some unsettling aspects of American culture, such as our excessive concern with credentials but seeming lack of concern with competence. Competition and the grading system are taken to task, as is our market orientation in learning—trying to get the highest grade for the least investment.

Andrei Toom grew up in Russia (then the Soviet Union). He taught mathematics and did research for nearly twenty years at Moscow University. He came to the United States in 1989 and taught mathematics at Rutgers University and at Incarnate Word College.

I am a Russian mathematician and teacher. For nearly 20 years I did research and taught students at Moscow University. Now I have moved to the United States, as have many other Russians. This article is about some of my experiences of teaching both in Russia and America.

Americans' ideas about Russia are as contradictory as Russia itself. For many years Soviet Russia was perceived as "The Evil Empire." On the other hand, there was a Sputnik movement in America, which claimed that the Russian educational system was much better than the American one. Obviously,

This article was originally published in the *Journal of Mathematical Behavior* and is reproduced here with permission.

these images did not fit together. A lot of effort is needed to give the real picture. I am just going to make a few comments to explain my background.

Communist rule in Russia emerged from the collapse of the obsolete Tzarist autocracy, under which most people were deprived of education. Early Communists enthusiastically sang the *"Internationale,"* which claimed: "Who was nothing will become everything." Nobody ever knew what it meant exactly, but many were excited. Many Russian revolutionaries sincerely believed that it was their mission to redress all the social injustices immediately, but ignorance crippled all their efforts. A telling example is described in the novel *Chapayev* by the Russian writer Furmanov.

The hero Chapayev, a Red Army commander, insists on giving an official certificate of competence in medicine to a poorly educated man, naively thinking that having such a certificate really makes one a doctor.

Communists made promises that looked very democratic, particularly that children of "proletarians" would be given unlimited educational opportunities. Children of manual workers and poor peasants really were given privileges to enter all kinds of schools, and professors who gave them bad grades might be accused of antirevolutionary activity. Only a generation later, Russia had thousands of hastily coached engineers and scientists of proletarian descent. One of these "proletarian scientists," an academician named Lysenko, gave fantastic agricultural promises that he never kept. However, Lysenko impressed Soviet rulers from Stalin to Khrushchev because they also were pseudoeducated. A major branch of biology, namely genetics, was declared a "bourgeois pseudoscience" because Lysenko was against it.

The ambitions of pseudoeducated "proletarian scientists," their haughtiness toward bourgeois science, their pretensions of superiority because of having had poor parents and being led by "the world's truest teaching" (that is, Marxism) caused a lot of industrial and ecological disasters. However, Communists never admitted the true causes of these disasters; all of them were attributed to some "enemies'" sabotage. A number of alleged "enemies" were arrested and reportedly confessed. Masses of people, although declared "educated" by that time, believed these reports. But disasters continued, and to explain them away the authorities needed more and more "enemies." Meanwhile, Russia became the world leader in wasted resources and polluted environment: *Chernobyl* is just one (but not unique) example.

I was 11 when Stalin died. For many years all Soviet people, especially youngsters, had been indoctrinated that they should never doubt the Communist tenets. All media had been filled with verbose praises to Stalin, who was called "the greatest genius of all times and all peoples."

However, much of Russian and foreign literature was available, including American authors. Foreign authors were published under the pretext that they "criticized bourgeois society" Mark Twain, Jack London, Ernest Seton, O. Henry, Edgar Allan Poe, Paul de Kruif, Ernest Hemingway, and Ray Bradbury were among my favorite authors.

I vividly remember reading a book about a scientist who proved that insects have no reason; they only have instinct. What he actually proved was that the behavior of insects was effective only in situations usual for them. When the experimenter artificially arranged unusual situations, the insects did the same standard movements although they evidently could not be of any use in that new situation, because it was different from those to which the insects had become accommodated through evolution. I was impressed: I understood that propaganda tried to turn us into some kind of insects. I thought then and think now that it is a most important duty of a teacher of humans to teach them to be humans; that is, to behave reasonably in unusual situations. When I taught in Russia, I was thanked most explicitly for this. But I met a lot of resistance from some of my American undergraduate students especially when I tried to give them something unexpected. On tests, they wanted to do practically the same as what they had done before—only with different numerical data. This is why I decided to write this article.

I always believed that really good education is the most valuable contribution that intellectuals of a country can make toward its democratization. Remember that the great French Revolution was prepared by the Age of Enlightenment. It was evident that the worst features of Soviet rule were connected with the power of the pseudoeducated who got their certificates for being "proletarians," but cared only for their careers. Understandably, Soviet authorities always were suspicious about independent thought and real intellectuals.

In return, good teaching, intended to develop real competence of students, always had a flavor of resistance to Soviet authorities, as it involved realism, open-mindedness, and critical thinking. When a good mathematics teacher tried to move his students to think independently, he was aware that his real influence went far beyond mathematics: He tried and succeeded to keep alive the critical spirit. Learning recipes without thinking was associated with the Communist tyranny; learning to solve nontrivial problems was associated with independence and criticism. For this reason, for example, George Pólya's writings on teaching were perceived in Russia as books on openmindedness and critical thinking rather than just on the teaching of mathematics. We knew that Pólya was not alone: He referred to other scientists, for example to Max Wertheimer's notion of "productive thinking."

In the years of Khrushchev's liberalism, some new foreign books also became available in Russia. Russian thinkers read very attentively all the foreign authors they could find. Many valuable ideas came from Americans: authoritarian personality (Theodor Adorno); group pressure (Solomon Asch); obedience to authority (Stanley Milgram). Eric Berne's *Games People Play* moved us to see which dirty games our rulers played with us. Thomas Kuhn's book about scientific revolutions was about ideological revolutions for us. Milton Rokeach's idea of open and closed minds opened our minds. John Holt's criticism of American schools made us understand that our schools deserved much harsher criticism.

My parents belonged to artistic circles, and pressure of censure [censorship] was a constant theme of conversations. If trimming a tree went too far, they would say with regret: "Look, how we have edited this tree!" Exact sciences provided the greatest available degree of independence from authorities, and my parents spoke with envy about mathematicians who could afford to say the exact truth and even be paid for it rather than punished. They could not guide my study of sciences, but they expected intellectual efforts of me, and it was important.

Later, my school teacher of mathematics, Alexander Shershevsky, helped me a lot. He strived to become a mathematician, but could not obtain a research position because in his student years he had gotten into some political trouble. (The trouble must have been minor; otherwise we would never have seen him again.) I was especially impressed by his responsible attitude to his mission. He urged me to attend informal classes in mathematics at Moscow University. The main business of these classes was solving nonstandard problems. Students were free to drop in and out; using this, I changed several groups until I found a teacher, Alexander Olevsky, whom I liked most. Every year students at Moscow University arranged a competition for high school students in solving problems. Every problem was new and unlike others and demanded a nontrivial idea and a rigorous proof to solve. There were five problems and five hours to solve them. Typically, everyone who solved at least one problem was rewarded. In this way I got several prizes. This convinced me that I could succeed as a mathematician. When I moved from high school to the mathematics department of Moscow University, solving problems naturally led me to research.

From my first year in the university I took it for granted that a competent mathematician should participate in the teaching of mathematics because I had excellent examples to follow. The famous Kolmogorov organized a mathematical college affiliated with Moscow University, and I taught there. Academician Gelfand organized a School by Correspondence, and I instructed its teachers. In the computer club I headed the teaching program.[1] Aleksandrov, Arnold, Boltyansky, Dobrushin, Dynkin, Efimov, Kirillov, Postnikov, Sinai, Tzetlin, Uspensky, the Yaglom brothers, and other first-class mathematicians were willing to lecture and to communicate with students. A lot of new and original problems from all branches of mathematics and at various levels of difficulty were invented for all kinds of students from young children to graduate students and young professionals. Now, I was among those who invented problems. When I advised Ph.D. and other students, I gave them problems that interested me, and we solved them together.

The main pressure that students put upon teachers was to tell them something new. A vivid example was Leonid Vaserstein (then a student), who would declare in the middle of a talk: "All this is trivial." Taken out of situational context this may seem impolite, but actually this was quite *productive*. He pressed lecturers for more competence. Soon he had to emigrate. (Now he is a professor at Penn State University.) His fate is typical: Top officials of Moscow University, very poor scientists but bombastic Communists, used all pretexts (notably anti-Semitism) to get rid of competent young scientists to ensure their own positions. Now, they do the same without Communist paraphernalia; they recently elected a notorious hardliner, Sadovnichy, president of Moscow University.

Whenever the purpose of learning was real competence, it had nothing to do with good standing with the authorities, who were feared and despised by intellectuals. Grades were just a nuisance, like any extraneous control. For example, when I taught in the college organized by Kolmogorov, I simply gave an A to every student because all of them deserved A according to average Russian standards, and I wanted to save them the trouble of dealing with the authorities. But they knew perfectly well that we expected much more of them than of the average student, and they worked very hard.

Every advanced school, where independent and creative thought was cultivated, became a breeding ground for political dissent. The mathematics department of Moscow University was no exception. From time to time there were political clashes, and I took part in them. This caused me problems with the Soviet authorities and eventually led to my emigration.

Most of my sixty publications are in mathematics; the others pertain to education and humanities. Not one article of the latter part was published as I wanted it, because of censure [censorship] restrictions. Most of them would never have been published without the willingness of a particular editor to take a certain, well-calculated risk. Whenever I brought an article to the newspaper *Izvestia*, my cautiously courageous editor, Irina Ovchinnikova, exclaimed: "Oh, Andrei, do you really think that this is publishable?" And she had to cross out the most critical statements to save the others.

My research in mathematics could not improve my position in the university because Communist bureaucrats always (and correctly) understood that I would never *solidarize* with them. The adviser of my Ph.D., Ilya Piatetski-Shapiro, emigrated to Israel and thereby became *persona non grata* for the Soviet establishment: Even referring to his papers was not easy. My papers were known abroad, but were not recognized as anything valuable by my supervisor, because I gave him too few chances to appropriate my work. I received several invitations from foreign universities, but the authorities never allowed me to go abroad. Only by chance, I got to Italy in 1989 and decided to accept all the invitations I had, without going back and subjecting myself to the same arbitrariness. From Rome I went to Rutgers University, then to other American universities.

It is a common opinion that the United States of America supports democracy. Democracy always was connected in my mind with good education for all people, and I knew that American thinkers also believed in this connection. Thus, when I came to this country, I expected to have rich opportunities to teach students to think critically, independently, and creatively and to solve nonstandard problems without hindrance from authorities.

My first experience in teaching in this country did not contradict this expectation. It was proposed that I give a course called "Analysis of Algorithms" to graduate students of the computer science department of Boston University (BU). The textbook *Introduction to Algorithms* by Cormen, Leiserson, and Rivest was excellent. The department applied to me a wise rule—to give full freedom to the lecturer—and I used it to the benefit of my students as I understood it. In one semester I covered most of that rich book. I believe that the mathematical introduction was especially useful: I filled many gaps in my students' former education. My nineteen students came from all over the globe, and most of them collaborated with each other in an excellent way. After every lecture they came to one room, discussed the problems that I gave them, and solved them together. Some problems I gave them were from the book; some were invented by me. I tried to miss no opportunity to make my students think, and they accepted it. Also there was no problem with grades. The department gave me *carte blanche,* and I used it benevolently: Almost all of my students learned a great deal, and I rewarded them with good grades.

But in the next year, when I came to a huge state university and started to teach the so-called business calculus[2] to undergraduates, I got into an absolutely new situation. All my ideas about teaching students to think became completely out of place. Never before had I seen so many young people in one place who were so reluctant to meet challenges and to solve original problems. All they wanted were high grades, and they wanted to get them with a conveyor belt regularity. Suppose that a worker at a conveyor belt gets inspired by some interesting idea and tries to implement it into his work. You can guess that he will get into trouble. This is what happened to me when I started to teach American undergraduates.

In my student years, I hated teachers who simply repeated textbooks: It seemed to me that they wasted my time. Naturally, as a teacher, I avoided that practice. This worked well until the last year, when I started to teach business calculus. Then I found quite a different attitude among my students: Many of them would be most satisfied if the teacher simply repeated and explained what was written in the textbook. It seems that some of them have problems in reading by themselves what is written there, although most textbooks are quite elementary (but verbose). At first I failed to understand this, and one student wrote about me: "He should teach from the text and give exams based on the text or similar problems."

The voluminous book I had to use in teaching the business calculus course may impress nonprofessionals, for example, parents of students. Its chapters are named after really important mathematical theories. But everything nontrivial is carefully eliminated. In fact, every chapter contains a recipe, as in a cookbook, and problems do not go beyond straightforward applications of the recipe. The book carefully avoids connecting the material of different chapters, presenting the subject from different sides, giving problems in which a student should choose which method to apply. And this book was chosen among others, some of which were quite usable. Why? I see one explanation: Because this book perfectly fits the *max-min* principle of the market: maximal pretensions with minimal content. All the other textbooks are not so perfect in this respect.

I was astonished by the fact that I could find absolutely no nonstandard problems in the textbook. But I said to myself: This is a good case for me to show what I can do! *I can* invent nonstandard problems! And so I *did!* And my first test was a total failure. It turned out to be so difficult for the students that most of them got very low grades. I had to learn that every technical calculation, which I was used to ignoring, was a considerable obstacle for my students. It took a considerable amount of time for me to understand how poor they were in basic algebraic calculations. Every time I prepared another test, I tried to make it as easy as possible, and still several times I failed: The tests turned out to be too difficult. As time went on, I came to the following rule: As long as a problem was interesting for me, it was too difficult for the students; only when a problem became trivial, might it be given in the test.

It was good luck for me that one of the students auditing my precalculus course, Robert Tufts, was a retired engineer who had lived much in Europe and Japan and had an extensive experience of learning and teaching. For him my style of teaching was not unusual; in fact, he liked it and told other students about it. Thus, they chose the label, "European teacher," for me, and this softened their shock. Still, another student wrote:

> Please inform Mr. Toom about the grading system and instruction methods of THIS country. Mr. Toom assumes that his students were taught as he was. I earned a grade of A in my college algebra and trigonometry courses so it makes no sense for me to be doing so poorly in this course. Please straighten this man out.

In the next semester I straightened myself out: At every lecture I took the textbook into my hand and explained some examples from it. And nobody complained.

As I had often done before, I gave out to students lists of additional problems arranged by me, and as before, these problems were useful as they moved many students to think. But I had not got used to caring about grades, and this time grades—not math problems—were the center of attention. My carelessness created a lot of trouble for myself and for the department. Those students who solved my problems wanted extra credit, while those who did not solve them wanted full credit also. Several times I was called to the official in charge to clarify my grading system. In the next semester I decided not to give any extra-credit problems, and no trouble arose. The less I teach, the less trouble I have. In Russia we used to joke: No initiative will remain unpunished. Now I saw this rule working in American education.

I had to learn by trial and error how much of elementary mathematics was taboo in the business calculus course. It took a while before I realized that

I was lecturing about exponential functions to students who were not required to know about geometrical progressions. Also I confused my business calculus students by trying to explain errors in the textbook. Many of them would prefer to accept every word of it without criticism.

Another mistake made by me was to include a trigonometrical function in a test problem. I could not imagine that students who take "calculus" were not supposed to know trigonometry, but it was the case. Of course, I was called to the official in charge and rebuked. Thus, I could discuss the equation $y'' - y = 0$, but not $y'' + y = 0$. In addition, I received a telephone call from someone who had graduated from the school of law; referring to a decision made by the authorities, he accused me of wasting taxpayers' money by teaching students what they did not need to know (trigonometry). After several lapses of this sort, the department decided not to invite me for the next year, although they knew that I was a competent scholar, that I was interested in teaching, and that I needed a position. All they wanted was not to have problems with the students.

I noticed that research mathematicians treat the business calculus courses like Russians treated Communist meetings: Nobody dares to criticize openly, but everybody tries to sneak away. That is why foreign lecturers such as myself are needed to do this dirty job. But foreigners adjust to the system pretty soon, so that American students have almost no chances of becoming aware of their ignorance. For me, a few months were sufficient: The pressure from those students who wanted good grades with minimal learning, which was supported by university officials, made me care more about my safety from complaints and less about the real competence of my students.

One foreigner, experienced in teaching Americans, advised me in a friendly manner "Listen, don't ask for trouble. Education in this country is not our concern. Nobody will care if you fall short of the syllabus, but never go beyond."[3] And he went home with dollars earned honestly; that is, by doing to Americans just what they—both students and officials—wanted him to do. Of course, he teaches in a much more productive way in his own country.

Suppose you fly in a plane. What is more important for you: the pilot's real competence or his papers that certify he is competent? Or suppose you get sick and need medical treatment. What is more important for you: your doctor's real competence or his diploma? Of course, in every case the real competence is more important. But last year I met a large group of people whose priorities were exactly the opposite: my students. Not all, but many. Their first priority was to get papers that certify that they are competent rather than to develop real competence. As soon as I started to explain to them something that was a little bit beyond the standard courses, they asked suspiciously: "Will this be on the test?" If I said, "no," they did not listen anymore and showed clearly that I was doing something inappropriate.

I had to learn also that American students want to be told exactly from the very beginning of the course what percentages of the total score comes from homework, from tests, and from quizzes. First I thought that it was some nonsense, as if I were requested to predict how many commas and colons I would use in a paper I was going to write. But later I understood that these percentages make sense for those students who do not care about the subject and take a course just to get a grade with minimal learning.

Of course, students are different. Many really want to learn, because curiosity is inherent in human nature. But selfless curiosity is illegal (at least in the business calculus course) in the sense that it is neither expected nor supported officially. On the contrary, officials cater to those who want to learn as little as possible, and percentages are a telling example of this.

It seems that some parents urge their offspring to get high grades by any means, but fail to add that they care about actual competence, too. I understand that some students are the first in their families to get a higher education. Their parents did monotonous work all their lives, tried to make more money for less work and were right, of course. Now, their offspring do monotonous exercises at universities, try to make more grades for less work, and nobody in the family sees anything wrong with it. Indeed, parents may perceive this as a great achievement when their offspring graduates, and they may think that they now have an "intellectual" in the family, while this is simply someone who bought a discounted degree at a university sale! Discounted not in the sense of money, but in the sense of intellectual effort and development.

The grade looks like the ultimate value, and neither students, nor parents, nor university officials see anything wrong with this. In fact, all officials completely support the top priority of official records. It seems to be generally taken for granted that students normally learn as little as possible for a certain grade. Only by a misunderstanding may they learn more, and when this happens due to an undetailed syllabus, they blame the teacher like people who blame an official whose neglect caused them a loss.

It is the basic principle of the market that everybody tries to get as much as possible and to pay as little as possible. There is nothing wrong with this: When I buy something, I try to save money, and everybody does the same. What is wrong is that some students apply the same rule to learning: They seem to think that they *buy* grades and *pay* for them by learning. And they try *to pay* as little as possible! In other words, some students seem to think that it is a loss whenever they learn something. This looks crazy when put in such straightforward terms, but there are students who behave as if they think this way. (I do not know what they really think.) And there are officials who take this behavior as normal and arrange the learning environment according to it.

The attitude "learn as little as possible" is not totally wrong, however, because a good deal of the stuff students are taught indeed deserves minimization (business calculus, for example). A good deal, but not all—there are excellent books and teachers—but many students are not sophisticated enough to discriminate.

After every test, I explained correct solutions. Many a student said: "Now I understand." I was glad: The purpose of my teaching was achieved. But some said it with regret, which meant: "This understanding is useless because it came too late to provide me a good grade." To me, tests were just a means to promote understanding; to them understanding was just a means to get a good grade. To some students it made no sense to understand anything after the test.

Some students are so busy and anxious counting points on tests and predicting grades that they have no "mental room" left to think about mathematics. It seems even irrelevant both for them and for the university whether they have learned anything at all: What matters for both sides is that the students overcame another barrier on their obstacle race toward graduation (and wasted some more months of their young and productive years).

At one lecture I wrote a theorem on the blackboard and said to the students: "Look what a beautiful theorem it is!" Some laughed. I asked what was the matter. Then one explained: "Professor, it is nonsense, a theorem cannot be beautiful!" And I understood that these poor devils, who had always learned under the lash of grades, never from natural curiosity, really could not imagine that an abstraction might be beautiful.

Any creative activity (including learning) needs at least temporary independence from external rewards and pressures. Peaks of creativity (which are essential in learning and solving nontrivial problems) need so much concentration on the subject that any sticks and carrots can only disturb them. Only when the intimate work of creative faculties is over and has produced a finished result, may one think how to sell this result most profitably. Pushkin, a Russian poet, said: "Inspiration is not for sale, but a manuscript may be sold." The same applies to learning: Those who lack intrinsic motivation and are guided only by external rewards, learn poorly. They are never carried away by the subject's charm for its own sake, as they believe that they must be "practical"; that is, never forget their points and grades. As a result they never use the powerful potential of creativity given to them by nature. Everybody's natural abilities are rich, but their use depends on individual priorities.

It seems that some students just cannot imagine that learning might be of intrinsic value, besides official graduation. And they might go through many years of schooling, communicate with teachers and officials, graduate from an elementary school, middle school, high school, and a university, and never have a chance to question this! Unless they meet some irritating foreigner!

Foreigners, however, soon understand that to survive in this country they have to adjust to the system rather than to criticize it. At various levels and in various ways, newcomers are shown clearly that this country wants intellectuals, but not those who are too independent. This may be one reason why so many immigrants who were excellent mathematics teachers in Russia have done much less than their best to reform American education.

In my case, pretty soon the pressure from students made me deviate from my principle to do my best: I was forced to care about my safety from students' complaints at the expense of their own best interests. Although my personal experience is limited, I think that this situation is typical. In another state, students complained about their mathematics teacher, another newcomer from Russia: "We pay as much as others, but have to know more than they for the same grade." Still in another state, another newcomer from Russia found an effective way to calm his students; when they asked how he would give them grades, he answered that he would do it "on the curve." I asked him what he meant, and he answered that he did not know: What mattered for him was that the students got relaxed and became willing to listen to lectures and solve problems.

Well, I can imagine a situation in which learning for a grade makes sense. If students are ultimately disappointed with the teacher, if they have given up any hope of learning anything valuable from him, if they not only disrespect, but actually despise him—then, and only then, it makes sense to learn for a grade—to get at least this if there is nothing better to get. In the final analysis, learning for a grade is the deepest offense to the teacher, because it implies the thought: "I know in advance that nothing valuable will come from real contact with the teacher; so let me at least get a grade." But, according to my experience, students who learn for grades do it in all courses. They seem not to be aware that they offend teachers; they simply take this mode of behavior for granted. (And most American teachers and officials also take it for granted.)

At one of my lectures on business calculus, when asked why I gave problems unlike those in the book, I answered: "Because I want you to know elementary mathematics." I expected to convince students by this answer. In Moscow, a university student who was told that he or she did not know elementary mathematics, got confused and checked into the matter immediately. Elementary mathematics was normally taught to children who looked like children. Now imagine my astonishment when right after my answer, an imposing train of well-grown adults stood up and tramped out. They decided (correctly) that they could graduate from the university without knowing elementary mathematics. And they knew that they would easily find a lecturer who would teach them from the text.

And the one who had to change was me. In the next semester, I never scared students away by checking into basics. I understood perfectly that teaching an advanced subject like calculus without filling gaps in basics was like building on sand. But I could not afford to care about my students because I had to care about my safety from their complaints.

I have examined the American Constitution and found no statement that guarantees the right of ignorance for students. Nevertheless, some students behave as if such a statement existed. And some officials behave as if they had no other choice than to comply with them. Why? One official explained to me that some students had sued universities for better grades and won. (I have never heard of a student who sued a university for better or more knowledge.) Now the main concern of officials is not to have this trouble again. One evident result of this is that bright students lose a lot of opportunities to learn more, but they never complain (regretfully), and officials do not need to care about them.

I do not propose to put all the blame on students. In fact, their priorities reflect the cynicism of educators who design courses not for the sake of students' best interests, but for other aims: for example, to put another artificial obstacle in their way, to keep teachers busy, etc. The business calculus course seems to be deliberately designed just as an obstacle for those who want to graduate in the business school.

I understand that I have very little experience with the bulk of the Russian population. Most of my students in Moscow were children of intellectuals, because in Russia (as in most countries) a much smaller percentage of youngsters than in the United States go into higher education. In fact, what is going on in America is an experiment: to give higher education to those strata of society which remain deprived of it in most other countries. My concern is that this should be really an education, not an imitation.

I was astonished to find that many of my American colleagues, although very competent as scientists and quite decent as persons, had absolutely different ideas about education and teaching than I had. When I spoke to them about education, they answered something like: "This is not my concern. There are special people to care about all that," as if I spoke about some important but remote activity. According to my experience, the prevailing attitude among American mathematicians is to avoid teaching. When these American mathematicians say that they have a "good position," this typically means that *they do not have to teach.* And if a mathematician with (substantiated or not) research ambitions has to teach, he often tries to do it as mechanically as possible. And students take this for granted, and they try to learn as mechanically as possible. The result is a tit-for-tat between teachers and students, which may reduce mathematical education to wasteful bureaucratic mirages. And the system (as any system) is robust: If a recent immigrant, inexperienced in American ways, happens to be different (for example, to love teaching), he or she does not fit into the system and only causes troubles.[4]

The attitudes of some mathematicians toward teaching form a perfect counterpart to the attitudes of some students toward learning. Some, but not all. It certainly is not exciting to teach those who invest more efforts into pushing for grades than for understanding. But, on the other hand, students as a whole are not nearly as hopeless as some smug teachers pretend.[5] It is true that there are a few nasty students who can put anybody off teaching, and it is true that some indifferent bureaucrats prefer to yield to their pressures (at the expense of those who want to learn). But in every course there are students who are really interested, and I think that these students are the most valuable. In every one of my courses there were students who were excited by those very nontrivial problems that moved others to complain. My former students came to my office to thank me. They said that after my course the next courses were easy for them. Some asked if I was expected to teach something in the next year and advised me to publish the problems I had invented. But bright students never complain (regretfully), and officials do not care about them. More than once I had to say to one student or another: "You did very well in my course, and I gave you an A. But this does not mean much, because what I teach you is not really mathematics."

Some people excuse bad teaching by saying: Since students buy it, it is OK to sell it. But pushers of drugs say the same. It is the responsibility of specialists to do the right things even if laymen cannot discriminate between right and wrong. It is the responsibility of teachers to teach in a way that really develops students' intellect. Imagine that a noneducated person is sick. Is it fair to prescribe him a fake medicine just because he cannot tell it from a good one? Of course not: This is not only inhuman, but also dangerous for the reputation of the medical profession. The same about teaching: Fake teaching is unfair and breeds anti-intellectualism. The moral status of those who designed the business calculus course is like that of colonial-time hucksters who sold cheap beads, mirrors, and "firewater" to ignorants, whose role is now played by students. (I do not blame rank-and-file teachers, because many have no choice.)

For many years, the Soviet authorities tried in vain to reduce scientists' concerns to their job and were irritated when someone interfered with public affairs. Sakharov is the most well-known example of a Russian scientist directly involved with politics, but I am sure that educational efforts of many others were equally important. In this respect, the free American job market seems to intimidate dissenters more effectively than Soviet despots ever could: Most American mathematicians try to deal with education as little as possible, because of the existing system of rewards.

Most students are young people. They are not yet quite mature, and their priorities are in the process of formation. Every school not only teaches particular subjects, but also suggests certain ideas of what learning and mental activity should be. In the present situation, the idea most often promoted by authorities is that official records are the most important results of learning. Many students are not independent enough to defend themselves against this bad influence and get phony education at the expense of real time and money. Their motivation shrinks to external sticks and carrots, and they fail to develop independence from external rewards of the social system.

I love to start my courses at the precalculus level by asking students to vote on the following question:

> Take the infinite decimal fraction 0.999. . . . [T]hat is zero, then decimal point, then an infinite row of nines. Is this fraction less than or equal to one?

Often the majority votes that the fraction is less than one. Then I ask, how much less, and students give different answers according to which calculators they use. This starts a useful discussion in which all the students participate because they feel that this really pertains to them. Every student tries to prove that his answer is correct, which allows me to convince them that all are wrong: This fraction equals one.

You may ask me: Why do I start my courses by provoking students into making a wrong decision in such a dramatic form? Because it is absolutely necessary for a teacher to keep his or her students alert and critical of themselves. If I simply informed my students that this fraction equals one, they would easily agree, but forget it by the next lecture. This is just one example. In fact, when I teach as I want, I try systematically to show that something that seems evident may be wrong. Experience of this sort, I believe, is essential as a psychological prerequisite for studying rigorous mathematics. In Russia, students were delighted whenever I succeeded to bamboozle them. Even children understood that it was a pedagogical device to make their knowledge and thinking more robust. My graduate students at BU also were excited when I proved that no algorithm can solve the sorting problem in linear time and right after that presented an algorithm that seemed to do this.

This is understandable: Wise nature has made people, especially young people, in such a way that they love challenges. That is why people (especially children) enjoy performances of magicians whose job is to cheat. Many love mysteries and detective stories whose authors intentionally mislead the reader. Why shouldn't the teacher use the same device? Creative students are happy to meet something puzzling or misleading, because it gives them a chance to become tougher as thinkers.

But many undergraduate students are oversensitive to everything that they perceive as a failure, even a small one. Whenever intonations of my voice led them in a wrong direction, students took it as a violation of some gentlemen's rules. It looks like some American students cannot afford the natural human love for intellectual challenges because of the pressures of grades and formal records. If the teacher's recommendations do not lead them straight to the right answer, they perceive it as the teacher's fault, not as a pedagogical device. But with this attitude one cannot develop intellectual independence.

Some seem to think that they should be perfect from the very beginning, and if they are not, this is a fatal failure—like an incurable disease. They seem to feel obliged to give the right answer as quickly as cowboys shoot in Westerns, and if they miss, they just feel themselves to be losers and have no ways to deliberately and systematically develop themselves.

Officially, certain prerequisites are requested for every course. I wanted to check students' actual prerequisites and found that many of them could not solve simple, almost arithmetical, problems.

I included in my courses a problem that I had solved in middle school:

Tom and Dick can do a job in two hours. Tom and Harry can do the same job in three hours. Dick and Harry can do the same job in four hours. How long will it take for all three of them to do this job?

This problem can be solved by elementary algebra and a few arithmetical calculations. Most of my students could not solve it. One of them wrote the following system of equations:

$$T + D = 2, T + H = 3, D + H = 4$$

The student got a bad grade and asked me why. I asked in return, which parameters she meant by T, D, and H—time or something else. She said that she meant no parameters, just Tom, Dick, and Harry. I replied: "This is illiterate." A Russian student would grasp the chance to learn something new, but the American took this as a fatal failure, left the room with tears in her eyes, and dropped from my course. I regret this even now, but what else could I say?

This case is typical in the sense that many students avoid discussing their mistakes; it looks like a useless pain for them. If you learn for competence, which is valuable for you as such, you can benefit from your mistakes. But if you learn for grades and your self-esteem completely depends on external evaluations, it is plain masochism to keep in mind lost opportunities.

At the last lecture of my business calculus course, I gave a problem:

When 1,000 pounds of cucumbers were brought to the shop, they contained 99 percent water. But while they were kept unsold, some water evaporated, and the percentage of water dropped to 98 percent. How many pounds do they weigh now?

The students grabbed their calculators, but seemed not to know what to calculate. After a while, one produced a complicated and wrong answer. And it was pretended that these students had learned to solve differential equations! Of course, they had not! All they had learned was to follow a few recipes without thinking—a bright start for their careers!

Well, let us admit that most people can manage without being able to solve differential equations. But why did the students waste their time? The syllabus, the textbook, all the course design aped those for future professionals, but with one *small* change: applying recipes instead of solving problems. But this change annihilated the whole enterprise.

Thus, students lost several months, but had not learned to solve any problems at all, because to solve problems means to think productively, that is, to produce ideas that are not given in advance. And this is what they were completely deprived of.

The problems given above should be solved in high school or even middle school. Solving problems like these and writing down the solutions are a valuable experience of productive formal thinking that is hardly avoidable for every man or woman in modern civilization. All normal teenagers have brains mature enough to solve such problems, and those who solve them at 14 really can learn calculus at 18. But most of my students seemed to have no such experience. What had they done throughout their many years of schooling?

It seems that to a great extent they had filled in boxes, that is to say, chosen the right answer among several ready-made ones. Multiple-choice tests are convenient because their results are easy to process. This seems to be the main reason why such tests are so often used. Perhaps such tests give valuable information to educators, but they grossly limit students' initiative, fragment their activity, and deprive them of self-organizational experience.

Suppose that you are an average student. If you write solutions, even wrong ones, you can analyze them and learn something from your mistakes. But if you just put tallies into boxes, you don't remember why you made the choice; so you cannot analyze your mistakes and cannot benefit from them. All you hope is that your conditional reflexes will gradually improve, but you cannot control this process, like an animal in a problem box.

Well, better late than never, that is why I gave the problems mentioned above to my students. But I could not give more than just a few problems of this sort, because I had to follow the syllabus.

Nowadays, throughout the world, every youngster is assigned to learn some mathematics, but most of those who are in charge of this huge enterprise cannot explain in reasonable terms what all this is for and what is meant by "mathematics" in this context. What is the purpose of mathematical education for those many who will not become professional mathematicians? This is an enormously important question, but too comprehensive to discuss here in detail. Let us at least understand that it has no straightforward utilitarian answer. Very little of mathematics is used by most people in their work or other activities. Managers and lawyers, social workers and police officers, drivers and farmers, politicians and officials, doctors and nurses, cooks and barbers, writers and artists, sportspeople, businesspeople, salespeople and showpeople do not solve quadratic equations, do not use set theory, the theory of numbers, functions or algorithms, analytical or projective geometry, and do not differentiate or integrate.

Please, do not think that I am *against* teaching mathematics. I am *for* it. What I want to emphasize is that a teacher should never expect that students will have a chance to apply recipes literally. If you teach nothing but recipes, you teach nothing. This is especially true when teaching such an abstract subject as mathematics: It makes sense only when it is teaching one to think, to learn, and to solve problems. When this takes place, teaching mathematics may be enormously useful for everybody.[6] Here (as elsewhere in this paper) I do not pretend that my opinions are original. A lot has been said in the same vein, for example: "In mathematics 'know-how' is the ability to solve problems, and it is much more important than mere possession of information."[7]

But thinking and solving nontrivial problems are conspicuous by their absence in many developmental courses. (Nobody knows what these courses actually develop.) Many courses of mathematics in liberal arts settings are made up by the following simple rule: Take the professional course, keep the shell, and eliminate the kernel. That is, keep the pretensions, terms, even some formulations, but eliminate everything that needs thinking. At first sight, it may seem easy to avoid this, because there are lots of problems in various textbooks; solving these problems would certainly benefit students much more than business calculus, which is neither business nor calculus. But this won't do because of the market pressures. Suppose that some author writes a textbook with problems that need thinking for their solution, and some college gives a course using this book. Instead of learning recipes with bombastic labels, students who take this course will have to adopt the modesty that is required for concentrating on the real difficulties of a subject. The college will have to admit that its students simply learn to solve some mathematical problems and thereby just become more intelligent. Which parents will send their offspring to it? Which firm will hire the students? What will they boast of?

To survive against competition, every university and every college has to pretend that it gives something modern, advanced, and immediately marketable. But is it possible to give advanced courses to students who are ignorant in elementary mathematics? Of course not. What to do? Very simple! Emasculate the course by excluding everything nontrivial, reduce the students' task to applying ready-made recipes without understanding—and you will survive and succeed. Your pretensions that you teach something advanced will allow the students to pretend that they are educated, and this will allow the firms and departments that hire them to pretend that they hired educated people. But at some point, this chain of pretensions will have to break.

The American ability to get things done has become proverbial. The question is what should be done. I have no panacea, but I invite Americans to at least see the problem. Many seem not to see any problem at all. I tried to figure out what political leaders of this country think about the quality of education and concluded that they think nothing about it. They speak of giving everyone an opportunity to obtain an education, but they say nothing about the quality of that education.

Now many Americans say: "We have won the Cold War." This is wrong. The Soviet rulers certainly lost the Cold War, but this does not yet mean that Americans won. The Soviet bureaucrats lost because they lived in the lunatic world of "advantages of the Soviet system," "Soviet type of democracy," "building of Communism," "enthusiasm of the Soviet people," and other slogans of their own propaganda. Lack of realism, fear of any independent opinion, enormous discrepancy between reality and official versions undermined the Soviet rule. Much can and will be said about the collapse of the Soviet Union, but I am sure that the dominance of bureaucratic fictions at the expense of reality certainly played a major role.

Regretfully, all the same can be said about some part of American education. There are people among students, their parents, teachers, and officials who do not understand what education is about. They anchor their aspirations and priorities to the bureaucratic form rather than to the substance of culture. Let me repeat that there is nothing special about Americans in this respect. There are lots of countries where the average education is worse than in America (in Russia, for example).

There is rule *by* the people in America, but not always *for* the people. People command to the intellectuals, in a sovereign way, something like the following: "Give certificates of competence to our offspring without any delay! And don't waste taxpayers' money by teaching students too much! And don't you dare to discriminate against ignorant ones." Intellectuals obey implicitly and give out bombastic graduation papers with an open hand. Everybody is glad: Scientists return to their research having paid as little effort and attention to teaching as possible. Bunches of youngsters get impressive certificates that are the most marketable results of their studies. Parents have realized their dream to "educate" their children. Some of the richest and smartest parents are also glad: They find special ways for their children to get *real* education, so their future is ensured. But what about the future of others? Is it ensured as well?

Those who learn for grades expect to succeed in their business. *Today* they are right insofar as almost every American who has a degree, however ignorant, can live better than even competent people in much poorer countries around the world. A person with a diploma should not fail to find a job in his or her field of competence: This is a common belief in this country. But this cannot last long in the situation when "competence" and a diploma tautologically mean each other. The advantages enjoyed by Americans are the results of real competence and real efforts of previous generations, whose heritage is now getting devaluated as a result of the bureaucratic character of the educational system. And someday, ignorant people with degrees and diplomas may want power according to their papers rather than their real competence. We Russians have some experience of this sort, and it is not unique. In all countries (including America) activists of ignorance try to dictate their will to universities, and sometimes they succeed—at the expense of those who really want to learn.

How much of American education really develops students' competence and how much—like business calculus—comes to pretentious trivialities? I don't yet know. And I don't know who knows. I am learning about it by experience, and it will take a long time to learn. But it is clear to me right now that the winners in the modern world will be those countries that will really teach their students to think and to solve problems. I sincerely wish America to be among these.

Study Questions

1. What were some critical problems in postrevolutionary Russia once education was opened to the children of "proletarians"?

2. What does Professor Toom believe the first duty of a teacher to be? Why did he find resistance to this in Russia?

3. What had incompetent Russian scientists traditionally done to rid themselves of competent young scholars?

4. What are the basic faults that Professor Toom finds with the attitudes and expectations of American university students?

5. What happened to this "European teacher" when he attempted to teach his students to think?

6. What distinctions does the author make between competence and the American value of high grades at minimal effort? What are the dynamic consequences of such values in learning?

7. What are Professor Toom's sincerest wishes for the focus of American education?

Notes

[1] Many thinkers were read with interest in our club. Reading Seymour Papert's *Mindstorms*, we thought: "If small children are taught to think with such care in America, they must develop into tremendously competent university students."

[2] Full title: *Calculus II for Business and Economics.*

[3] Remember that throughout my business calculus course, I never went beyond into something more advanced; I simply tried to cover up gaps in my students' basic knowledge. And exactly this caused all the trouble.

[4] Most advertisements about positions request what they call "commitment to excellence in teaching," especially teaching undergraduates. But what does it mean: commitment to teach thinking or commitment to waste one's time for pseudoteaching? And according to my experience, if an applicant claims that he or she loves teaching, he or she only moves others to think that he or she is failing in his or her efforts to do research.

[5] A typical game (in Berne's sense): "It is profanity to make such a genius as I am, waste my precious time on teaching."

[6] One small example of a successful solution of a practical problem: Once my daughter (who was 12) needed a dictionary, and we went to a bookstore. She chose one but could not find any printed indication of the number of words it contained. Then she chose a page that looked typical, counted the number of words in it, looked at the number of the last page, rounded both numbers to the first digit and mentally multiplied them. Thus in a few seconds, she obtained an adequate estimate of what she needed. I was delighted. This may be called "mathematical common sense." What a contrast with most of my business calculus students who were helpless without their calculators and without a detailed instruction of what to do and in which order!

[7] George Pólya, *In the Curriculum for Prospective High School Teachers.*

8

Life and Cultures
The Test of Real
Participant Observation

E. L. Cerroni-Long
EASTERN MICHIGAN UNIVERSITY

Studying other cultures from afar, from books and in the classroom, should prepare one for the contrastive principles of living in a new culture. However, when Professor Cerroni-Long, an Asian Studies scholar from Italy, visited Japan, she discovered that intellectual preparation does not protect one from culture shock. For her the need to understand, to lend predictability to the cross-cultural encounter, became a necessity for mental equilibrium. The conscious application of cultural anthropological techniques provided her with the foundations for both survival and understanding.

From having earned a PhD in Anthropology at an American university, in combination with her experiences in many other cultural settings, Professor Cerroni-Long is able to explore some American culture patterns from an entirely different perspective.

E. L. Cerroni-Long is a professor of Anthropology at Eastern Michigan University in Ypsilanti. She was born and raised in Italy, where she received a Doctorate in Oriental Studies from the University of Venice (1970). She was a postdoctoral student at the University of Kyoto, Japan, from 1970 to 1972. She received a PhD in Anthropology from UCLA in 1986. Dr. Cerroni-Long specializes in the study of intercultural relations and in the last twenty years has conducted research in various areas of Europe, Asia, and North America.

One of the students in my field methods class—slightly exasperated by the seeming intricacies of the ethnographic enterprise—said it best: "It's easy for you to be an anthropologist! . . . You are a *foreigner!*" Indeed, I have been a foreigner much of my life, and I consider myself a "professional stranger," not just because of my disciplinary specialization but truly as a result of life experiences that came about quite fortuitously but that I think have contributed in a crucial way to the depth of my anthropological perspective.

Growing up in northern Italy, in a family of artists and scholars passionately dedicated to the study of Italian intellectual traditions, I had a limited experience of "foreignness." Italy is an ethnically homogeneous society, poor enough not to attract—until recently—any sizable groups of immigrants from abroad and bourgeois enough to create extremely effective regional and occupational cleavages, so that differences in behavior are seldom experienced within one's own social circle. When differences do arise, they can be easily explained away. Actually, my own extended family harbored sharp regional differences—with my father's side being committedly Roman, my mother's side just as adamantly Friulian, and various other members having allegiances to the Venetian region in which we lived. But I always attributed the continuous conflict in styles of behavior to personality factors or simply to the tiresome unpredictability of grown-ups, and I spent little time analyzing it. I was too busy dreaming of faraway times and places—Asia, ancient Arabia, Africa—places I had never visited but with which I felt a great affinity, possibly having been inspired by family lore of glorious colonial experiences in Libya, by the exotic Northern African heirlooms I played with as a child, or by the intangible but very real "Oriental" flavor one can still find in Venetian architecture, art, history, and traditions.

Also, coming of age in the heady 1960s, when the West was enthusiastically rediscovering the "wisdom of the East," I could strengthen my interest in Eastern civilizations with a growing appreciation for their aesthetic and spiritual expressions. I can now see that my love for Zen Buddhism was stimulated by the prose of Alan Watts, my understanding of Islamic civilization was built on Burton's and Lawrence's descriptions, and my fascination with Indian thought was heavily dependent on Eliade's popularizations. But, my interest in Eastern civilizations was genuine, and when the time came to choose a graduate program of study, I was very excited to enter the newly created "Oriental Institute" of the University of Venice. There I spent several blissful years exploring all sorts of arcane areas of knowledge, with the freedom of choice and the instructional guidance that are the mark of truly outstanding academic programs. As time went by, I restricted my interest to the "Buddhist area" of Asian civilization, and later I decided to specialize in Japanese studies, writing a dissertation on the relationship between certain aspects of contemporary Japanese literature and the Japanese philosophical tradition. When I obtained my doctorate, in 1970, I felt I was quite knowledgeable about Japan, and when I received a two-year research scholarship to be pursued at the University of Kyoto, I left Italy without the slightest doubt about my ability to adjust easily to my research setting and to work on my project—the analysis of Japanese social change through literary expressions—easily and successfully.

Discovering Anthropology

It took all of three days in Japan, the time necessary for me to make my way to the foreign researchers' dormitory to which my sponsors had assigned me, to change my outlook in a most dramatic way. My excitement about exploring "the Orient" started to dim by the time the plane landed at the Hong Kong airport, on its last stopover before reaching Japan. I had been flying for many hours and tiredness was certainly affecting me, but I remember looking around the transit lounge and having the distinct feeling of being on a different planet. It was not just that the physical appearance of the majority of the people surrounding me was so markedly different from what I was used to, it was also that they acted so strange! To begin with, so many people were squatting down—rather than sitting or standing—that I automatically scrutinized the floor to see if they were looking for something. Also, it disturbed my sense of propriety that so many people had taken off their shoes or were wearing them as if they were sandals, their feet halfway in and with the heels flattened out. Above all, though, I could not shake the feeling that people's gestures, their facial expressions, the interpersonal distances they kept, and the overall noise level their interactions created were somehow "all wrong."

Things did not get any better when I finally arrived in Japan and spent a short orientation period in Tokyo before proceeding toward my assigned destination, Kyoto. The fact that people seemed to have the greatest difficulty in understanding what I thought was fluent Japanese puzzled and irritated me— I discovered only much later that I was using linguistic expressions as obsolete as Chaucerian English. But what I kept finding most disturbing was the general noise level characterizing public places, the size and density of the crowds, and the frequency with which people waiting for a bus, using a public phone, or simply hanging out would adopt a squatting position.

By the time I finally made it to my room in Kyoto, exhausted by the long trip and in the grip of what I later came to recognize as a classic case of severe culture shock, I was determined never to leave it again, unless it was to go to the nearest airport, homeward bound. Two days later, my despondency diminished by ample rest and my determination somewhat weakened by the dictates of hunger and thirst, I decided that I could at least check out the place before leaving, and I timidly started exploring my surroundings. This brought me in contact with another resident, and the severity of my culture shock can be gauged by the fact that in realizing that he was a "fellow European" I felt such a sense of joy, relief, and gratitude that I practically never again left his side, and three months later we were married.

In retrospect, I think that my culture shock was actually amplified by this experience, since it compelled me to try to contemporaneously negotiate two cultural realities that were both quite alien to me: the Japanese one of day-to-day living and the English one my husband represented. At the same time, though, having a partner providing continuous emotional support gave both of us the opportunity to dispassionately analyze our reactions to the Japanese milieu, while the discovery of cultural differences between us increased our sensitivity to nuances of behavior and schooled us in the tolerance for diversity and sense of humor that alone can successfully lead to overcoming culture shock.

In my case, though, the reactions I found myself experiencing in Japan touched off an intellectual chain reaction. My culture shock filled me at first with surprise and then with indignation. How could a Japan "expert," as I still considered myself, find herself so totally lost in a culture lovingly studied for years? How could my knowledge of Japanese language, history, literature, and philosophy be of no use in helping me adjust to a setting I thought I was quite familiar with? How could I react so negatively toward a society I considered a sort of spiritual "second home"? But, above all, how was I ever to find a way to sort out the blooming, buzzing confusion that seemed to surround me and try to get on with the research required by my project?

The answers to these questions did not come quickly or easily, but I increasingly found help through a disciplinary approach I had known only vaguely before arriving in Japan, the approach of cultural anthropology. By becoming familiar with some of this discipline's concepts, not only did I start to understand and resolve my culture shock, but I also began formulating strategies through which I could successfully negotiate the reality of Japanese culture. As I began to recognize the cultural matrix of particular patterns of behavior, I came to see their connectedness and to accept their "necessity," and all the frustration and irritation I had experienced in dealing with them became diluted in the sheer pleasure of solving an intellectual puzzle. As time went by, I actually found myself looking for circumstances that would test my understanding. As I gradually trained myself in the fundamental anthropological skills of "attending, observing, registering, and correlating," I discovered that I could now look on cultural misunderstandings as a pleasurable challenge rather than a source of stress.

Predictably, the area in which I had experienced the greatest difficulties—much more serious than the discomfort initially created by the noise and the crowds—had to do with role expectations, particularly in relation to my scholarly activities. I had arrived in Japan as a young professional, with specific projects to accomplish. I expected to fit easily into an academic community where mutual intellectual stimulation would be freely exchanged, on a collegial basis. Instead, I soon found that my comparatively young age and the circumstances of my residence in Japan had automatically labeled me as an "apprentice." As such I had been assigned to a number of senior scholars whose role was not only to aid my learning but also "to look after me" in every sense of the word. Furthermore, their instruction would not be imparted through the scintillating intellectual exchanges I had so often engaged in with my Italian professors but through what first looked to be endless, aimless sessions of small talk, typically shared with a group of other "disciples," who seemed chiefly interested in providing a passive audience and were not even trying to discuss their knowledge, opinions, or ideas.

Although I felt it my duty to fulfill my hosts' expectations and I tried to play the "disciple" role to the best of my ability, for almost two years I found this experience utterly bewildering. It was only when my anthropological investigations led me to see the connection between socialization practices, sense of self, and definition of social role that I began to see how the Japanese teaching/learning style—through personal contact in the context of a hierarchical, paternalistic relationship—fitted so well with other aspects of Japanese society. In fact, I then became convinced that in Japan the teacher–student relationship encapsulates so many facets of the overall cultural "script" that it is perceived as a general model for interpersonal relations. Consequently, I believed its study would provide critical insight into the fundamental characteristics of Japanese culture, and I started to study it in earnest by becoming an "apprentice" to a number of "masters." In this area of behavior, as in several others that had created profound puzzlement, anthropology had led me from frustration to understanding, and I felt privileged to have found such a useful "key."

I really believe that the way I discovered anthropology gave an unusual twist to an experience that could have been lived very differently. Not having been formally trained in this discipline, I was able to explore it in an idiosyncratic way, picking and choosing concepts and approaches totally on my own and having the opportunity of immediately testing them in a "total immersion" situation. Being in Japan not as an anthropologist doing field research but as an Orientalist pursuing a literary project, I never developed the type of ambiguous rapport with "the natives" that cultural investigations often engender. My desire to understand Japanese society was not a requirement of research but a prerequisite for mental equilibrium. Thus I never resented the enormous investment of time and effort it required, and I never tired of doing it. Above all, I never perceived any aspect of Japanese culture as a "problem" to be studied; rather, I clearly recognized *myself* as the problem, insofar as I needed to learn to fit into Japanese society to be able to pursue my scholarly project. I did a lot of participant observation in Japan, but it hardly was the application of a particular disciplinary technique; I was as a child growing up, badly wanting to participate in the culture in which I found myself. Observation and relentless analysis were simply the only ways to earn an admission ticket.

As a consequence of all this, I never looked at cultural anthropology merely as an academic subject or as a field of professional specialization. Rather, I came to consider it a sort of "intellectual life preserver," an eminently applied science through which I could understand my husband, get on with my studies, and learn to live comfortably in a foreign country. At the same time, I also think that the fact that I "discovered" anthropology in Japan colored my disciplinary orientation. First, it strongly biased me toward a "cultural" rather than "social" approach, and second, it called my attention to the overall homogeneity and integration of cultural patterns, particularly as expressed in nonverbal and paraverbal behavior. Because I had to figure out the organization of Japanese culture "from the inside," through description and interpretation of details rather than through the abstract comparison of general characteristics, I found the model of culture originally developed by Boas, and still at the basis of the American anthropological tradition, much more useful than any other. Furthermore, this model proved especially effective because Japanese culture lends itself particularly well to an inductive, behaviorally focused analysis.

Japan is a very homogeneous society in which strict conformity to standardized rules of behavior is highly valued and commonly practiced. Partly because of this, the Japanese are experts at carrying on "silent dialogues" through the sophisticated modulation of nonverbal behavior, and they are extremely skillful at extracting symbolic meaning from the most varied aspects of experience. Japanese behavior is simultaneously so ritualized and rich in symbolic nuances that an outsider observer cannot escape an overpowering feeling of being in the midst of a high-level balletic performance, where everyone knows exactly how to contribute to the overall effect. As a result, in becoming increasingly familiar with Japanese culture, one comes to associate it with the image of a *tableau vivant,* a pattern of patterns, the best possible illustration for Ruth Benedict's concept of "cultural configuration." Furthermore, in dealing with the Japanese, someone with a growing interest in anthropology as a discipline—like me at the time—is strengthened in the belief that a culture can truly be studied and understood simply by observing and analyzing the behavior of its members.

Encountering Ethnicity

While the insights of cultural anthropology helped me considerably in adjusting to Japan, just as the experience of Japanese culture molded my basic anthropological perspective, what finally convinced me to pursue this discipline professionally—and to do so in the United States—was a trip to Hawaii. I went there from the East, since at the expiration of my scholarship I had decided to stay on in Japan to teach and do research. I stayed on for more than seven years, and the trip to Hawaii was just a holiday. But again, a chance experience gave a powerful spin to the trajectory of my life and of my intellectual growth. What I found in Hawaii was the phenomenon of ethnic variation. Obviously I was already aware of the reality of ethnicity, but it was only by seeing it correlated to minority status in the context of a truly multiethnic society that I perceived its great relevance to the understanding of culture.

Arriving in Hawaii from Japan made me look at the Japanese-Americans I came to know there with particular interest. Clearly they were neither Japanese nor American but something new and unique. What particularly struck me, though, was that what made them unique was not the superimposition of new patterns of behavior on the Japanese but rather the subtle way their Japaneseness had been—in my eyes at least—both subtly transformed and reinforced.

This conclusion was reached, I believe, because being attuned to Japanese nonverbal behavior I could see it reproduced faithfully, albeit in a simplified form, in the behavior of the Japanese-Americans I met in Hawaii. What *had* changed, in some cases quite dramatically, was verbal behavior, especially as a vehicle for the expression of values and beliefs. However, it seemed to me that a recognizable Japanese behavioral style was very much present and that among in-group members the decoding of its underlying symbolic meaning proceeded undisturbed by possible superimposed verbal disclaimers, as if it were operating below awareness and ahead of any conscious labeling process. I would see, for example, Japanese-American women forcefully argue for female equality and independence just as they nonverbally gave out messages of docility, other-directedness, and submission to male authority—messages that seemed to set the "tone" of interaction with other Japanese-Americans much more strongly than their verbal counterpart.

The observations I gathered during my visit to Hawaii considerably strengthened my inclination toward looking at culture as a system of communication and also gave me some basic ideas on how to define ethnicity in relation to culture. In particular, I remember becoming very excited about thinking that if indeed the original patterns of nonverbal and paraverbal behavior are maintained across generations of people born and raised in a culture different from their ancestral one, then they may constitute the very core of cultural behavioral style and thus be the key to understanding the dynamics of cultural membership and identity.

Subsequent research experiences in various parts of Asia, England, and Italy confirmed my original feeling that no matter what level of assimilation an ethnic group achieves, group identity is essentially maintained through the perpetuation of a set of microbehavioral patterns that are learned during the very early years of life. Although largely unrecognized as bonding factors, these patterns seem to determine both self-identification and group cohesion by generating a recognizable behavioral style that can be called on to establish group boundaries when necessary for ideological reasons. I also concluded that if we could trace the trajectory by which behavioral style changes during the process of acculturation, we would reach a better understanding of how it comes into being in the first place. As time went by, I increasingly felt that to test many of these ideas I needed to do firsthand research among ethnic groups living in a typically multiethnic society; that is when I decided to come to the United States.

Ethnic diversity is not, of course, a peculiarly American phenomenon, but the type of ethnic groups one finds in America and the ideological definition of ethnicity that has been developing within the context of American society warrant special attention. Most of the latent, emerging, or established ethnic groups I had occasion to study in Asia and Europe have not experienced relocation. They live in areas ancestrally theirs, and the characteristics of the land they inhabit are very much a part of their sense of uniqueness. Often, as the advocates of separatism among them argue, they are simply "nations without states," groups that have become part of larger national systems to which they do not feel they really belong. The situation I found in the United States is very different. With the exception of the Native Americans and of the Mexicans originally living in what has now become the American Southwest, all of the ethnic groups one finds in the United States are the result of migration. Furthermore, as a consequence of the civil rights movement and the nationwide social unrest of the 1960s and early 1970s, there has emerged in the United States a "minority group" ideology. According to this, the political elite has recognized the cultural diversity of a few ethnic groups, has regulated their existence through the creation of well-defined boundaries around them—first and foremost by declaring them "official minorities"—and has institutionalized the presumptive process of their assimilation through a program of majority-selected incentives for socioeconomic advancement. As a result, ethnicity and minority status—with all the socially uncomplimentary connotations of these terms—have become equated in the minds of many Americans, just as the latent consciousness of ethnic heterogeneity leads many to believe that there is no such thing as an "American culture." These contradictions seem to *demand* anthropological analysis, and from my first days in America I believed that any kind of research conducted here would prove particularly rewarding. Furthermore, having decided to formalize my interest in anthropology by entering a graduate program at UCLA, I found that my excitement about doing research in the country in which Franz Boas had developed the anthropological approach I considered so attractive was compounded by that of studying in an academic setting that had actually produced a number of distinguished Boasian anthropologists. Because of all this, I saw coming to America not only as an opportunity for exciting research but also as both the fulfillment of a fantasy and the repayment of an intellectual debt. I did not know, though, that this experience would lead me to insights that entirely redimensioned my views of culture and of anthropological research.

Cultural Participation and Analysis

After leaving Japan and before coming to the United States, I had gone back to Italy for a while, and I had lived for a period in my husband's home country, England. Also, over the ten years preceding my journey to America, I had visited a score of Asian and European countries. With this experience to back me up and with the knowledge provided by years of anthropological study and research, including professional involvement in intercultural training, I fully expected to be "vaccinated" against culture shock, but I learned soon enough that this is one reaction not assuaged by training. Besides, if now I at least had the consolation of being familiar with the symptoms of culture shock, this time they were combined with a psychological crisis for which I was not at all prepared.

My decision to study anthropology in the United States had not been anchored to any amount of practical knowledge of the American educational system or even of the current characteristics of American intellectual life. With the ethnocentrism typical of someone making an emotional choice, I had expected that my study experience in America would closely resemble those I had already undergone in Italy and Japan, with all their characteristics of elitism and exclusiveness I took so much for granted. I most definitely was not prepared for the atmosphere of an American public university campus, set by what seemed to me an incredibly large number of incredibly young undergraduates. I was not prepared for the frank and democratic American acceptance of the characteristics of mass education, including what I considered an enormous amount of bureaucratic complexity. I was not prepared to find that educational quality could be so openly and directly linked to its financial cost. I was not prepared to see such a large portion of both the undergraduate and graduate student population consist of foreigners. I was not prepared for the businesslike, impersonal way students were treated by campus staff and even by many professors. Most especially, I was not prepared for being considered "just another foreign graduate student" and to have to deal on a daily basis with people who were unknowingly belittling my background and experience—including years of fieldwork and university teaching—and whose behavior I so often found either patronizing or dismissive.

With hindsight I now think that this was an extremely useful experience, but its value was paid in frustration, humiliation, and exasperation. Again, I was lucky in being able to share it with my husband—who had also entered a graduate program—and in having the help and support of an outstanding group of academic mentors. The chair of my sponsoring committee, the late Professor Hiroshi Wagatsuma, was particularly instrumental in helping me maintain a measure of mental health. He himself, Japanese-born and trained at the most elite Japanese institution, Tokyo University, had undergone experiences similar to mine when first entering the United States, and after many years of teaching and living here, he was still vividly aware of the difficulties created by cultural dissonance.

Talking with Professor Wagatsuma was excellent therapy, but more important, in listening to the anecdotes with which he could so brilliantly exemplify his analyses of American culture, I started to realize that my problems were essentially *cultural* and that this experience, albeit painful, was also providing me with a great chance for reaching new insights about the craft of anthropology itself. After I had suffered greatly from what I considered attacks to my sense of personal worth, I finally realized that this was happening only because I had not framed this experience in anthropological terms. Why was I taking "native" definitions—of friendship, scholarly work, or success—so very seriously? Had I not learned the lesson of relativism and of the inevitability of ethnocentrism? Where was my use of the fundamental anthropological skill of balancing the emic and etic points of view? Why was I getting irritated by the Americans making fun of my accent when I had taken perfectly in my stride the Japanese incessantly pointing and laughing at my Roman nose or at my overall foreignness? These were all questions I found myself "stonewalling," until I realized that I was embarrassed by their simple answers. The fact was that, because American culture was typically Western, I had related to it as if it were my own and was then cut to the core by its "betrayal."

The whole problem emerged from the question of participation: Since I had come to America as a student, I wanted to fully participate in the culture in this role, but according to my own culture-specific definition of it. Thus, I had encountered great problems in areas of behavior particularly related to the definition of that role. The quantification drive underlying the educational system baffled me; the profound anti-intellectualism of even the most dedicated American student bewildered me; and the prevalence of anecdote over analysis, of simplicity over complexity, of concreteness over abstraction, and of detail over depth in the teaching and studying of social science vexed me. Here I was, in one of the best anthropology programs in the country, and all my peers would talk about whenever we met socially were other people, sports, money, or sex. If professional matters were ever discussed, they would concern grades, number of publications, or job prospects. If one became involved in a research project, people seemed interested in knowing only who funded and administered it. If one took a new course, people would want to know what the instructor was like.

While my initial adjustment problems in Japanese academia had to do with the acceptance of my role as the feudal retainer for munificent intellectual lords, now I felt plunged back into the nervous, immature atmosphere of my junior high school days. But whereas in Japan I had managed to detach my sense of self from the behavior that was required from me, and I had in fact taken pride in becoming an "impeccably cultural performer," now I could not seem to do the same. This realization led me to a long process of cultural self-analysis, at the end of which I came to better understand not only the salient characteristics of my cultural background but also all the hidden epistemological agendas that had colored my research until then. In turn, this made me look at the ethnographic enterprise from a new point of view, and I came to see in sharp relief some of its more common limitations: the concentration on the study of exotic, marginal, or socially deviant groups, clearly different from the ones we, the researchers, belong to; our common practice of "the field trip," always implying a physical demarcation between "our" territory and that of the people to be studied; and the use we make of our study of cultural specificity to acquire prestige within academic worlds that are themselves culture-specific. Indeed, a certain kind of anthropological research started to seem to me at this point a rigged intellectual game with limited possible returns. On the other hand, I also came to appreciate that once the test of *real* participant observation is successfully negotiated, anthropological analysis can provide the deepest understanding of the human experience.

Now I fully realized for the first time that culture is not a sort of house we can enter and leave at will. Culture defines the parameters of all human expressions, and, like a chronic disease, we always carry it with us. Thus, there are no extracultural standpoints from which to do cultural analysis. My understanding of Japanese culture had been filtered through the lenses of my Italian background, and the whole process was being repeated in America. However, both in Japan and in the United States I had not had the wish and the opportunity to distance myself emotionally from the setting of my cultural analysis. In Japan, for a variety of reasons—including the extreme physical "foreignness" of the setting—I had managed to become a real participant and to maintain an ethnographic detachment. But in America I had fallen into the trap of fully validating native categories and then resenting them.

Understanding the dynamics of this process helped me resolve most of my day-to-day frustrations and made me realize that anthropological practice, per se, does not necessarily lead to overcoming ethnocentrism. In fact, by "institutionalizing" the distance between the researcher and the people being studied, anthropological practice may subtly reinforce ethnocentrism. But, if anthropological practice is supplemented by the test of real participant observation, one can begin to comprehend the enormous scope of cultural constraints. At this point the anthropologist truly becomes an impeccable "professional stranger." From this point, however, one neither can "turn off" the anthropological lenses through which all experiences become framed nor "go home again," simply because the very concept of "home," as a privileged native culture, has been totally deconstructed through ethnographic detachment.

Exploring American Culture

Figuring all this out took the best part of my first four years of residence in the United States, including a lengthy trip to Italy at the end of the third year. By the end of this period I had completed my coursework and taken my doctoral qualifying exams, and I was doing exciting research on several fronts.

As I mentioned previously, my original project had to do with trying to trace the trajectory of change affecting the communication patterns of ethnic group members living in a multiethnic society. Because of my previous experience, I had initially planned to study the acculturation of the Japanese-Americans. However, the very hypothesis at the basis of my research—that ethnicity is perpetuated through the maintenance of microbehavioral patterns acquired so early in life that they become almost unconscious—led me to consider the necessity of selecting for my analysis an ethnic group not labeled as a minority, to demonstrate that retention of an idiosyncratic ethnic style has nothing to do with social labeling or group militancy. Also, particularly under the influence of Professor Wagatsuma, I had become increasingly interested in the issue of "native anthropology," and I was intrigued by the way it related to the study of ethnicity. Specifically, being Italian myself, I started wondering what it would be like to study the Italian-Americans. Would my perceptions of this group be different from those of Italian-American scholars, and if so, how? And how would my observations compare with those gathered by researchers of totally different ethnic backgrounds, such as, for example, members of the Anglo majority?

While I was still trying to decide the focus of my research, I was lucky enough to become involved with a project investigating the health maintenance practices of various American groups of Asian ancestry. As I was able to use my "Asian expertise" within that context, I decided to concentrate on the Italian-Americans for my doctoral dissertation research. For the next several years, these were the two areas of investigation in which I was formally engaged. At the same time, however, the exploration of American culture as a whole remained my informal, but no less exciting or demanding objective. I soon learned that revealing this objective to American fellow anthropologists-in-training was not a good idea. In particular, my asking for their professional insights into their own culture seemed to create great embarrassment. In line with this, the unwritten rule about anthropology graduate work in most of the academic institutions I came to know during this period was that "real" anthropological research is done abroad. On the other hand, foreign students—especially from "exotic" Asian and African countries—would be encouraged to study aspects of their own cultures. Furthermore, I noticed that even discussing the topic of my formal research on ethnicity would create quite a bit of uneasiness; Americans, including American anthropologists, simply did not seem to expect that a foreigner may be here to study their culture, and ethnicity was certainly one of the aspects of the culture they least wished to discuss.

As for my Italian-American research subjects, while fully informed of the aim of my project and of the observation techniques I would employ, they were quick to let me know how they thought ethnicity should be studied. Although they always put up very graciously with my observation sessions, they also ended up "convincing" me that I should really interview them about their values and beliefs. In effect, all through my explorations of American culture, I repeatedly found a common popular concern with the ideational realm, an attitude almost opposite to the Japanese preoccupation with behavioral norms. A great many Americans seem to believe that "ideas make the person" and because ideas can and do change, people can continuously reinvent themselves. Perhaps because of this belief, the idea of American culture as a stable configuration is not commonly accepted, and even members of minority groups feel that their identity is a matter of "negotiation."

On my part, however, I found that applying a complex set of microbehavioral observation techniques, I not only could document the remarkable retention of an ethnic-specific behavioral style across generations of Italian-Americans, but I was also able to find relevant commonalities in the behavior of people observed in random social settings, from a doctor's visiting room to a barbecue party and from a department store to a university campus, thus gathering evidence of a system of recognizably American behavioral patterns. Also, the academic program I had joined gathered a large number of advanced foreign students, and it was very instructive and therapeutic to exchange notes with them on American culture in general and on the subculture of American academia in particular.

I especially enjoyed monitoring the reactions of Asian students, since I was often able to predict them, and I sometimes came to share these reactions. One of these had to do with American humor; neither I nor my Asian fellow students—especially the Japanese among them—could get used to the constant barrage of sarcastic put-downs Americans seem cheerfully to accept as "joking." After being caught in a particularly virulent exchange of wisecracks, one of these friends once told me he privately referred to it as "jockeying," as in jockeying for power and control, and I still think this is an accurate definition of what goes on behind the smiles. I recognized a distinct continuity between American humor and its Anglo-Irish counterpart. I had experienced problems with a certain brand of British joking all through the time I had lived in England. But what I found most surprising in the American penchant for sarcasm is its use by people who seem typically characterized by great personal vulnerability and a very shaky sense of self-worth, so that humorous repartee becomes a sort of voluntary "social flagellation."

Actually, I have often wondered whether Americans do harbor a streak of Puritan masochism; "No pain no gain" sounds profoundly suspect to my Mediterranean ears. Certainly the dictates of extreme individualism, combined with ideological rigidity *and* social heterogeneity, seem to lead almost inevitably to a "culture in pain." During my years in graduate school, I observed many casualties of the enormous pressure people live under. After maintaining a decent GPA while putting up with all the wisecracking, the showing off, the self-promotion, the undercutting of potential competitors, and the sexual and ethnic tensions, some students would just suddenly "disappear." "Oh, he moved to the Coast. . . . She has found a good job. . . . He ran out of money. . . . She just dropped out," people would say, and in a few days, the person would apparently be totally forgotten. When confronted about this cavalier attitude toward evident casualties of a ruthlessly competitive system, people would reply, "You gotta learn not to care too much. People move, start new lives, don't keep up. If you care you get hurt." To me it all sounded like the rationalizations of people hardened by life in a war zone.

Foreigners often comment favorably on the "energy" one senses in this country. It is certainly real, but its flip side is tension. When I first came here, one of the things that particularly struck me was that strangers who accidentally make eye contact—in the street, in shops, on public transportation—will speak or at least smile to each other, something unthinkable in either Europe or Japan. Americans say it is just a way to be friendly, but to me this always seems a touching effort at establishing an amicable truce with potential enemies, as if to avoid a likely confrontation. Similarly, I now find it "normal" that American public speakers almost inevitably begin their presentations with a little joke, but from a European point of view, this is a strategy that seems to betray both performance anxiety and a clumsy attempt at courting favor. It is certainly a very different opening gambit from the British one, which requires a strong statement of fact, or the Italian one, which can be either an idiosyncratic statement of opinion or an outright complaint.

Once I started to teach, the level of performance anxiety American students live with really became evident. To comfort my classes, I often tell them that in Italy examination results are always publicly posted, that most university exams involve a personal interview—at which the professor frankly expresses her or his overall opinion of you, whether positive or negative—and that most of these interview sessions are large public events, so that there may be a lot of witnesses to your downfall. They listen in disbelief and groan in real pain. Certainly, the characteristics of American society that critics traditionally bemoan—the personal isolation, the psychological insecurity, the ruthless competition, the liability of social status, and the intolerance for diversity—justify this anxiety. But, in my view, there are two factors that uniquely handicap the pursuit of a contented life in this culture. One is the commitment to ideological integrity over interpersonal harmony, and the other is the lack of cultural self-awareness. Obviously these perceptions are strongly influenced by my comparative framework, in turn created by my Italian background and Japanese experience. However, the "natives" themselves are ready to admit that ideas, values, and beliefs are taken very seriously in this country, and, in so doing, the human factor is repressed or trampled over and much personal unhappiness results. Shortly before arriving here, I briefly visited the Soviet Union, and I cannot shake the impression that American and Soviet cultures are unexpectedly similar in this respect. At a deep level not influenced by political changes, they share a penchant for "radical utilitarianism," a tendency toward measuring everything in relation to ideological goals, disregarding human and aesthetic values in the process.

What seems to me uniquely American, however, is a profound disbelief in systemic social constraints and, in particular, in the reality of an indigenous culture. For years I have been systematically polling students, acquaintances, and miscellaneous informants on their perceptions of American culture, and I must conclude that denying that an American culture exists seems to be one of the most consistent local cultural traits. But Americans are very interested in themselves, and if a foreigner asks about seemingly peculiar cultural characteristics—Why do people eat popcorn at the movies? Why do coffee cups often get refilled free in restaurants? Why do people always get invited to social events in couples? Why is ethnicity only recognized in minority groups? Why is youth considered better than maturity? they take pause and seem willing to start looking at their behavior from a new perspective. That is when teaching anthropology becomes truly exciting. By openly discussing my perceptions of American culture and by encouraging students to analyze how these perceptions may be related to my cultural background, I can lead them to turn their ethnographic lenses to various aspects of their own daily experience.

The point of all this is that I have come to believe that the anthropological perspective is a "way of life," as well as the outlook of a specific discipline. Being an anthropologist can simply mean getting a certain type of diploma and performing certain prescribed activities according to the expectations agreed on by a certain professional community. But it can also mean trying to understand the very matrices of our behavior and being able, if not to escape the mazeways our native culture has trained us to walk, at least to analyze the entire process, dissect its formulation, and contemplate its results. Anthropological knowledge can certainly increase mutual tolerance but only if we are prepared to train the field glasses on our own cultural peculiarities and define them as such. To achieve this, it helps to undergo the test of real participant observation, but I believe that with the right guidance, aspiring anthropologists can be trained to reap the rewards of "continuous ethnographic alert" without having to suffer the pain of prolonged cultural dissonance.

There is, however, one potentially disturbing fact that must be taken into serious consideration when embarking on the ethnographic enterprise. That is the realization that if culture determines the framework of all our expressions, it must also affect our cognitive processes. This implies that any intellectual endeavor, including anthropological theorizing (or writing about anthropological experiences, as in this article), is culturally colored. Fortunately, human beings have an adaptive capacity for thinking they understand each other even when they are instead steadily mistranslating incoming messages. But this does not have to be the only way to keep intercultural interaction open. I am quite convinced that if anthropological research methods can be clarified and systematically applied, if we develop careful guidelines for the cultural self-analysis of aspiring anthropologists, if we relentlessly explore the process by which behavioral style emerges, and if we find a way to elucidate the boundaries between culture and ethnicity, our discipline can live up to the promise its founders felt assured it had.

I also believe it is particularly important to analyze cultural settings not usually considered "for anthropological consumption." Ethnographic reports on French or American culture have a very different impact on the Western reader than, say, descriptions of the Ik or Yanomamo cultures. Whether we want to admit it or not, the latter tend to become, at best, abstract metaphors for the human condition. The pervasive reality of culture can only be truly appreciated when you call people's attention to its local expressions, and if this can be done by native and nonnative researchers in a position of real participation, so much the better. Bronislaw Malinowski once said that anthropology is the discipline of the sense of humor. This is a particularly nice definition, I think, if we complement it with the lesson of real participant observation. If we can identify our own cultural foibles and still smile at ourselves, we can also learn to live with the strangeness of assorted "cultural others," since we will be able to see the culture as just a reflection of our own. This is the perspective I gained from my exploration of American culture, and how much value I give to it is self-evident: I am still here.

Study Questions

1. Aside from the fact of having to adjust to distinctly different cultural surroundings, how did having a partner from another culture effectively help the author in adjusting after her initial culture shock?

2. What problems relating to the applicability of studying a culture from afar and then finding oneself totally enmeshed in that culture became evident to Professor Cerroni-Long?

3. How were anthropological principles, the author's "intellectual life preserver," helpful in leading to the understanding of Japanese culture?

4. What did the author learn from her research in Japan, Hawaii, England, and Italy about the bonding factors of cultural identity?

5. If the author is correct, what can we presume are the social consequences of institutionalizing minority statuses?

6. Do you believe that anyone can ever completely overcome ethnocentrism?

7. What does the author imply by "a culture in pain"?

8. Do you believe that it is true that Americans live at a level of performance anxiety? What features of American culture does the author indicate to support this view?

9. In what novel and insightful ways does the author view anthropological perspective as a "way of life"?

9

Shifting Borders

Laura Macia
University of Pittsburgh

Recently arrived from a one-year period in South Korea, a young graduate student from Colombia faces for the first time life in the United States of America. Adjustment to the new country is harder than expected. She describes her difficulties with local newscasts and a bus ride still vividly remembered years after it occurred. In the process she discusses how these episodes relate with different ways of understanding national pride, and different expectations in the interaction with the world at large.

Laura Macia was born and raised in Colombia. She received her degree as a Lawyer with an option in Mathematics and Masters in Anthropology from the Universidad de los Andes in Bogotá (2001, 2003) and her PhD in Anthropology from the University of Pittsburgh (2012). She is a postdoctoral associate at the Graduate School of Public Health at the University of Pittsburgh.

As a young Colombian woman who during her childhood watched canned American TV shows dubbed into Spanish, Hollywood movies, and traveled to meet Mickey Mouse in person, I was not concerned when I moved to the United States to study. In my mind, all these prior experiences counted as valid previous exposure to the American culture. Besides, popular culture in Colombia was heavily influenced by the US, which should have also given me some cultural advantage: Michael Jackson and McDonald's were well-known icons, and for better or for worse (although mainly for worse), Colombian fashion during the eighties included big hair and neon colors. Adding to my confidence was that I had been living during the previous eight months in South Korea where food, religion, and toilets, to name just a few, were clearly truly different from everything I had experienced before. As I saw it, moving to the US was going to feel like a return to the familiar, right? Well, not quite. Two interrelated issues proved particularly challenging during those early days.

My biggest source of culture shock came wrapped in a seemingly harmless disguise: the evening newscast. Shock built slowly and inconspicuously night after night as I watched the evening news. I wasn't even fully aware that it was there, until one day I found myself talking desperately on the phone with my husband (who was still living in South Korea), telling him about what could be best described as a claustrophobic attack. I felt like I had been stranded, unable to communicate, on a faraway island or an isolated corner of the globe. As words came out of my mouth, I realized most of it came down to the evening Pittsburgh news. Every night I had been watching the "local news," and every night it offered me a picture of the world around me. It was not a very big world. Most of the reports were on fires, crashes, and lost cats—all less than 50 miles away from the bed in which I was hearing about them. These 50 miles comprised the core of this new world I was living in. A few reports were from the United States beyond these local borders, mostly on the presidential election. From how the election campaigns were reported, I got the impression that what occurred in this broader space known as the United States remained relevant, but was nonetheless removed from where I was. Most of what occurred beyond this second border was unaccounted for, with one main exception: events taking place in a faraway place called Iraq where only war, death, and heroism existed. Immersed as I was in figuring out my new routines and my new city, and in academic books, articles, and writings, this was the main version of the world that I digested on a daily basis. Night after night, and week after week, this was the only world presented to me. Colombia and South Korea started to feel simply as distant figments of my imagination.

My second source of surprise about the American culture was presented to me in a much clearer and sudden form. Just a few weeks after arriving in my new home, I took a bus ride that remains vivid in my memory more than a decade later. I was sitting near the front of the bus, near a group of people who did not appear to know each other but were talking animatedly. At first I was not paying attention to their conversation, as their looks intrigued me. In particular, I was noticing their poverty: their much worn clothes, their missing teeth, their ailing bodies. At this point what was most surprising was not that they seemed poor, but rather that they were not the only ones or the first I had seen in my short stay. Since I had arrived in the US poverty had been staring at me constantly, everywhere. Coming from Colombia I had seen poverty. A lot

of it. But after living in South Korea where, perhaps in part due to my own difficulties in reading that culture, I had been unable to readily recognize poverty,
I was expecting to see much less of it in the US, a much wealthier country.

As I was thinking about all of this, I started to pay attention to the conversation that was taking place among my neighboring bus riders. It was then
when my surprise became absolute confusion. In varying versions of the same
theme, all these people were expressing their gratitude for their luck in having
been born in the best country in the world, which offered them endless
opportunities and freedom. I found this conversation astonishingly paradoxi-
cal in part because it contradicted my own interpretation of their personal situation: where they saw "opportunity and freedom" I had been reading
"marginalization, oppression, and gross inequality." But what made the conversation most bewildering to me was that it went completely at odds with my
own experience of citizenship in Colombia. While usually very passionate
about the country's many assets, Colombians are also masters at finding fault
in most everything in the Colombian government or society. Complaining is
common and widespread in Colombia, and a national pastime is to *arreglar el
país*, or "fix the country," which entails discussing all that is wrong about it.
Everybody fixes the country: those at the top and those at the bottom, the
haves and the have-nots. Colombians do take pride in their luck in citizenship
often. However, it is not an unquestioning pride. Even among those fortunate
Colombians who have received access to prime education, work opportunities, and health care, there is always much in need to be changed. Conformity
is somewhat of a scarce resource, and national pride is something to be
achieved, to strive for.

A commonly used expression in Colombia (and Latin America in general) when questioning social or political conditions is *por eso estamos como
estamos,* which translates as "that's why we are as we are" (Elizondo 2011).
This expression summarizes what surprised me most on that bus. *Por eso estamos como estamos* assumes that "how we are" is not ideal. "How we are," in
this expression, is always lacking, lagging, at fault, behind, in need of change.
But on that bus and for those people, "how we are" was free and endowed
with opportunity, unhesitatingly faultless. Despite my own observations,
despite the ragged clothes and the missing teeth, "how we are" was good and
grateful. I have no way of knowing how much the people sharing my bus ride
were interested in what happened beyond the US borders. My guess, however,
was that most of their information came from the same newscasts I was
watching. And yet, in that moment and on that bus, they were glad they were

not on the other side of that border. How can luck be assessed, I wondered, when the outcome for the others playing the lottery of life is not truly known? Can unwavering pride go hand in hand with no knowledge about the alternative? Or more disquieting, can it exist alongside that knowledge?

It is possible that this difference in how national pride is understood and lived has at least some of its roots in what I perceived as different intensity in the nurturing of nationalism in both countries. Despite what may seem from how common self-criticism is among Colombians, it does not mean that Colombians are not proud of their country. However, this pride does not constrain reproach. That is, unless it is uttered by an outsider or to outsiders. In such cases Colombians tend to come together. Airing the dirty laundry is a privilege available to insiders, among insiders. National pride in the United States of America, on the other hand, is omnipresent and intensely stimulated. Flags are present everywhere you turn: in public buildings, in malls, on trucks, on sweaters. Events and everyday activities that exalt national pride are also common. Children pledge allegiance to the flag daily, the national anthem is sung at the beginning of most important gatherings, and many national holidays are strongly American. Out of ten national holidays, at least five seem to reinforce national identity and pride: Presidents' Day, Memorial Day, Independence Day, Veterans' Day, and, although in a somewhat different vein, Thanksgiving. None of these situations are the case in Colombia. Colombian flags fly abundantly only during important sporting events and relevant national holidays. Only two holidays out of 18 clearly fit this criterion, both related to the independence from Spain: Independence Day and the *Batalla de Boyacá*. Knowledge of the pledge of allegiance to the flag is not widespread, and there are no common civilian spaces for reciting it. Singing of the national anthem is also reserved for very select occasions; once again, sports seem to be the ones that offer most opportunities for unabashed nationalism.

After more than ten years living in the US since that bus ride, I have developed a more nuanced vision of this seemingly blind and unquestioning patriotism. In recent years social demonstrations against oppression and marginalization in the US, especially along racial lines, have become more common. Expressions of discomfort about the existence of second-class citizenship are public and common in many circles. While newscasts haven't changed, I am more aware that many Americans do not allow them to fully delimit their world; these people are not only truly interested in what occurs outside their borders but also go to great lengths to learn about it. These interests range from the everyday experiences of food and sports (yes, I am talking about *futbol*—soccer—here), to curiosity about politics and social dynamics in other countries. And it appears that Americans themselves are also changing how they perceive themselves, and how they understand their love for their own country (Tyson 2014).

At times the world still seems somewhat smaller and the other side somewhat blurrier when standing in this new American home of mine. Plus, I still enjoy "fixing" both my country of birth and my country of residence. Often. But some thoughts and feelings have changed. Although unreserved conformity has eluded me, I have learned that unhesitating criticism can be equally blind. I have treated claustrophobia by opening windows to that bigger world that in the beginning was so elusive. Turning the television off certainly helps. I have also learned to appreciate some of the benefits of living in a smaller world, particularly in how quickly action that would be difficult to achieve in bigger worlds can emerge: the victims of fires and crashes tend to receive immediate tangible support from their local communities, and lost cats are often found. In time, this new reality, within the boundaries of a smaller world that I try to make bigger, and with much to complain about but much to appreciate as well, has become my new familiar.

Study Questions

1. The author titled this piece "Shifting Borders." Explain which borders she found shifting as she moved to the United States.

2. What does the expression in Spanish *por eso estamos como estamos* mean? What is its importance for the author?

3. Compare national pride, including its construction, in Colombia and the United States.

References

Elizondo, C. 2011. *Por eso estamos como estamos: la economía política de un crecimiento mediocre*. Madrid: Random House Mondadori.

Tyson, A. 2014. Most Americans Think the U.S. Is Great, but Fewer Say It's the Greatest. *Pew Research Center*. http://www.pewresearch.org/fact-tank/2014/07/02/most-americans-think-the-u-s-is-great-but-fewer-say-its-the-greatest/ (Accessed July 1, 2015).

—— 10 ——

First Impressions
Diary of a French
Anthropologist in New York City

FRANÇOISE DUSSART
UNIVERSITY OF CONNECTICUT

*Moving from the solitude of the Australian outback, where she had been
studying Australian aboriginal culture, a French anthropologist finds herself living in New York City in a multiethnic neighborhood characterized by
poverty, homelessness, and drug dealing. From reflections of seven months,
excerpted from her diary, she not only describes the neighborhood, the
apartment complex, and some of its residents but also comments on some
aspects of the culture of the neighboring, wealthier residents of "The City."*

Françoise Dussart was raised in France, Africa, England, and the United
States. She received her BA and Masters in Anthropology from the Sor-
bonne University in Paris (1980, 1982) and her PhD in Anthropology
from the Australian National University at Canberra (1989). She is Professor of Anthropology at the University of Connecticut at Storrs.

Anthropologists are, by nature, note-takers. What follows are slightly neat-
ened excerpts from the diary I kept when 1 first reached New York City in the
fall of 1988.

Arrival

The plane will be touching down soon. After five years of working in an Australian aboriginal community, I suspect I am prepared to handle the "exoticism" of New York. How much stranger can the ceremonies of Manhattanites be than those of the Warlpiri Aborigines? Certainly the system of kinship will be a lot easier to handle. Here you do not have to marry your mother's mother's brother's daughter's daughter. I will try to suspend judgment. But is that possible?

The plane banks over New York. I have to stop thinking of the city's geography in terms of aboriginal culture. I look out the plane's oval window and, seeing the sparkling skyline, recall the fires burning in the central Australian desert. This kind of obsessive comparison-making is the observer's kiss of death. Still, the temptation is always there.

On landing, I am confronted by more differences. Stopped by an immigration official, I am asked to prove that I have adequate funds for my stay in the United States, and then I am questioned about my profession. I respond in the most general terms that "anthropology is the study of people, their history, their habits, and their rituals." The official seems satisfied with my answers. I have money and a profession, the twinned necessities of American acceptance. (I guess that's why they call the man at the airport a customs official!) Back in Yuendumu, the settlement at which I conducted my fieldwork, those questions would have had little meaning. Arrival would have been marked by a long and involved interrogation about my family genealogy.

The ride into Manhattan is marked by general discussion of "The City," as if there were no other city in the world. In this regard, residents of Manhattan seem particularly geocentric. (I am taught over time the specialized lexicon of the region. Brooklyn, the Bronx, and other boroughs are part of New York City but are never referred to as "The City," a term restricted to the borough of Manhattan.)

I am told what I should do ("The museums are nice, and the art galleries are fantastic") and what I should not do (a much longer list that includes not going to Harlem alone, avoiding confrontation, and carrying enough money to satisfy muggers, robbers, and other petty criminals).

Two words linger in my head as we snake through the traffic into New York: danger and inequity. The danger arises from all the talk of robbery, burglary, and rape. I am told to fear the city before I've even had a chance to explore it. The inequity arises from the scenes outside the window: the shelterless populations next to neatly kept homes. These two words figure into the storytelling tradition of the city's residents. Real estate and crime are the subject of many conversations. Perhaps this is the modern-day legacy of the fireside storytellers of central Europe.

First Day

I will be staying in the very part of town I was told to avoid: the southern tip of Harlem. As I walk around the neighborhood (the environs of West 107th Street), I am confronted by the speed with which the affluence of neighborhoods changes. From one block to the next, you can switch from doorman apartments to tenements populated by people of predominantly Central American origin. My accommodations are found in the second form of habitation.

The rectilinearity of Manhattan is an impressive quality of this city. All the streets are on a grid that denies natural geography. Local residents do not understand notions of uphill and downhill. Their awareness of which way is north or south is based on the numbering of the streets, not on any geographical sense of the terrain. This is so unlike aboriginal culture, where location is defined by terrain. (The urge to compare, I guess, is inevitable.) "Go to the water hole and walk east until the mulga trees area" is replaced by the simplicities of consecutive numbering (though I am told that lower Manhattan rejects the grid completely).

Even before I arrive, I am told of the drug addicts and mentally disabled homeless who walk the streets. In my new neighborhood, I discover that the homeless situation is quite depressing. Unwed mothers with children also make up a part of this migrant army of despair. The scenes remind me of the "Courtyard of Miracles" in the French novel *Notre Dame de Paris,* but we are not in the sixteenth century. How can it be that such a rich city has so many beggars? Perhaps that is why it is so rich.

I have already started to notice that different ethnic groups dominate different street activities. It is obvious that the Koreans run the fruit stores on Broadway. There are also other groups overseeing specialized markets. A small group of South American Indians sells flowers out of shopping carts they roll around the West Side of Manhattan. One Peruvian woman sells native sweaters and dolls from the inside of a heated car. Dozens of impoverished black men sell castaway clothing, books, shoes, lamps, and junk salvaged from the garbage of wealthier locals. Even in junk selling there are differences to be observed. The better-off vendor uses a table and has prices marked with little stickers, whereas the more desperate street people line up their wares on the cement and take pretty much what is offered. The homeless tend to avoid corners because corners are too windy, and their clothing is ragged at best. The slightly more upscale salesperson, on the other hand, will gladly set up a stand on a corner.

I observe more links between ethnicity and occupation. Most of the taxi drivers in New York seem to be Haitian. A driver named Jean Jean from Port au Prince describes the difference between being a cabbie in Haiti and being a cabbie in New York. "The passengers are much more trusting in Haiti," he tells me in French. He says that New York passengers, fearful of being over-charged, almost always provide detailed instructions of exactly what route they wish to take. I let him choose the path he wishes, all the time trying to test myself on the orientation of east, west, north, and south.

First Week

I have settled in the top-floor apartment of a five-story walk-up on the Upper West Side of Manhattan, just south of Columbia University. The univer-sity's presence is not felt. This is a Spanish-speaking world. Most of the residents come from Central and South America. The food, the smells, the language, and the way in which life is played out on the streets are all wholly Latino.

The rent in the apartment where I am staying is low, and this fact domi-nates much of the conversation I have with native New Yorkers. Sometimes I feel that real estate and safety are the only two topics of conversation. Safety is discussed because a number of nonminority acquaintances are made nervous by the "unsafe" nature of my new neighborhood. When I ask what constitutes "unsafe," they seem to associate predominantly white neighborhoods with protective environments, even though they admit to having been confronted in those areas as well.

Back at my apartment building, I ask a Puerto Rican neighbor (as best as I can without speaking Spanish) where he feels safe. He points to our build-ing. Safety, clearly, is relative. In this "dangerous" neighborhood, he can buy food, pitch pennies, and go to church. He says he would never go to Brooklyn.

I could picture a map of New York City with "safe" areas shaded in by dif-ferent ethnic groups. I suspect that the whole of the city would be covered. Likewise, "unsafe" shading would produce similar results.

Second Week

I have been spending my time trying to map out the cultural geography of my neighborhood. Never have economic discrepancies been so dramatically defined. Stepping out of my building, I am surrounded by a Spanish ghetto with all the cover-story problems (crack, unwed mothers, welfare dependency), but walking west just half a block brings me to a solidly middle-class row of cooperative apartments, and just another hundred yards more brings on distinctly wealthy residents. In a three-minute walk, I have moved from poverty to Crabtree & Evelyn, a fancy goods store specializing in luxury soaps. I am told that if I were to move east from my building entrance (to Columbus Avenue), I would find myself among the notorious crack dens of the city. I have not yet walked on that avenue.

I can't think of a European city in which wealth and poverty exist in such close proximity. There are, of course, ethnic distinctions to be made. When I note "poor," it is a poor Hispanic and black population, and when I write "rich," it is predominantly white, though Japanese investment has made its presence felt here, too. (The buzzers on every other door of the co-ops along Riverside Drive have signs written in *Kanji*.)

I have started asking some of the older residents (often a gold mine for the fieldworker) about the evolution of the neighborhood. I learn that until the late 1960s this was a predominantly Irish neighborhood. It is hard to believe that all traces of that presence have been eradicated. After strolling around, I find one last defiant marker of that Irish legacy: the Kennedy Funeral Home. (I guess it's appropriate that the last establishment to stay deals in the dead and dying.) The establishment stands out. It has a faux Cape house façade with white embroidered curtains. The owner is still a Mr. Kennedy, but he has hired a Hispanic consultant to maintain ties to the community.

I have been feeling many of the same frustrations in New York that I had during the first few months of fieldwork in Australia because I cannot speak the language of the streets. I keep thinking about the halting conversation I had earlier in the week with my Puerto Rican neighbor, Tony. He has an English vocabulary of perhaps fifty words. English does not get one very far in the *bodegas* and *carnecerias* that dot Amsterdam Avenue.

Fluency in the neighborhood is generationally distinguishable. The younger population speaks English and Spanish fluently, so I converse with them. But for Tony and other first-generation immigrants, communication with English-speakers is almost all gesture. Once in a while whites need to talk to the superintendent, whose command of English is practically nonexistent. Usually one of his children comes to help everyone reach some kind of understanding.

A typical view from my window includes clutches of young women (girls, really) tending to babies, the heads of older women poking out of windows, and men on the street pitching pennies, fixing unfixable cars, and drinking beer out of green bottles or rum from a shared brown bag. It is rare to see groups of men and women together.

Third Week

I went to a number of social events this week. As usual, everyone at the gathering was, like me, white and middle class. I was amazed how tight a network of friendships and professional links emerged during the meal. I have clearly stumbled into the American equivalent of the French intellectual elite. The same schools, the same vacation spots, and the same books are constantly mentioned. There are differences, however. French intellectual life is played out on a more intimate scale, so that in France the country's top lawyers, actors, writers, and filmmakers often intersect at various social events. That is not the case here in New York. There are book parties for writers, museum openings for art critics and artists, and movie screenings for specialists in cinema. Of course I am moving in a slightly less stylish circle, but the point remains that there is a professional and ethnic homogeneity in the social gatherings I have attended.

I must now add another topic of obsession to the list that previously included only real estate and security. The obsession surfaces in the question asked before all others and pursued with the greatest intensity: What do you do? It seems that acquaintances need to know the nature of your professional life in order to feel at ease. In France it would be considered rude to initiate a conversation on such a topic. Conversations in France are introduced by discussions of family origins. White Americans seem less concerned by such genealogical inquiries.

I had an interesting conversation with a group of five women all roughly my age. I say "interesting" not because there were any overlapping interests but because I felt so alien. Most of the discussion centered around their bodies. I was amazed to find them absolutely at ease discussing their weight, how much they were going to lose, and how they were going to lose it. There was a detailed conversation on the relative merits of aerobics, swimming, and tennis, all activities that had as their goal weight loss. I wrote to a friend of mine in

France about the discussion, and in the correspondence that followed we agreed that such intimacies would never be revealed in such a setting. Talk about the imperfections of one's body is limited to closest friends and mothers.

The commitment to keeping fit is visible everywhere in the neighborhood outside the Spanish community where I live. Athletic supply stores can be found every few blocks, and the reservoir a mile from my building is regularly circled by joggers in various states of fitness (I once saw a father jogging while pushing a baby carriage).

Although the American women I talked with are comfortable talking about the physical condition of their bodies, discussions of sensual condition are taboo. Again, comparison with the French experience is inevitable, where strangers are perfectly comfortable talking about the satisfaction and the limitation of their sexual liaisons. Maybe such discussion makes my American women friends uncomfortable because it suggests prefeminist roles. I know that my more traditional "feminine" interests such as cooking and knitting have frequently gotten me into trouble with professional women who find such activities frivolous and counterproductive.

These last few weeks in New York recalled the first lecture I had in cultural anthropology. The professor stressed the need to avoid cultural relativity that denies the uniqueness of the community under investigation. The more I learn about New York, the less comfortable I become with the terms and conclusions I have made. I suspect that if I gave the community in which I live the same attention I applied to the Warlpiri Aborigines, it would take many years to find answers to the questions that constantly confront me. What is the relationship between "black-magic candles" sold at the Haitian botanica and the Catholic religious figures? Why do my neighbors play the illegal numbers games on the street that pay much lower dividends than the state-sanctioned lotteries? But on a more theoretical level, I would like to know how much this Hispanic community adopts the values of white America, how it resists assimilation, and how it adapts elements of the society that surrounds it. Each question provokes twenty more questions.

First Month

I gave my first dinner party. I was fascinated to see what people brought in the way of gifts: two bottles of wine, a dessert, and even a head of broccoli the guest thought I might want to toss into the salad. Each of these gifts, different as they are, share one common element—consumption during the meal. In France, such gift giving would be considered somehow inappropriate. Flowers are the most common offering to the host or hostess.

A few guests expressed surprise that I actually cooked the meal instead of ordering from a restaurant or preparing some microwaved delicacies. When I asked them if they ever cooked, they said proudly that they had never turned on their oven (they had been living in the same apartment for the last three years). After the party I had expected some reciprocal invitations, but none came. When I asked why the party was received so unilaterally, I discovered that many New Yorkers are reluctant to reveal where they live. The reasons are complex and diverse. One fellow I spoke to admitted he was embarrassed by the size of his apartment: It was too small a space in which to entertain. Another woman made a point never to invite anybody to her apartment. "It is my sanctuary," she said, "why would I reveal it to anyone?"

Subsequent dinners with these acquaintances were held at restaurants (except once in the home of close friends). The guests, each on separate occasions, called me up and proposed that we get together again with other friends in a restaurant. The effort of getting together for a meal at a restaurant is one facet of New York hospitality among people in their twenties and early thirties. But we often all share the bill!

Second Month

I attend my first women's studies seminar at a New York university. I have no idea what to expect and so arrive early to gather my thoughts. The participants start to enter, and I quickly realize that no men will be attending. The mood is warm and supportive, with a lot of high-pitched salutation and kissing. The seminar starts, and the speaker begins her lecture on "The Roles of German Jewish Women During the Second World War." The woman next to me shakes her head while the paper is being delivered. Another woman sucks her tooth, and still a third objects out loud. When the lecture is over, the listeners begin an open assault on her ideas, challenging not only her data but her premises as well. I am surprised by the vehemence of these condemnations. In seminars I attended in Britain and Australia, I never saw anger and argumentation. In France, where the pleasures of disputations are legendary, such a conflict would have been the start of a long-standing feud. That's not what happened here in New York. The seminar ended, smiles returned to the faces of the participants and the lecturer, and the women kissed one another good-bye.

Third Month

Although the poverty is sometimes unnerving, I am constantly surprised by the intensity of community spirit among people in the neighborhood. Most of middle-class Manhattan exists on the nuclear family level, while West 107th Street is always displaying the entanglements, jealousies, and affections of the extended family. I have very little to do with these interactions, but increasingly the residents are recognizing that my stay may not be temporary. The triumphs of neighborliness are small ones. Yesterday Tony helped me carry a heavy shopping bag to the front door of my fifth-floor apartment.

Fourth Month

The temperature has dropped well below freezing. The men who linger on the street corner have retreated into cars they keep heated, into the lobby of the nearby funeral home, into grocery stores, and into basements that reveal the glow of old color TVs. Bottles of rum are generally passed around.

There is clearly a generational separation in the male population. Rum is not an adequate stimulant for the younger men of the community. I regularly walk over the tiny plastic envelopes in which crack is sold. The dealing can be observed from my living room window. The transaction itself is a complex pirouette marked by drop-offs, cash exchanges, coded negotiations, and the ultimate sale.

One young entrepreneur has hung a pair of shoes over a lamppost. This marker is to alert out-of-town drug buyers to the availability of his wares. The cars stop, and after brief discussion he pulls the little plastic bag from his sock.

Missing from the street life are the women. They can be seen at the windows of their kitchens throughout the neighborhood. The apartment two floors below, which is occupied by the family of the building's superintendent, has no fewer than four generations of women coming and going. Disposable diapers, baby carriages, and small children are carried up and down the staircase. Women spend most of their time in kitchens with their children and female friends and relatives. Each sex relies on the emotional support of their friends and relatives of the same sex and the same generation level.

Fifth Month

I spend the day taking a casual survey of the building's thirteen apartments. The ground-floor apartment is occupied by three Columbia college students with a serious commitment to hard-rock music. There is a sort of music war that takes place between Led Zeppelin and the Latino tunes. The second floor is occupied by a young, low-paid editor at a publishing house and a family from the Dominican Republic living in two apartments. The nature of this family must be defined in the anthropological literature as matrifocal. The third floor has an extended family from Ecuador, another one from Cuba, and three brothers from Puerto Rico. The fourth floor is occupied by a white American actor, a nuclear family of jazz musicians, and an extended family from Bolivia. The fifth floor is occupied by three Puerto Ricans, a white student from Columbia University, a freelance journalist, and a cultural anthropologist. One apartment is empty now. It used to be a "crack house," as white people refer to it here. One morning, the police raided the apartment. The only objects left in the apartment are a sword and Latino American saints, the heads and bodies lying separately on the floor. Maybe the police pulled the statues apart because they thought that the drug dealers were hiding the white powder inside them.

Sixth Month

The windows of my office look out on a Spanish funeral home. Quite often I see grieving women. They scream, roll in the street, and sob uncontrollably. They show their grief to the entire community. The men tend to be less demonstrative. Once the coffin is brought out of the funeral home, it is quickly taken away. Death is not allowed to linger in New York. When a woman in a building adjacent to mine committed suicide by jumping off the roof, her body was taken away by the police less than fifteen minutes later. I am amazed to discover that there is no place to be buried in Manhattan.

There are two churches on 107th Street. One is a Catholic church, which is the most popular, and the second is called the Kingdom Hall of the Jehovah's Witnesses. Proportionally, white people attend the Pentecostal services more than the Catholic services, though they represent a small proportion of the people who attend services in both places. White people go elsewhere.

People cross themselves as they pass the statue of Jesus Christ that stands outside the Catholic church. Often several coins lie at the feet of the statue, and they are later picked up by homeless people. I have seen this done in Italy or Spain and even in some parts of rural France. But people's religious habits are not so simply defined and limited. In fact, within a few yards both from the church and from the Kingdom Hall, there is a strange store in which they sell all kinds of natural or health food and all the necessary apparatuses for magic religious practices as performed in parts of Latin and South America and the West Indies. Their collection of objects and of statues of saints (like those lying on the floor across the hall from me) is impressive. There, one can also buy candles to keep black cats away or to charm a lover. The Korean grocery store had to adapt, and they are now selling spray cans against black cats (considered bad luck among the Spanish-speaking people).

Seventh Month

It is much warmer outside. The men both young and old are back in the streets rolling dice, listening to loud music, fixing cars, and selling drugs. The women in the community emerge briefly in the late afternoon to join in the streetside discussions. Chairs and even a couch have been put on the sidewalk in anticipation of summer.

I am amazed by the variety of street games that are played by the older men. They can pitch pennies and roll dice for hours at a stretch. (Dice are played when the men of the street are cash rich; pennies are pitched when they are poor.) Occasionally a checkerboard or sets of dominoes will make a brief appearance. There is one man—the fellow who brought out the couch—who comes every day and calls out for mates to play with him—to play for money, of course. He seems to live off his winnings from the games. The only time of the week he cannot be found is on Sunday when he attends mass.

The increase in temperature marks a switch from rum drinking to beer drinking. The men in the neighborhood have a strong preference for Heineken, and though none of the men is rich, the bottles are never returned for deposit. Monday mornings are marked by dozens of empty brown bags littering the sidewalk. When the men are low on money, they pitch pennies and drink Budweiser.

The bottles are usually picked up by the neighborhood Hispanic homeless man named Junior. The people who live here also give him food, drinks, and money. One of the superintendents has given him access to a basement so that he and his dog can seek shelter for the night. Once in a while, often under the influence of crack or heroin, he becomes violent and insults some of the men who look after him. The victims usually ignore him and to get rid of him give him money or a beer. Here people take care of their "mads" and drug users.

Each time I try to characterize the community in which I now live, I am struck by the diversity within what is often perceived to be Latino cultures. I am referred to by the Spanish-speaking people on 107th Street as one of *los Americanos;* they do not even know that I am French.

I live in a building not of Hispanics but of Bolivians, Ecuadorians, Dominicans, Puerto Ricans, and Cubans. They are not fully integrated in the larger American society, and they are not fully integrated in their homeland either. They seem to be very aware of what is happening in their respective countries through radio programs, television, news that new migrants bring with them, and visits home every two years or so. They seem to construct their identities in relation to both environments, here and there, and so construct a unique environment that includes other cultural groups they may never have met in other circumstances.

The tendency to judge must still be fought. I still make comparisons, but less often.

Study Questions

1. In reading this personal account, try to totally immerse yourself in Professor Dussart's situation, a foreigner in New York City moving into a mixed ethnic area of questionable personal safety. How comfortable would you be in this area? How would you feel about your sister or girlfriend living in such an area?

2. What topics of conversation tended to prevail among the author's neighbors and female acquaintances that were markedly different from appropriate topics in France?

3. Why was the author not invited to any of her dinner guests' apartments as a polite gesture of reciprocity?

References

Banton, M. 1983. *Racial and* Ethnic *Competition.* Cambridge: Cambridge University Press.
Bastide, R. 1966. *Les Ameriques Noires.* Paris: PBP, Payot.
Bourdieu, P. 1979. La *Distinction.* Paris Les Editions de Minuit.
Hall, S. 1985. Religious Ideologies and Social Movements in Jamaica. In R. Bocock and K. Thompson (eds.), *Religion and Ideology.* Manchester: Manchester University.
Levi-Strauss, C. 1961 (1955). *A World on the Wane.* New York: Criterion Books.

————11————

Arranging a Marriage in India

SERENA NANDA
JOHN JAY COLLEGE OF CRIMINAL JUSTICE

During her first visit to India, Professor Nanda discovered the common practice of arranged marriages to be very puzzling in terms of her own American culture. The extensive and complex cultural contrasts became even more evident as the researcher soon learned that her own expectations in matchmaking were equally puzzling in India. Dr. Nanda did eventually find a wife for her close friend's son, but not until she learned to search in ways that were culturally new to her. Much of what is described in her classic article still holds true for contemporary India, though Indian arranged marriage now includes many modern features such as Internet dating websites.

Serena Nanda, Professor Emeritus of Cultural Anthropology at John Jay College, City University of New York, has carried out extensive fieldwork in India. Her publications include *Culture Counts*, an introductory textbook, *American Cultural Pluralism and Law*, *Gender Diversity: Cross-cultural Variations*, and most recently, two culturally based mysteries, *The Gift of a Bride* and *Assisted Dying*.

Sister and doctor brother-in-law invite correspondence from North Indian professionals only, for a beautiful, talented, sophisticated, intelligent sister, 5'3", slim, M.A. in textile design, father a senior civil officer. Would prefer immigrant doctors, between 26–29 years. Reply with full details and returnable photo.

A well-settled uncle invites matrimonial correspondence from slim, fair, educated South Indian girl, for his nephew, 25 years, smart, M.B.A., green card holder, 5'6". Full particulars with returnable photo appreciated.

—Matrimonial Advertisements, *India Abroad*

In India, almost all marriages are arranged. Even among the educated middle classes in modern, urban India, marriage is as much a concern of the families as it is of the individuals. So customary is the practice of arranged marriage that there is a special name for a marriage that is not arranged: It is called a "love match."

On my first field trip to India, I met many young men and women whose parents were in the process of "getting them married." In many cases, the bride and groom would not meet each other before the marriage. At most they might meet for a brief conversation, and this meeting would take place only after their parents had decided that the match was suitable. Parents do not compel their children to marry a person who either marriage partner finds objectionable. But only after one match is refused will another be sought.

As a young American woman in India for the first time, I found this custom of arranged marriage oppressive. How could any intelligent young person agree to such a marriage without great reluctance? It was contrary to everything I believed about the importance of romantic love as the only basis of a happy marriage. It also clashed with my strongly held notions that the choice of such an intimate and permanent relationship could be made only by the individuals involved. Had anyone tried to arrange my marriage, I would have been defiant and rebellious!

At the first opportunity, I began, with more curiosity than tact, to question the young people I met on how they felt about this practice. Sita, one of my young informants, was a college graduate with a degree in political science. She had been waiting for over a year while her parents were arranging a match for her. I found it difficult to accept the docile manner in which this well-educated young woman awaited the outcome of a process that would result in her spending the rest of her life with a man she hardly knew, a virtual stranger, picked out by her parents.

"How can you go along with this?" I asked her, in frustration and distress. "Don't you care who you marry?"

"Of course I care," she answered. "This is why I must let my parents choose a boy for me. My marriage is too important to be arranged by such an inexperienced person as myself. In such matters, it is better to have my parents' guidance."

I had learned that young men and women in India do not date and have very little social life involving members of the opposite sex. Although I could not disagree with Sita's reasoning, I continued to pursue the subject. Young men and women do not date and have very little social life involving members of the opposite sex.

"But how can you marry the first man you have ever met? Not only have you missed the fun of meeting a lot of different people, but you have not given yourself the chance to know who is the right man for you."

"Meeting with a lot of different people doesn't sound like any fun at all," Sita answered. "One hears that in America the girls are spending all their time worrying about whether they will meet a man and get married. Here we have the chance to enjoy our life and let our parents do this work and worrying for us."

She had me there. The high anxiety of the competition to "be popular" with the opposite sex certainly was the most prominent feature of life as an American teenager in the late fifties. The endless worrying about the rules that governed our behavior and about our popularity ratings sapped both our self-esteem and our enjoyment of adolescence. I reflected that absence of this competition in India most certainly may have contributed to the self-confidence and natural charm of so many of the young women I met.

And yet, the idea of marrying a perfect stranger, whom one did not know and did not "love," so offended my American ideas of individualism and romanticism, that I persisted with my objections.

"I still can't imagine it," I said. "How can you agree to marry a man you hardly know?"

"But of course he will be known. My parents would never arrange a marriage for me without knowing all about the boy's family background. Naturally we will not rely only on what the family tells us. We will check the particulars out ourselves. No one will want their daughter to marry into a family that is not good. All these things we will know beforehand."

Impatiently, I responded, "Sita, I don't mean know the family, I mean, know the man. How can you marry someone you don't know personally and don't love? How can you think of spending your life with someone you may not even like?"

"If he is a good man, why should I not like him?" she said. "With you people, you know the boy so well before you marry, where will be the fun to get married? There will be no mystery and no romance. Here we have the whole of our married life to get to know and love our husband. This way is better, is it not?"

Her response made further sense, and I began to have second thoughts on the matter. Indeed, during months of meeting many intelligent young Indian people, both male and female, who had the same ideas as Sita, I saw arranged marriages in a different light. I also saw the importance of the family in Indian life and realized that a couple who took their marriage into their own hands was taking a big risk, particularly if their families were irreconcilably opposed to the match. In a country where every important resource in life—a job, a house, a social circle—is gained through family connections, it seemed foolhardy to cut oneself off from a supportive social network and depend solely on one person for happiness and success.

Finding a Suitable Wife

Six years later I returned to India to again do fieldwork, this time among the middle class in Bombay, a modern, sophisticated city. From the experience of my earlier visit, I decided to include a study of arranged marriages in my project. By this time I had met many Indian couples whose marriages had been arranged and who seemed very happy. Particularly in contrast to the fate of many of my married friends in the United States who were already in the process of divorce, the positive aspects of arranged marriages appeared to me to outweigh the negatives. In fact, I thought I might even participate in arranging a marriage myself. I had been fairly successful in the United States in "fixing up" many of my friends, and I was confident that my matchmaking skills could be easily applied to this new situation, once I learned the basic rules. "After all," I thought, "how complicated can it be? People want pretty much the same things in a marriage whether it is in India or America."

An opportunity presented itself almost immediately. A friend from my previous Indian trip was in the process of arranging for the marriage of her eldest son. In India there is a perceived shortage of "good boys," and since my friend's family was eminently respectable and the boy himself personable, well educated, and nice looking, I was sure that by the end of my year's fieldwork, we would find a match.

The basic rule seems to be that a family's reputation is most important. It is understood that matches would be arranged only within the same caste and general social class, although some crossing of subcastes is permissible if the class positions of the bride's and groom's families are similar. Although dowry is now prohibited by law in India, extensive gift exchanges took place with every marriage. Even when the boy's family does not "make demands," every girl's family nevertheless feels the obligation to give the traditional gifts, to the girl, to the boy, and to the boy's family. Particularly when the couple would be living in the joint family—that is, with the boy's parents and his married brothers and their families, as well as with unmarried siblings— which is still very common even among the urban, upper-middle class in India, the girls' parents are anxious to establish smooth relations between their family and that of the boy. Offering the proper gifts, even when not called "dowry," is often an important factor in influencing the relationship between the bride's and groom's families and perhaps, also, the treatment of the bride in her new home.

In a society where divorce is still a scandal and where, in fact, the divorce rate is exceedingly low, an arranged marriage is the beginning of a lifetime relationship not just between the bride and groom but between their families as well. Thus, while a girl's looks are important, her character is even more so, for she is being judged as a prospective daughter-in-law as much as a prospective bride. Where she would be living in a joint family, as was the case with my friend, the girl's ability to get along harmoniously in a family is perhaps the single most important quality in assessing her suitability.

My friend is a highly esteemed wife, mother, and daughter-in- law. She is religious, soft-spoken, modest, and deferential. She rarely gossips and never quarrels, two qualities highly desirable in a woman. A family that has the reputation for gossip and conflict among its womenfolk will not find it easy to get good wives for their sons. Parents will not want to send their daughter to a house in which there is conflict.

My friend's family was originally from North India. They had lived in Bombay, where her husband owned a business, for forty years. The family had delayed in seeking a match for their eldest son because he had been an Air Force pilot for several years, stationed in such remote places that it had seemed fruitless to try to find a girl who would be willing to accompany him. In their social class, a military career, despite its economic security, has little prestige and is considered a drawback in finding a suitable bride. Many families would not allow their daughters to marry a man in an occupation so potentially dangerous and which requires so much moving around.

The son had recently left the military and joined his father's business. Since he was a college graduate, modern, and well traveled, from such a good family, and, I thought, quite handsome, it seemed to me that he, or rather his family, was in a position to pick and choose. I said as much to my friend.

While she agreed that there were many advantages on their side, she also said, "We must keep in mind that my son is both short and dark; these are drawbacks in finding the right match." While the boy's height had not escaped my notice, "dark" seemed to me inaccurate; I would have called him "wheat" colored perhaps, and in any case, I did not realize that color would be a consideration. I discovered, however, that while a boy's skin color is a less important consideration than a girl's, it is still a factor.

An important source of contacts in trying to arrange her son's marriage was my friend's social club in Bombay. Many of the women had daughters of the right age, and some had already expressed an interest in my friend's son. I was most enthusiastic about the possibilities of one particular family who had five daughters, all of whom were pretty, demure, and well educated. Their mother had told my friend, "You can have your pick for your son, whichever one of my daughters appeals to you most."

I saw a match in sight. "Surely," I said to my friend, "we will find one there. Let's go visit and make our choice." But my friend held back; she did not seem to share my enthusiasm, for reasons I could not then fathom.

When I kept pressing for an explanation of her reluctance, she admitted, "See, Serena, here is the problem. The family has so many daughters, how will they be able to provide nicely for any of them? We are not making any demands, but still, with so many daughters to marry off, one wonders whether she will even be able to make a proper wedding. Since this is our eldest son, it's best if we marry him to a girl who is the only daughter, then the wedding will truly be a gala affair." I argued that surely the quality of the girls themselves made up for any deficiency in the elaborateness of the wedding. My friend admitted this point but still seemed reluctant to proceed.

"Is there something else," I asked her, "some factor I have missed?" "Well," she finally said, "there is one other thing. They have one daughter already married and living in Bombay. The mother is always complaining to me that the girl's in-laws don't let her visit her own family often enough. So it makes me wonder, will she be that kind of mother who always wants her daughter at her own home? This will prevent the girl from adjusting to our house. It is not a good thing." And so, this family of five daughters was dropped as a possibility.

Somewhat disappointed, I nevertheless respected my friend's reasoning and geared up for the next prospect. This was also the daughter of a woman in my friend's social club. There was clear interest in this family and I could see why. The family's reputation was excellent; in fact, they came from a subcaste slightly higher than my friend's own. The girl, who was an only daughter, was pretty and well educated and had a brother studying in the United States. Yet, after expressing an interest to me in this family, all talk of them suddenly died down and the search began elsewhere.

"What happened to that girl as a prospect?" I asked one day. "You never mention her any more. She is so pretty and so educated, what did you find wrong?"

"She is too educated. We've decided against it. My husband's father saw the girl on the bus the other day and thought her forward. A girl who 'roams about' the city by herself is not the girl for our family." My disappointment this time was even greater, as I thought the son would have liked the girl very much. But then I thought, my friend is right, a girl who is going to live in a joint family cannot be too independent or she will make life miserable for everyone. I also learned that if the family of the girl has even a slightly higher social status than the family of the boy, the bride may think herself too good for them, and this too will cause problems. Later my friend admitted to me that this had been an important factor in her decision not to pursue the match.

The next candidate was the daughter of a client of my friend's husband. When the client learned that the family was looking for a match for their son, he said, "Look no further, we have a daughter." This man then invited my friends to dinner to see the girl. He had already seen their son at the office and decided that "he liked the boy." We all went together for tea, rather than dinner—it was less of a commitment—and while we were there, the girl's mother showed us around the house. The girl was studying for her exams and was briefly introduced to us.

After we left, I was anxious to hear my friend's opinion. While her husband liked the family very much and was impressed with his client's business accomplishments and reputation, the wife didn't like the girl's looks. "She is short, no doubt, which is an important plus point, but she is also fat and wears glasses." My friend obviously thought she could do better for her son and asked her husband to make his excuses to his client by saying that they had decided to postpone the boy's marriage indefinitely.

By this time almost six months had passed and I was becoming impatient. What I had thought would be an easy matter to arrange was turning out to be quite complicated. I began to believe that between my friend's desire for a girl who was modest enough to fit into her joint family, yet attractive and educated enough to be an acceptable partner for her son, she would not find anyone suitable. My friend laughed at my impatience: "Don't be so much in a hurry," she said. "You Americans want everything done so quickly. You get married quickly and then just as quickly get divorced. Here we take marriage more seriously. We must take all the factors into account. It is not enough for us to learn by our mistakes. This is too serious a business. If a mistake is made we have not only ruined the life of our son or daughter, but we have spoiled the reputation of our family as well. And that will make it much harder for their brothers and sisters to get married. So we must be very careful."

What she said was true and I promised myself to be more patient, though it was not easy. I had really hoped and expected that the match would be made before my year in India was up. But it was not to be. When I left India my friend seemed no further along in finding a suitable match for her son than when I had arrived.

Two years later, I returned to India and still my friend had not found a girl for her son. By this time, he was close to thirty, and I think she was a little worried. Since she knew I had friends all over India, and I was going to be there for a year, she asked me to "help her in this work" and keep an eye out for someone suitable. I was flattered that my judgment was respected, but knowing now how complicated the process was, I had lost my earlier confidence as a matchmaker. Nevertheless, I promised that I would try.

It was almost at the end of my year's stay in India that I met a family with a marriageable daughter whom I felt might be a good possibility for my friend's son. The girl's father was related to a good friend of mine and by coincidence came from the same village as my friend's husband. This new family had a successful business in a medium-sized city in central India and was from the same subcaste as my friend. The daughter was pretty and chic; in fact, she had studied fashion design in college. Her parents would not allow her to go off by herself to any of the major cities in India where she could make a career, but they had compromised with her wish to work by allowing her to run a small dress-making boutique from their home. In spite of her desire to have a career, the daughter was both modest and home-loving and had had a traditional, sheltered upbringing. She had only one other sister, already married, and a brother who was in his father's business.

I mentioned the possibility of a match with my friend's son. The girl's parents were most interested. Although their daughter was not eager to marry just yet, the idea of living in Bombay—a sophisticated, extremely fashion-conscious city where she could continue her education in clothing design—was a great inducement. I gave the girl's father my friend's address and suggested that when they went to Bombay on some business or whatever, they look up the boy's family.

Returning to Bombay on my way to New York, I told my friend of this newly discovered possibility. She seemed to feel there was potential but, in spite of my urging, would not make any moves herself. She rather preferred to wait for the girl's family to call upon them. I hoped something would come of this introduction, though by now I had learned to rein in my optimism.

A year later I received a letter from my friend. The family had indeed come to visit Bombay, and their daughter and my friend's daughter, who were near in age, had become very good friends. During that year, the two girls had frequently visited each other. I thought things looked promising.

Last week I received an invitation to a wedding: My friend's son and the girl were getting married. Since I had found the match, my presence was particularly requested at the wedding. I was thrilled. Success at last! As I prepared to leave for India, I began thinking, "Now, my friend's younger son, who do I know who has a nice girl for him . . . ?"

Further Reflections on Arranged Marriage

This essay was written from the point of view of a family seeking a daughter-in-law. Arranged marriage looks different from the perspective of the prospective bride and her family. Young women do get excited about the prospects of marriage, but there is also ambivalence and increasing uncertainty, as the bride contemplates leaving the familiarity of her own home, where as a "temporary guest" she was often indulged, to live among strangers. She will now come under the close scrutiny of her husband's family: how she dresses, how she behaves, how she gets along with others, where she goes, how she spends her time, her domestic abilities—all of this and much more—will be observed and commented on by a whole new set of relations. Her interaction with her family of birth will be monitored and substantially curtailed. Not only will she leave their home, but with increasing geographic mobility, she may also live very far away, perhaps even on another continent. Expressed desires to visit her natal family may be interpreted as an inability to adjust to her husband's family and may be a potential source of conflict. Even in the best situations, the burdens of adjustment in an arranged marriage are heavier for a woman than for a man.

The new bride may be a target of resentment and hostility from her mother-in-law or her husband's unmarried sisters, for whom she is now a source of competition for his affection, loyalty, and economic resources. Even if she is psychologically or physically abused, returning to her parent's home is a highly stigmatized option, as is divorce, which is still rare, though increasing, particularly in urban areas. Marriage and motherhood are still considered the essential roles for a woman, both for lower-class working women and even middle-class and professional women. Most families still consider "marrying off" their daughters as a compelling religious duty and social necessity. This increases a bride's sense of obligation to make the marriage a success, at whatever cost to her own personal happiness.

The vulnerability of a new bride may be intensified by the issue of dowry. Although illegal, dowry is an increasingly pressing issue with the increasing value of consumerism as a source of status. If a groom's family is not satisfied with the dowry, the young bride may be harassed to get her parents to give more. In extreme cases, she may even be murdered, with her death claimed as an accident or suicide (see "Rising Number of Dowry Deaths in India," https://www.wsws.org/en/articles/2001/07/ind-j04.html). A "dowry death" offers the husband's family an opportunity to arrange another match for him, thus bringing in another dowry.

Changes in Indian marriage patterns diverge within the contexts of class, rural/urban location, generational differences, and divergent gender perspectives. Arranged marriage continues to be preferred in India, though more by men than by women, and more by the older than the younger generation, as it continues to provide a source of stability and security. Additionally, the traditional Indian orientation to the family and kinship group, of which arranged marriage is an essential component, provides many women with an "Indian" cultural identity they wish to maintain, in contrast to the values of individualism associated with globalization, Westernization, and modernization.

An emerging alternative to arranged marriage, is what are called "love marriages" but this simple opposition obscures a more complicated picture, in which there are actually a range of alternatives. In a "love marriage" the initial contact between the couple does not involve traditional matchmakers and choices dictated by family members, and may—or may not—be accepted by parents; this is particularly true where the potential couple's free choice of a spouse crosses religious, caste, or social class lines.

Another alternative to traditional arranged marriages are "self-arranged" marriage, where the individuals meet on their own, but then seek their parents' approval. If the parents agree, the process follows that of a traditional arranged marriage. Middle-class parents sometimes adjust to the changes in the marriage landscape by arranging for their marriage-ready children to meet several potential partners (though this is done covertly), giving them the right of refusal.

The changes in contemporary Indian marriages must be understood in the context of globalization of values, and also, perhaps even more importantly, in the increasing number of women in the workforce. Whether for call center professionals, or poor garment factory workers, it is mainly the workplace that has opened up opportunities for men and women to meet each other and develop intimate relationships. Also important is the diffusion of "modern" cultural values regarding "love," reflected in the Indian media and discussed endlessly by young women. Even within traditionally arranged marriages, there is an emerging expectation of what scholars call "companiate" marriage, in which the traditional emphasis on familial obligation is slowly giving way to an idealization of intimacy, trust, and equality between the conjugal couple.

Partly because of geographic dislocation, in both arranged and "love" marriages, partners are increasingly sought through newspaper advertisements and the Internet, though the traditional criteria of similar caste, ethnicity, professional status, religion, and physical qualities and sometimes horoscopes, remain important. After an exchange of "bios" and photos, a short list is created, with some attempts to verify the information and for the potential spouses to contact each other. These channels increase the possibilities for exaggeration and outright fraud, resulting in an emerging profession of private detectives hired to check the backgrounds of the potential spouse and their family.

Abetted by both global values and the importance of women's earnings to their families, Indian women today are increasingly asserting their autonomy. They are, however, still more powerless than men, and particularly among the poor, vulnerable to marital abuse, often related to alcoholism, and abandonment. If they choose a "love match," they almost always live in nuclear families, even if their families become reconciled to their choice. This deprives them of the support—however tenuous—of their own families. Poorer working women often use their wages to amass a dowry, hoping that this will encourage their families to find them a suitable mate or that it will cement a "love match." The traditional Indian folk saying that a woman leaves her home twice in her life, first when she marries and the second time when she dies, no longer holds true, bringing with it changes that are both welcome and a new source of concern.

Study Questions

1. What are three aspects of American culture that would seem to be the greatest obstacles to arranged marriage?

2. Would you ever consider an arranged marriage for yourself? Why or why not?

3. If you were asked to arrange a marriage for a male friend, what qualities or characteristics would you look for in a possible mate? For a female friend?

4. How is arranging a marriage different for a boy than it is for a girl in India? How do these differences relate to gender roles and identities in Indian culture?

5. Marriage, like other aspects of culture, is intertwined with many cultural values and practices. What do you see as the major aspects of American culture linked to American marriage practices? What do you see as the major aspects of Indian culture linked to the Indian practice of arranged marriage? Consider such things as geographical mobility, the role of kinship groups, economic factors, attitudes toward divorce, and gender roles, among other factors.

Suggested Readings

Kapur, Cari Costanzo. 2010. Rethinking Courtship, Marriage, and Divorce in an Indian Call Center. In Diane P. Mines and Sarah Lamb (eds.), *Everyday Life in South Asia*, 2nd ed. Bloomington, Indiana.

Lessinger, Johanna. 2013. "Love" in the Shadow of the Sewing Machine: A Study of Marriage in the Garment Industry of Chennai, South India. In Ravinder Kaur and Rajni Palriwala (eds.), *Marrying in South Asia: Shifting Concepts, Changing Practices in a Globalising World*. Delhi: Orient Blackswan.

Nanda, Serena, and Joan Gregg. 2009. *The Gift of a Bride: A Tale of Anthropology, Matrimony, and Murder*. Lanham, MD: Altamira/Rowman and Littlefield.

Films

Provoked. Jag Mundhra, director. Distributed by Private Moments Ltd., UK, 2007.

Monsoon Wedding. Mira Nair, director. Distributed by Mirabai Films, Inc. USA. 2001.

12

An Outsider's View of American Culture

Janusz L. Mucha
AGH University of Science and Technology—in Kraków, Poland

A frequent visitor to America, Professor Mucha compares his European idea of the "city" to what he discovered in the United States. The immediate and informal cordiality of Americans is also discussed, as is urban anonymity, the profane naturalness of violence, patriotism, education, ethnocentrism, and the American potluck dinner.

Janusz L. Mucha is a professor of Sociology at AGH University of Science and Technology in Kraków, Poland. He received an MA in Sociology, an MA in Philosophy, a PhD in Humanities, and a Habilitation Degree from the Jagiellonian University of Kraków, Poland. He also studied as a postdoctoral fellow at the Johns Hopkins University; the Bologna Center in Italy; the Taras Shevchenko University in Kiev, Ukraine; the University of Wisconsin; and the University of Chicago. His primary fields of interest are sociobiological and anthropological theory, ethnicity and migration.

It is quite difficult to look at American culture with a fresh eye. One can easily become bewildered or upset, especially if one comes from a country where America has been treated as something special. And, in my case, having an education based on American sociology, cultural anthropology, and social psychology, having read all the classics of American literature, and having watched many movies, both classic and modern, directed by both foreigners and Americans, confusion about the culture persists. Further, this being my

136

fifth time in the United States, having lived for months in big cities like Chicago and New York, in small towns like Stevens Point, Wisconsin, and South Bend, Indiana, I have had an opportunity to view, firsthand, the diversity of American culture.

Having the experience mentioned, liking America, and being rather flexible, I see how one can easily lose the sense of novelty of first contact and view this initial contact through later experiences. Ultimately, one too easily begins to treat everything as normal; one attempts to understand everything, perceive the causes of everything that is going on, and frame one's observations and experiences into some structural and functional context.

Nothing bewilders or upsets me in America. After all these years I still see things that are different here than they are in both my native Poland and the many other countries that I have visited. Unfortunately, these observations are neither novel nor original: They are, or at least should be, obvious to many people, foreigners and Americans alike.

I love nature, but I am a city boy. I was born and raised and had lived for forty years in Cracow, a medieval university town of a half million inhabitants in southern Poland. An urban environment is very important to me. This is something I miss in America. The idea of the "city," as I conceive it, hardly exists in America. My idea of "city" can be found in parts of three American cities: San Francisco, New York, and New Orleans. There is a noticeable lack of an urban environment in America. I do not refer here to the fact of the deserted, burned-out, or depopulated parts of cities. I have noticed many empty, run-down apartment houses that would be put to good use in Poland. What I refer to is the physical and social structure of the towns and cities of America. It is the exception in America to have the excellent public transportation found in Vienna, Paris, London, and even Warsaw. In many American cities there are not even sidewalks: The people rarely walk, so why invest in sidewalks? If one jogs, one can use the street or roadway. American drivers understand the use of the roads for exercise and, unless a driver is drunk, there's not much risk.

Not only are there no sidewalks, there are no squares where people can safely gather, meet other people, talk, or buy flowers. There are no coffee shops like in Vienna, Rome, or Budapest. If you want coffee, you must drive to McDonald's or go to a restaurant. If you walk beyond the environs of "downtown," or the shopping mall, you will most likely be stopped by a police officer who will, if you are white, offer to assist you. But how can the officer be of assistance? Can he or she give you a ride to a real café? Can he or she return you to the "downtown" that, after dark, is most often both unsafe and deserted? There is no such thing as a real theater, and the movie theaters are back at the shopping mall, far removed from the empty downtowns of America.

Numerous sociologists and cultural anthropologists tend to identify American urban life with anonymity, the lack of primary groups and face-to-face contact, with only superficial and formal relationships. How do I see America? I have experienced a lot of friendliness and kindness in America. Everyone wants to help me, to thank me for calling or for stopping by. Everyone seems to care about me. When I make new acquaintances, including the dental hygienist, everyone addresses me by my first name, and I can be certain that he or she will make every effort to pronounce it as correctly as possible. Very soon, I discover that I am learning many intimate details of the personal lives of the people I have just met. I find myself a bit embarrassed, but I doubt that they are. They become my friends so quickly, and as quickly they begin to share their problems with me. There are, in the English language, the nouns *colleague,* and *acquaintance,* but I do not discover them to be in popular use. In America, when one meets someone, he or she immediately becomes a friend. Does this mean, for instance, that you can expect to be invited to his or her home for dinner or to just sit and talk? Absolutely not. I have often been invited to dinner, but perhaps I have been fortunate in meeting a different type of American. My brother, who teaches Russian and Polish at a Texas university, had not been invited to anyone's house for dinner during the entire academic year. My American friend, who teaches history in a New England college, had not been invited to anyone's home during her first year in the small college town. Therefore, I am forced to conclude that quality friendships in the sense of lasting, intimate, emotionally involving relationships are more difficult to develop.

In reference to the anonymity of urban life, as I have mentioned earlier, urban "life" hardly exists. There are neighborhoods, however, and "urban villagers" reside therein. Is this anonymity a feature of these neighborhoods? I do know, at least by the faces, everyone who lives in my own neighborhood in South Bend. If I do not recognize someone, I can tell whether that person "belongs" to my neighborhood. If a nonresident is in the neighborhood, he or she will be singled out immediately. It is possible that a patrol car will stop and a police officer will kindly ask the stranger to produce identification. A black person obviously cannot rely on anonymity in a predominantly white neighborhood. Neighborhoods do not want anonymity. The neighbors, in this instance, want to know everyone, to be able to address everyone by his or her first name, to be able to say "hello," and to ask how one is doing. And, as I've learned, they prefer the answer to be brief and positive: "I am fine, thank you."

An obvious reason for this fear of urban anonymity is the problem of security. However, the lack of anonymity does not imply that the relationships are truly friendly in the deeper sense of the word. The neighbors know each other, but they do not visit each other's homes to sit and talk, to exchange recipes, to borrow household tools, or to help if the automobile is not running. In this age of telephones, neighbors do not ordinarily just stop by unexpectedly.

American society is famous for the brutality of social life. The high rate of violent crime is incomprehensible. Rapes, female battering, child abuse, and molestation are the lead stories for local television and the print media. This information about violence has many positive consequences. If we wish to fight something, if we want to prevent crime, we must be aware of it. However, the constant forced awareness—the information on why and how someone was killed or raped—accustoms Americans to violence. They treat it as something natural, as just another case of a person killing or being killed. Violent death or abuse belongs to the profane, ordinary world of America. There is nothing sacred about it, unless it is the residual fear that it can also happen to you. On the other hand, death of natural causes is almost completely removed from everyday lives. Old people die in nursing homes or hospitals, and even this type of death, in being generally ignored, does not belong to the sphere of the sacred.

The fact of violence in everyday American life has numerous social consequences. One consequence is the decline of urban life. Americans have now accepted the fact that downtown areas, after dark, belong to the criminals or misfits. Americans accept the fact that strangers may be dangerous. Americans, thus, try to avoid downtown areas and strangers, especially at night.

Patriotism is another feature of American life that appears to differ from many European countries. I have been exposed to patriotism for the greatest part of my life. However, Polish patriotism, or nationalism, is different. Poland was, for forty-five years, under Communist rule, which was, to some extent, accepted, although the majority of Polish society treated it as alien domination. The Communists monopolized the use of national symbols. In the mid-1970s, the ruling party made it illegal to use these symbols without special permission by the state authorities. I can recall the unauthorized use of national symbols only within the religious context. I have never seen a Polish national flag in a private residence. Only once in my life did I see an eagle, the Polish national symbol, in a private residence. From my interpretation, the old national symbols became identified with a state that was not treated as the true embodiment of the national institutions. In America, state and nation are symbolically identified, and, moreover, nearly everyone feels the necessity to emphasize his or her identification with nation or state. I will not elaborate on the yellow ribbons in evidence during the Persian Gulf War, but it seems to me necessary to mention the presence of the American flag in most residences, offices, and clubs I have visited. Further, Lions Club lunches, university graduations, basketball games, and so on all begin with the singing of the national anthem.

Is there anything wrong with these public displays of patriotism? I do not believe so. However, the use of national symbols on an everyday basis has, in my opinion, two questionable consequences. First, the meanings of these symbols are shifting from the sacred to the profane, ordinary, everyday sphere of life. Second, the public display may indicate a strong degree of ethnocentrism. Excessive patriotism, pride in country and its achievements, may signify—and I am convinced that this is true in America—a very strong and blinding conviction that the American ways are much better than the ways of other countries and peoples. After all these years, after all these arrivals and departures, and after all these meetings with many Americans in Poland and in other countries of Europe, my impression is that American people, especially as visitors to foreign areas, are friendly but arrogant. They are arrogant in the sense that they do not understand non-American customs and habits, they do not even try to understand, and they are convinced that other customs "must" be much worse simply because they are not American. Americans are friendly in the sense that they would sympathize with other people; they would pity them and give them advice on how they should elevate themselves . . . to become more American.

What are the reasons for this general behavior and attitude? One reason is that the American educational system does not promote general knowledge about the United States and other countries. Personally, I am not of the opinion that education is the best solution to *all* social problems. Moreover, I believe that the significance of education is often exaggerated by politicians and mass media. However, American students at the grade school, middle school, and high school levels do know much less than students their ages outside of the United States. How can students learn more if no one demands that they learn more? I used to participate in monthly faculty meetings of the College of Liberal Arts and Sciences at a state university. Each month, a part of the agenda was a discussion of the admission policy. Should we accept candidates who cannot read, write, and calculate? Eventually, we continued to accept these deficient students . . . to a university! Their knowledge of their own country is minimal and inadequate. Their knowledge of other parts of the world is practically nonexistent. This may be the foundation for Americans' deep convictions that their ways are superior. They know little of their own country and less about other countries. What little they know is evidently the basis for their unquestioned views.

Another reason for the "friendly arrogance" of Americans may be their relative parochialism. The United States is so large and diverse that it is very difficult to learn much more than something of one's own state and, perhaps, neighboring states. Geographically and culturally (regions, ethnic groups), the United States is indeed so diverse that one can travel and study it for years, always learning something new and interesting. But, from my point of view of the whole of humankind, this big and diverse nation is only one relatively homogeneous spot on a map, a spot in which nearly everyone speaks the same language, can stay at the same type of hotel or motel, eat in the same type of restaurant, and shop at the same kind of supermarket. People living in Europe have a much better opportunity to appreciate the world's cultural diversity and to become much more relativistic than Americans. Europe remains a continent of natural cultural diversity, and the differences in the European educational system help in developing a relativistic attitude toward other peoples and customs. Naturally, not all Europeans take advantage of their educational opportunities, and they too often remain as rigidly ethnocentric as many educated Americans.

A third reason why the American is generally more ethnocentric than the average European is the nature of mass media. Reading American dailies (with perhaps the exception of the *New York Times*, *Chicago Tribune*, *Washington Post*, *USA Today*, and a few others), we get an impression that the entire world consists of some extension of the United States. In weekday editions, we rarely learn of the world beyond the Atlantic and Pacific Oceans, or even north and south of the nation's borders. In the case of an assassination of a public figure, a revolution, a minor war, or a significant natural catastrophe, we may learn something of the world beyond the borders. On a regular basis, we learn very little of other countries. I have discovered that educated people are not certain if Poles use the Latin or Cyrillic alphabet, if the Polish language is distinct from Russian, or if the Poles had their own army during the Communist regime. Even interested people are often of the opinion that Hungarians are Slavs and that Lithuanians and Latvians speak Polish or Russian.

These facts are common knowledge to the people of Europe, but how could Americans know these things? Schools do not teach them, and the newspapers are more interested in a recent rape in Florida than in the economic, political, and cultural situations of their neighbors in Mexico or Canada.

American television does not help much. "Headline News" and "CNN" provide information about the rest of the world on a regular basis, but the major networks do not, unless, as we discover in the print media, there is news of a sensational nature. Local television stations inform mostly on local crimes or local economic and political happenings, such as the daily whereabouts of the president or governor. For local television, the world is further restricted, ending at the borders of the county.

Every teacher can provide many examples of the blatantly inadequate knowledge of many Americans about the world beyond the country. I offer two examples. An intelligent female student in a course, Principles of Sociology, was very active during the discussions and once volunteered to present a report based on a selection from Émile Durkheim. She came to me before the presentation and complained that it was too difficult. She had happened on a foreign word, *solidarity*. She was even unable to pronounce the word correctly. She did not understand and was curious to know why Durkheim had used the word, which was coined much later, somewhere in Eastern Europe, to describe a political movement. She could not recall the context in which she first learned of the word and, further, in her own town, there was no such thing as "solidarity"

A second example is about another intelligent female, a minority student enrolled in my course, Race and Ethnic Relations. After two weeks of the semester she came to me with a problem: How is it possible that some other students are able to answer some of my questions about racial and ethnic situations in the United States if these particular issues were not presented in the textbook? She was very sad because she knew everything about her town and actually believed that nothing was different than it was in her own social milieu.

During my current visit to the United States, I have, in addition to teaching at the university, been studying a Polish community in a relatively small town. Both as a university professor and as a researcher, I participated in many parties of a more-or-less formal nature that were organized by individuals and various institutions. Nearly always, I went to these parties with my wife. Two things stand out from these gatherings. One was the way people greeted us. Sometimes we simply said hello, but most of the time we shook hands. But, by "we," I mean only myself and the host. Never that I recall, during the entire year, was my wife offered a hand in greeting or farewell. At the beginning, she was quite offended but then began to accept it as a local custom. I am certain that no one intended to offend her. Everyone was friendly to both of us. Why was she treated differently? Was it sexism? I inquired to learn if someone could explain and was told that this was a kind of custom. We do have different customs in Poland.

Another thing that surprised me was that private parties, but not formal dinner parties, were nearly always of the potluck character. The guests were expected to bring their own beverages and specialties. This does not happen in Poland. One may bring flowers (in the United States, women seemed to be deeply embarrassed when I brought them flowers) and/or a bottle of wine, vodka, or brandy. *No one* brings food. The host would be offended. But in America, not only do people bring food but they can take the leftovers home. Many years ago, the first time I experienced this custom, I did not know what to say. I had brought a bottle of very good Polish vodka to an American friend, but it was too strong for the participants of the party. The people tasted it, perhaps out of courtesy. When I departed, the host gave me the bottle, nearly full, to take with me. For a long time I did not know if I was given a message that I had brought something bad or improper. The next time, I brought a six-pack of beer and we drank all of it.

There was an additional surprise in store for me. My wife and I organized a potluck party for my departmental colleagues. One couple brought a home-made cake. Because they had to leave earlier than the other guests, they asked my wife to give them what remained of their cake. My wife was shocked. The fault was clearly mine. I forgot to tell her what to expect.

When I studied the Polish-American community, I participated in more formal dinners, as well. Some dinners were held by upper-middle-class associations of men and women. Sometimes, but rarely, these dinners were organized in restaurants. Mostly, however, dinners were served in large Polish-American clubs. Participants were dressed up: Men, mostly professionals or from the business community, were in suits; the women wore elegant dresses. The "equipment" was of a different nature. The tables were simple, the table cloths were of paper, and the plates were paper or plastic, as were the glasses. There were no separate plates for dessert. Dessert was thrown on next to the roast beef and potatoes. After dinner, the disposable plates and glasses were rolled into the table cloth and discarded. After dinner, coffee was drunk sitting at a Formica table.

This is obviously an example of American efficiency and convenience. Paper table coverings and plastic plates, knives, forks, spoons, and glasses are always in evidence. Now, here in America, we have potluck lunches at work, and now my wife and I also use the products of American chemical expertise when we throw a party. The difference is that, for us, the use of the fake stuff is a problem, especially when the real stuff is so readily available. And, having noticed the dish-washing machines in most of the private houses, we are further confused.

I am led to wonder. American ingenuity, from all quarters addressed to laborsaving devices, serves to free its citizens from the tedious and time-consuming labors of everyday life. This provides free time, perhaps more free time than available in any complex, industrialized society. Why don't Americans devote a portion of this free time to learning something more about the world within and without their own provincial borders?

Study Questions

1. What are the major human and structural differences that Professor Mucha discovered between American cities and cities in Europe?
2. How does the author justify the contention that "urban 'life' hardly exists"?
3. What may be an interpretation of American public displays of patriotism?
4. What is implied as the consequences of "friendly arrogance"?
5. What are some of the reasons why the author found Americans to be ethnocentric?
6. How does the potluck dinner differ from European dinner party customs?

Note

I would like to thank my wife, Maria Nawojczyk, and my brother, Waclaw Mucha, for their helpful comments on this paper.

13

Growing Up American
Doing the Right Thing

AMPARO B. OJEDA

LATE OF LOYOLA UNIVERSITY, CHICAGO

As a young student on her first visit to America, Professor Ojeda, a Fulbright scholar, was reassured that her adjustment to American life and culture would be easy. The orientation survival kit was of minimal help in adjusting to some American customs, especially those involving child-rearing. Years later, in returning to the United States with a daughter, Professor Ojeda was faced with a crucial conflict of values—American values versus the more familiar values of her own Philippine traditions.

Amparo B. Ojeda was born and raised in the Philippines. She completed her undergraduate degree and an MA in English Literature from the University of San Carlos, Philippines, and an MS in Linguistics from Georgetown University under the Fulbright program. Rudolf R. Rahmann, a Divine Word Missionary (SVD) and an anthropologist, encouraged her to pursue anthropology with a special emphasis in Southeast Asian anthropology and linguistics. She earned her doctorate at the University of San Carlos. Professor Ojeda conducted fieldwork in the Philippines and was involved in ongoing research on the adjustment of Filipino immigrants in Metropolitan Chicago. She retired from the Anthropology and Linguistics Departments at Loyola University, Chicago.

The earliest and closest encounter that I had with Americans, and a most superficial brush with their culture, goes back to my childhood days when an American family moved into our neighborhood. I used to gaze at the children, a boy and a girl, who were always neatly dressed and who would romp around their fenced front yard. Not knowing their names, I, together with a cousin, used to call them, *"Hoy, Americano!"* (Hey, American!), and they themselves soon learned to greet us with "Hey, Filipino!" That was as far as our "acquaintance" went because in no time at all they were gone, and we never again heard about them.

That brief encounter aroused my curiosity. I wanted to know something more about the "Americanos." What kind of people are they? What food do they eat? Where is America? As time passed, I learned about America—about the people and about some aspects of their lifestyle—but my knowledge was indirect. The opportunity to experience the world of the "Americano" directly was long in coming, and when it did I was gripped with a sense of ambivalence. How would I fare in a strange and foreign land with an unfamiliar culture? That was how I finally found myself on the plane that would bring me on the first leg of my cultural sojourn to Hawaii.

Excited as I was, I could hear my heart thumping, and apprehension came over me. Suddenly, the thought hit me: I have journeyed far from home, away from the comforts and familiarity of my culture. You see, in this trip, my first outside of my homeland, I did not come as an anthropologist to do fieldwork. I came as a graduate student to study linguistics. Seven years later I would be an anthropologist. But I am getting ahead of myself.

My host family during my brief two-week stay in Honolulu was waiting at the airport. The whole family was there! The children's beaming faces and the family's warm and gracious greetings gave me a sense of assurance that everything was going to be fine. "There's nothing to it," we Fulbright scholars were reassured during a briefing on aspects of adjustment to American life and culture. So there I was in Hawaii, the first leg of my cultural sojourn (I stayed in the Midwest for another four weeks of orientation, before proceeding east to do graduate work), equipped with a theoretical survival kit designed and guaranteed to work. I would later discover that there were discrepancies between the ideal procedures and techniques and day-to-day behavior.

The differences between my culture and American culture became evident in the first few hours after my arrival. On our way out of the air terminal, the children began to fuss: "I'm hungry," "I'm tired," "I'm thirsty," "I want to go to the bathroom!" Over the whining and fidgeting of the children, my hosts and I tried to carry on a conversation but to no avail. Amazingly, despite the constant interruptions, the adults displayed considerable tolerance and patience. No voice was raised, nor harsh words spoken. I vividly recall how, as children, we were reminded never to interrupt while adults were talking, and to avoid annoying behavior, especially when in the company of adults, whether these people were kin, friends, or strangers.

We left the main highway, drove on a country road, and eventually parked by a Howard Johnson restaurant. The children did not need any bidding at all. They ran inside the restaurant in search of a table for us. I was fascinated by their quite independent and assertive behavior (more of this, later). I had originally been feeling dizzy and drowsy from the long plane ride, but I wasn't anymore. My "cultural" curiosity was aroused by the children's youthful showmanship, or so I thought. As soon as we were all seated, a young man came to hand us menus. The children made their own choices. Not feeling hungry at all, but wanting to show appreciation, I settled for a cup of soup. When the food finally came, I was completely shocked by the portions each child had. I wondered if they could eat it all. Just as I feared, they left their portions only partially eaten. What a waste, I thought. I remembered one of my father's gems of thought: "Take only what you can eat, and make sure to eat the last morsel on your plate." I must confess that I felt very bad looking at mounds of uneaten food. How can so much food be wasted? Why were children allowed to order their food themselves instead of Mom and Dad doing it for them? Was it a part of independence training? Or were Mom and Dad simply indulgent of their children's wants? I did not have any answers, but I surmised that it wasn't going to be easy understanding the American way. Neither would it be easy accepting or adjusting to American customs. I realized later that my difficulty was brought about by my cultural bias and naivete. Given the situation, I expected my own familiar behavioral/cultural response. For instance, in the Philippines, as well as in many other Asian countries, children are rarely allowed, if at all, to "do their own thing" without the consent of their parents. Consultation with parents, older siblings, aunts and uncles, or grandparents is always sought. In America, I found out that from an early age, a person is encouraged to be independent, to make up his or her mind, and to stand up for his or her rights. Individualism is encouraged among the American youth, whereas among Asians, including Filipinos, group unity, togetherness, and harmony are valued.

Values such as obedience to authority (older people are vested with authority) and respect for elders are seriously observed and practiced. The young address their elders using terms of respect. Among the Tagalog, the particle *po* (sir, ma'am) or *opo* (yes sir, yes ma'am) is always used. Not to do so is considered rude. Children do not call anybody older by their first names. This deference to age contrasts sharply with the American notions of egalitarianism and informality.

American children, I observe, are allowed to call older people by their first names. I recall two interesting incidents, amusing now but definitely bothersome then. The first incident took place in the university cafeteria. To foster collegiality among the faculty and graduate students, professors and students usually ate lunch together. During one of these occasions, I heard a student greet a teacher, "Hey, Bob! That was a tough exam! You really gave us a hard time, buddy!" I was stunned. I couldn't believe what I heard. All I could say to myself was "My God! How bold and disrespectful!"

Not long afterward, I found myself in a similar scenario. This time, I was with some very young children of new acquaintances. They called to say hello and to ask if I could spend the weekend with the family. At their place, I met more people, young and not so young. Uninhibited, the children took the liberty of introducing me to everybody. Each child who played the role of "introducer" would address each person by his or her first name. No titles such as "Mr.," "Mrs.," or "Miss" were used; we were simply introduced as "Steve, this is Amparo" and "Amparo, this is Paula." Because I was not acquainted with the sociolinguistics of American communicative style, this took me quite by surprise. I was not prepared for the reality of being addressed as the children's equal. In my own experience, it took me some time to muster courage before I could call my senior colleagues by their first names.

A somewhat similar occurrence happened many years later. I had impressed on my little girl the proper and polite way to address older people, that is, for her always to say "Mr." or "Mrs." before mentioning their first names and family names. I used to prod and remind her often that it was the right thing to do. Imagine my surprise and embarrassment when one day I heard her greet our next-door neighbor saying, "Hi, Martha!" I asked her why she greeted her that way. She readily answered, "Mommy, Martha told me not to call her Mrs. _____, just Martha!" What could I say? Since then, she was always called Martha but I had qualms each time I heard my daughter greet her. In the Philippines, older people, regardless of their status in life, whether they are relatives or strangers, are always addressed using respectful terms such as *mang* (title for an elderly man), *iyo* (abbreviated variant for *tiyo*, or uncle, a title for a male relative but also used to address someone who is elderly), *aling* (respectful title for an older or elderly woman), and *manang* (a regional variant for *aling*). However, one gets used to doing things in a certain way after a while. So did I! After all, isn't that what adaptation is all about? But my cultural adventure or misadventure did not end here. This was only a prelude.

I was introduced into American culture from the periphery, which provided me with only a glimpse of the people's lifestyle, their passing moods and attitudes, and their values and ideas. I did not have the time, effort, or desire to take a long hard look at the cultural environment around me. I returned to the Philippines with some notions about American culture. If I have another chance, I told myself, I want to check it out judiciously and with objectivity. Seven years later, an opportunity presented itself. I was back in the "good old U.S.A.," this time to stay. I humored myself with the thought that I was smarter, wiser, and better prepared for challenges. I did not expect any serious problems. If there were problems, they would be inconsequential and therefore less stressful. This was far from the truth, however!

This time I was not alone against a whole new world. I had become a mother and was raising my child while virtually swimming against the current of cultural values that were not my own. True, there are clusters of universal human values to which everybody adheres. But it is likewise true that certain values are distinctive to a culture. Here lay the crux of an important problem that I needed to resolve. How was I going to bring up my child? Did I want her to grow up American, or did I want her to be a reflection and/or extension of myself, culturally speaking? The longer I pondered on these nagging questions, the more I began to realize that they were rather unfair questions. There were no easy answers.

There was, however, one thing of which I was certain: I wanted the best for my child, that is, the best of two worlds, America and my own. To do this, there were choices to be made. Predictably, I found myself straddling between two cultures, my right hand not knowing what my left hand was doing. At times, I found myself engaged in a balancing act in an effort to understand American culture without jeopardizing my cultural ways. Thus, alternatively, I would be strongly assertive and modestly defensive when my peculiar beliefs and actions were questioned.

Two incidents remain fresh in my mind. Briefly, someone made her observations very clearly to me by her remarks: "I see you always walk your daughter to and from school every day. . . . You know, many children in the neighborhood walk to school unaccompanied by adults. Why don't you let your daughter walk with them to school? She will learn to be on her own if you let go."

Another woman, some years later, asked me whether my daughter had started to drive, to which I answered "No." Surprised, she asked how my daughter could get around (to parties, movies, and so on). She remarked, "It would be easy for her and for you if she started taking driving lessons and got her own car." Forthright remarks! Fair criticism?

These two incidents bring into sharp focus the contrast between Filipino culture and American culture in the area of socialization. It is plain to see that in these instances, I am perceived as controlling and reprimanding, whereas the other person (American) is viewed as sociable, egalitarian, and indulgent. Because of the American emphasis on self-reliance and independence, relationships between the children and the (Asian) Filipino mother are often interpreted as overdependent. Mothers are often perceived as overprotective. This observation results from unfamiliarity with the traditional family dynamics of the (Asian) Filipino family. In order to avoid a distorted perception of one culture by another, it is extremely important that the uniqueness and cultural distinctiveness of a culture be explored, recognized, and respected for what it is. Otherwise, that which is not familiar, and therefore not clearly understood, would be viewed as "bizarre," although it is completely meaningful to members of another culture.

Among the Filipinos, life is governed by traditions that do not stress independence and autonomy of the individual. The family surpasses the individual. Hierarchical roles define each member's position in the network of relationships. These relationships are strictly prescribed, such as the relationship between children and parents, between father and children, and between mother and children. For instance, the mother plays a paramount role in the nurturance of the children. The burden of the child's well-being rests on the mother.

Going back to the heart of the problem—that is, the issue of child-rearing values—I have made a conscious choice, and in doing so, my values, beliefs, and actions have been brought into question. I have reassured myself that there is no need to worry as long as my child benefits from the quality of life I have prayerfully sought and arduously worked for.

At this point, I come full circle to the question: How am I doing as a parent, as a mother? Did I do the right thing? Is my daughter growing up American? My answer would have to be "It depends. Let's wait and see!"

Study Questions

1. What are some significant differences between child–adult relationships in American and Asian cultures?
2. If you were Professor Ojeda, how would you have raised your child in America? Why?

3. What are the important distinctions between Filipino and American child-rearing practices?
4. Can you perceive any problems with American children being raised with emphasis on individuality, self-reliance, and independence?

Note

I wrote this article not to discredit or minimize the significance of American child-rearing ideas, attitudes, and practices. I simply want to emphasize that there are cross-cultural differences in outlook, values, customs, and practices. Certainly, the socialization of the young is no exception.

Suggested Readings

McGoldrick, Monica, John Pearce, and Joseph Giordano, eds. 1982. *Ethnicity and Family Therapy*. New York: Guilford Press.
Mead, Margaret, and Martha Wolfenstein, eds. 1955. *Childhood in Contemporary Cultures*. Chicago: University of Chicago Press.
Whiting, Beatrice B., and Carolyn P. Edwards. 1988. *Children of Different Worlds*. Cambridge, MA: Harvard University Press.

––––––––––14––––––––––

My American Glasses

FRANCISCO MARTINS RAMOS
UNIVERSITY OF ÉVORA

From a Portuguese perspective, Professor Ramos examines a few American cultural traits, such as informal language use, social life, body ritual, football, and that great American shrine, the bathroom. In the style of Horace Miner, the author offers lucid and critical insights into many of the customs that Americans take for granted.

Francisco Martins Ramos was raised in the Alentejo, a southern rural area of Portugal. He lived in Africa and visited the United States several times. He received his BA in Anthropology from the Technical University of Lisbon and earned his doctorate in Anthropology at the University of Évora (Portugal). He was Professor of Anthropology at the University of Évora until his retirement in 2009. In 2010 he was nominated Professor Emeritus and continues his work at the university. His areas of interest are community studies, nicknames, tourism, and Africa.

The following text is a humble reflection on American daily life, resulting from my contact with American society. I must say that a foreigner's careful look is not necessarily more refined, precise, and detailed than that of the indigenous people. As paradigmatic examples I recall the famous articles Ralph Linton (1936) and Horace Miner (1956) wrote on aspects of American cultural reality. Inspired by the brilliant words and original ideas transmitted by these authors, respectively, in "One Hundred Percent American" and "Body Ritual Among the Nacirema," I will present a critical view of some forms of behavior, phenomena, and attitudes within American daily life that raised my interest or shocked me.

Half a dozen visits to the United States (totaling about eight months) allow me some insight, simultaneously close and distant, and have led me to the present reflections. The title I have selected simply reflects a new perspective resulting from a new angle of observation.

These comments do not pretend to reduce or caricature American culture or Americans, and they are not, surely, meant to express any superiority on the part of the author. Thus, the *chiens de garde* (guard dogs) of ethnocentrism will be warned, since this is a perspective that wishes to emphasize the richness of cultural differences and of people's identity and singularity.

When I mention American culture, the idea of diversity and heterogeneity is implicit, which is the consequence of a varied number of cultural inputs from the most diverse origins. American culture is the result of a multicultural amalgam that has been consolidating itself through the years and that is in permanent evolution, with a rhythm and a dynamic that surprises a European point of view.

The ideas expressed in this article correspond not only to my own personal opinions but also to those of many colleagues and friends who gave me help and important information. I assume total responsibility for their contributions.

The United States has always exercised a strange attraction for the spirit of the Portuguese: first, as the land of quick success; second, as the cradle of democracy; third, as an unrestrained jungle of competition; and, finally, as the model to follow. Perhaps for these very reasons there has never existed in Portugal the deep anti-American sentiment that characterizes other well-known European and world situations.

Nowadays, America comes to us, fresh and quickly, at the hour of TV news, ritually and arithmetically. Radio news programs or TV reports give information and news about the American nation every day. But the situation was not always like this.

Thirty or forty years ago, what we knew about America was mythologically overemphasized in the letters of some Azorean relative.

What we knew about America came from cowboy films and documentary movies that filled our eyes with the skyscrapers of New York or the memories of Al Capone's peripeteias.

What we knew about America was part of another world, distant, unreachable, almost abstract.

In Portugal, however, what used to confuse us were the inconceivable episodes of racial segregation. In fact, the Portuguese still had one foot (and its heart) in Africa and did not easily accept this business of ethnic discrimination—we who have mixed ourselves with African, Asian, and Amerindian peoples in the seven corners of the world.

Each Portuguese who learned on school benches that America separated herself from the British Empire had a secret and inexplicable sensation of joy and satisfaction at knowing the English were defeated. Because of an ancient treaty signed in the fourteenth century, we had to bear the British after their help against the French Napoleonic invasions, and this agreement has functioned more to their benefit than to ours. Thus, nations of colonial vocation vibrate with these pretty little joys!

We cried for John Kennedy and Martin Luther King, citizens of humankind, and, still today, we are commonly surprised how Ronald Reagan could become president of the greatest nation in the world.

With the development of modern media technologies, with the increase and improvement of the means of transportation, with the implementation of exchange programs and visits, with the increase of reciprocal tourism, America is today very close to us, and her mythology is no longer incomprehensible. She now generates other myths.

La recherche du temps perdu (the search for the lost time) is for a middle-class American the search for a history and for European roots. For that reason, Europeans are not badly treated in America. As Octavio Paz has said, "The United States drown themselves in the challenges of conceiving a country" (Santos 1989: 2). As Walt Whitman wrote, what has united Americans has not been a common history, which they did not have, but "the will to build a future: a common future where utopia blends with reality" (Santos 1989: 3).

I first visited the United States in 1982. For five months I lived in Madison, Wisconsin, a state with rural characteristics, which I was comfortable with. The Alentejo Province, where I was born and raised, was also rural, as are many of the areas of my country that lack the rapid advances of industrialization.

Later, during other visits, I had the opportunity to visit Milwaukee, Chicago, Washington, D.C., New York, Phoenix, Los Angeles, Dallas, Boston, and San Francisco, areas that offered examples of the rich urban vocation of the American nation.

What surprises us as Europeans is the fact that Americans could have done in less than 150 years what it took centuries for us to do. For better or worse, in this duel of contradictions, the struggle is between the old Puritan morality and a new hedonism. The paradox is the democratic identity of the United States—a collective project—and the constantly growing individualistic trend.

A Portuguese citizen arrives in America, conscious of his or her rural extraction, and the first thing that he or she realizes is that America is not a big megalopolis. We feel perfectly integrated in the rural world of a state such as Wisconsin—with an economy based on the primary sector, with conservative political horizons as in the majority of rural societies.

A less observant visitor can lose himself or herself in the complexity of multiple and contradictory cultural traits. First, we become submersed in the imperialism of material culture, in terms of shape, space, and time. After this comes the invasion of cultural behavior traits.

Unexpectedly, the first thing I found strange, even bizarre, was the use and abuse of the word *nice*, both in formal conversations and in colloquial language. I participated in the following dialogue at a family party on Thanksgiving Day:

"Nice to meet you. What's your name?"

"Francisco."

"Oh, nice! Do you have a family?"

"Yes, I have two children. . . ."

"Very nice! Do you like America?"

"Yes, but . . ."

"That's very nice! Do you like our weather?"

"It's a little cold for me. . . ."

"But today is a nice day! By the way, did you watch the football game last night?"

"I did, but I don't understand American football. . . ."

"Oh, it's a pretty nice sport!"

Some hours later:

"Bye-bye, Francisco. It was nice to meet you. . . . Have a nice stay in the States."

In fact, the abuse of the word *nice* shocks the hearing of an attentive interlocutor and of the visitor who is interested in dominating the meandering of North American language. Either a certain mental laziness exists that generates a simplification of the linguistic process of communication, or the English language does not have the vocabulary and the semantic richness to avoid abusive repetitions. "Pretty nice" and "It's nice to be nice" are expressions that capture the extreme of what I am referring to.

An American woman who has been introduced to us always hesitates in shaking hands and is not prepared to be kissed, even by another woman. I presume that this attitude derives from educational rules or is a self-defense mechanism. The compliment normally is "Hi! Nice to meet you!"

It is interesting to note the practical sense that Americans give to forms of address. They avoid the European or Portuguese formalities of titles: mister doctor, mister engineer, mister architect, and so on. In America, preferential treatment stresses the Christian name, which in Portugal is used only with the passage of time or between kin and friends. There is a difference between the practical meaning of social relations and the world of true formality.

In the States, social life is programmed to arrange a dinner, a party, a picnic, a visit, and so on. These are operations planned far ahead. Sociability is not improvised; it is highly programmatic, predictable, and repetitive.

America has no parallel in the cult of physical exercise: Gymnastics, athletics, and life in the open air are integral parts of the daily life of Americans of all ages. Physical exercise is just one more part of Miner's "body ritual."

American football, in spite of being a game of truly male orientation, also attracts women as spectators, fans, and strong participants in discussions about the game. Up to now, European women have not been attracted by European soccer at any level: participation, attendance at games, or club/team discussions.

Football is characterized by virility, difficulty, and risks and is considered to employ a combination of war and chess strategies. Such a combination of animation and subtlety and the equilibrium of the metaphor appease the American conscience against all those (Europeans) who consider American football an exercise in brutality.

When Portuguese citizens leave their native province and arrive in America, they are confronted with a series of strange situations. Some situations provoke laughter, and others are quite dramatic and embarrassing. Many situations generate stupefaction. As a matter of fact, Horace Miner (1956), who some time ago had already subtly played with some traits of North American culture, called our attention to the characteristics of the bathroom, the true ceremonial center of body ritual. A Portuguese who visits the bathroom in the home of an American friend faces some puzzling situations. For example, in the bathrooms of more than twenty American couples that time and friendship have allowed me to know, in dozens of hotels, motels, dormitories, bus and train stations, restaurants, and bars, no two water taps are alike. Consequently, I have encountered great difficulties in turning the water on, in adjusting cold and hot water, in regulating the faucet pressure, and in stopping the flow. The problem is that the tap mechanisms can be put into action by the pressure of a forefinger on a generally hidden button, by turning a screw that we wouldn't think to turn, by moving an appurtenance considered to be ornamental, or by using a masked hook, a secondary metal arabesque, or an invisible pedal.

If from the taps we move to showers, baths, and toilets, it is easy to recognize the embarrassment of a common Portuguese who is forced to make a detailed preliminary study of the sanitary equipment, which the circumstances do not always permit. We perfectly understand Americans' exemplary obsession with bad smells, as we can verify through the shape of toilets and the volume of water they consume in restrooms. However, the paraphernalia, mechanisms, and equipment are so different as to constitute a labyrinth for the rural European Portuguese.

In public restrooms, the Portuguese amateur in urbanities will certainly be quite surprised with a form of cultural behavior never dreamt of: The American who urinates in public initiates conversation with the partner at his side, even if he does not know the latter! Themes of these occasional dialogues are the weather, football, politics, and so on. We can guess at the forced pleasure of the Portuguese, who heretofore has regarded urination as a necessary physical function, not as a social occasion. The public restroom! Is it an extension of the barroom?

Next, I would like to comment on gastronomy. The first consideration is the diversity of American food, rich and varied as many others, as a form of cultural manifestation. In this case, the gastronomic contributions from different and distant cultures make American cuisine a true "melting pot," an opportune expression to describe so-called "ethnic" food. A Portuguese who has not traveled much will be faced with the dilemma of choice in a restaurant or at the supermarket. In fact, there are seemingly endless types of sauces, numerous varieties of bread, an immense number of different kinds of cheese, potatoes cooked in various ways, and so on. Another marvel is the fast-food system, which fits perfectly into the American way of life. Indeed, during weekdays, the fast-food system is oriented to the performance of work, in a real struggle against time.

My discussion of gastronomy would not be complete without reference to table etiquette. Americans normally use the knife very little but use the fork continually. Those of us who have been educated by the French bible of good manners at the table have always been told that it is good etiquette to use a fork and knife simultaneously: fork in the left hand, knife in the right. Thus, we find it difficult to accept as proper etiquette the use of the fork with the right hand, leaving the left hand under the table as a sign of good manners.

Speaking of manners, if an American cannot avoid belching in public (he burps and naturally apologizes), for a Portuguese this means a lack of good manners. However, the same Portuguese will be positively impressed with the kindness and amiability showed by American pedestrians or drivers, who are always willing to give the correct information any time it is requested. The paradox is that Americans think the same way about the Portuguese.

Whereas some differences amaze and delight us, others are true shocks. One difference is the idea of one's sharing a bedroom with an American woman, without being involved in sex. Indeed, it is normal and current among university students, participants at conferences, and friends to share a bedroom and a bed only for practical reasons. We can imagine how a Portuguese (or a Spaniard or an Italian) would conceive of such partition without generating conflict with his engraved honor as a Latin macho. Something that an American woman does, with the greatest naturalness, will be more than reason for a Latin man not to sleep a wink all night, if it should happen that he shares the same room only with the intent of having a good sleep and reducing expenses. The Latin caught in this trap will necessarily have his night replete with dreams, his imagination well fed, and a prolonged insomnia. . . .

The United States is a country where everything must be paid for, with two honorable exceptions: the ice vomited up by machines strategically placed in hotels and service stations, and matches, which are publicity tools offered by cigarette machines and free at any hotel or restaurant of any category. However, there is an institutionalized payment that surprises me: the tip. It is a quasi imposition that I consider contradictory in a society like the United States. In fact, the philosophy that informs American life is one of merit, of success, and of justice. It seems to me that in this society, to give a tip would be to humiliate someone who fulfills his or her duty, renders a service, or performs a task that does not need to be rewarded beyond the normal circuit. Tips pay favors, compensate insufficiencies and not duties, and are the embryo of corruption. They never will be just, even in societies where class differences are clandestine or hidden. Tips in the States are equivocal; they are a form of oblivion and in contradiction to American life and values.

A big country, from a geographical point of view, the United States is a country closed in on itself. Americans know little about the world except when a plane crashes in Germany, a revolution takes place in Portugal (located about seven hours away by air), or when the king of Spain dies. On the other hand, we always know when an American president has a toothache, when a Hollywood star gets divorced for the third time, or when there is a rally for legalizing marijuana. This focus can be understood by the fact that the United States is a country at an intercontinental level, with several dozen states that function almost like European countries. Isn't it true that a middle-class American will spend his or her vacation in another American state? This virtual autism derives from another important factor within American daily life—the television. The American TV, a complex and overwhelming hydra, reports live on car accidents at the street corner, interviews the storekeeper on our block, or covers the "League of Friends" of something or another. The only international issues reported, in fact, are those directly related to the United States of America. Besides these, only natural disasters, revolutions, and air accidents are covered. The world is too far away: Europe is too distant, South America is not very close either, and only the immediate geographical space is subject to attention. TV imperialism and the enormous publicity machine suffer from umbilical narcissism, exploitable at any moment.

The American family is an enigmatic institution, both protective and uncaring. When I reflect on the concept of family, the transmission of values, and the conveying of parental authority, which is simultaneously rigid and relaxed, I feel that something is wrong; that is, there is something essentially different from these concepts in Europe. I admit my bias and some ethnocentrism, but I question the attitudes of American youth. For example, the obsession for alcoholic drinks when one reaches the authorized or legal age (which varies from state to state) appears to be in contradiction with family values conveyed to youngsters. I had many opportunities to observe young people, boys and girls, who used to get drunk, mixing various types of alcoholic drinks. When I asked several groups the reason for such mixtures, the answer was always the same: "We mix the drinks in order to get drunk as soon as possible." It is true that not all American youths proceed in this manner, but it is also true that the great ambition of a youngster eighteen years of age is to leave his or her parents' home. The wish for autonomy and freedom, and the obsessive thirst for alcoholic drinks, seem too radical and are a strange rupture within family tutorship. That is the reason I suggest that something is not going well in the family educational system in the United States. I hope to be forgiven by those who think I am generalizing too readily.

During my first visits to America, I thought there was a kind of empty space in relation to social control. I thought in these terms because I was a foreigner and apparently anonymous. In fact, in this respect American society is not so different from others. In large urban centers, naturally, interpersonal relations are marked by a great indifference, but that happens all around the world. By the same token, in American rural areas, as in rural areas worldwide, there are forms of social control, more or less visible, more or less subtle. What happens to the foreign visitor and observer is the initial blindness in the face of novelty and the unknown. Such blindness does not allow us to focus our dispersed attention on the analysis of social phenomena in their real proportions and profundity.

My son Carlos went to Los Angeles to spend a vacation. It was agreed that he would stay one and a half months in the house of our friends. Before his departure, I gave him some advice and information about the American way of life. During his stay he used to call me, but the tone of his voice did not sound very convincing when he informed me that he was truly enjoying his "American dream." After twenty-nine days, I received an unexpected phone call:

"Father, meet me at the airport, I'm coming back tomorrow!"

"But why so early?"

"I'll tell you later."

The next day, I went to the Lisbon airport. As soon as he saw me he gave me a hug and sighed,

"I wanted so much to return, but I already regret having come!"

That's exactly what America provokes in us: an ambivalent sentiment of love and rejection, in a type of overwhelming anguish that generates the ambition to go to America and the wish to come back quickly.

My son's thirty days in America were a unique experience that is a dream for many Portuguese and European youngsters of his age and that had also been the unreachable ambition of my own youth. Carlos wants to return to the States, and nowadays he is showing his intercontinental behavior with the consumption of many liters of Pepsi or Coca-Cola and enormous portions of ketchup, popcorn, and French-fried potatoes.

Meanwhile, I notice that he makes a show of using slang phrases that he has taken to his English classes. Naturally, this has not helped him earn good grades.

Since Carlos returned, he systematically uses coded expressions. He now says, "It's really good over there; there things are better; when I was there . . . , there I could heat my orange juice in the microwave; there we can find everything." After some time, it was easy for me to conclude that for my son *there* means America.

A Portuguese of middle-class background can usually speak several languages. This situation is much appreciated by Americans, and we are normally well respected given our capacity to communicate in three or four languages: our mother tongue, English, French, and Spanish or German. For us, this was always a necessary or a natural thing: Besides our own language, it is not difficult for us to speak in Spanish; we have a long and great tradition connected with French culture and the French language; and in order to understand Americans, we need to speak English. Americans find themselves in an inferior position because neither history nor necessity has forced them to learn other languages. For some Americans, the ability to speak French is an indicator of incomparable prestige. I think that some Americans insist on enriching their vocabulary with French words and expressions, even if they cannot speak the language fluently. The Portuguese visitor wins some status and security given his or her role as a polyglot. However, in other situations, the Portuguese visitor gapes at the spectacular achievements (in terms of material culture and social pragmatism) of so-called American civilization.

We are amazed, for example, that the prestige of certain professions in America is not as low as is the case in Portugal. I think, in contrast, that Americans grant more dignity to the worker, regardless of the type of job performed. In the United States, a farmer, a taxi driver, or a traveling salesperson would not necessarily feel inferior; in Portugal, however, these are truly minor professions. In Portugal, too, an economist, an anthropologist, or a graduate in chemistry would almost never perform the aforementioned "lowly" jobs. "It does not become one" and "it looks bad" would be the first justifications.

In fact, this problem is linked either to the labor market or to the educational system, to access to the university, and to the total proportions of graduates, which are quite different both in quality and quantity in these countries.

The United States values community associations in a way we think exemplary. Cooperative projects, professional and sectorial associations, defense leagues, and friends groups proliferate in the heart of American society. In a land that has recently fomented excessive narcissism and individualism, it is interesting to note the conciliation of these two philosophies and postures.

Indeed, in the end, I know extremely little about the United States of America. Probably my American glasses have given me a blurred, out-of-focus image of reality.

The posture of a Portuguese can be ridiculous when in America. I remember that my son warmed his orange juice in the microwave to soothe his sore throat. Our difficulty in determining on which side a door opens is ridiculous. We Portuguese do not take showers after meals, we think it dangerous for our health to eat oranges at night, we make a lot of noise when we blow our noses, we rarely go to bed before midnight, and we spend enormous amounts of time at the table.

Any American, in turn, would grin at this strange behavior.

15

The Young, the Rich, and the Famous

Individualism as an American Cultural Value

PORANEE NATADECHA-SPONSEL
UNIVERSITY OF HAWAI'I, HONOLULU

From the point of view of a scholar raised in Thailand, Americans appear open and immediately friendly in their greetings. However, if one looks closely with a critical eye, these greetings are superficial and ritualized, and they tend to hide the more important aspects of American cultural values. The openness in greetings provides both contrast and contradiction to the closedness of social relations and family structures, especially when compared to traditional Thai cultural values. Further, the values of privacy and individualism and the attainment of wealth and fame are viewed as critical elements in relation to the nature of social relations and the kinship system.

Poranee Natadecha-Sponsel was born in the multiethnic region of Thais and Malays in the southern part of Thailand. She has lived in the United States since 1978. She received her BA with honors in English and Philosophy from Chulalongkorn University in Bangkok, Thailand (1969). She earned her MA (1973) in Philosophy at Ohio University, Athens, and her EdD (1991) from the University of Hawai'i at Manoa in Educational Foundations with an interdisciplinary focus on Anthropology and Environmental Education. She is retired from teaching at the University of Hawai'i, Honolulu.

"Hi, how are you?" "Fine, thank you, and you?" These are greetings that everybody in America hears and says every day—salutations that come ready-made and packaged just like a hamburger and fries. There is no real expectation for any special information in response to these greetings. Do not, under any circumstances, take up anyone's time by responding in depth to the programmed query. What or how you may feel at the moment is of little, if any, importance. Thai people would immediately perceive that our concerned American friends are truly interested in our welfare, and this concern would require polite reciprocation by spelling out the details of our current condition. We become very disappointed when we have had enough experience in the United States to learn that we have bored, amused, or even frightened many of our American acquaintances by taking the greeting "How are you?" so literally. We were reacting like Thais, but in the American context where salutations have a different meaning, our detailed reactions were inappropriate. In Thai society, a greeting among acquaintances usually requests specific information about the other person's condition, such as "Where are you going?" or "Have you eaten?"

One of the American contexts in which this greeting is most confusing and ambiguous is at the hospital or clinic. In these sterile and ritualistic settings, I have always been uncertain exactly how to answer when the doctor or nurse asks "How are you?" If I deliver a packaged answer of "Fine," I wonder if I am telling a lie. After all, I am there in the first place precisely because I am not so fine. Finally, after debating for some time, I asked one nurse how she expected a patient to answer the query "How are you?" But after asking this question, I then wondered if it was rude to do so. However, she looked relieved after I explained to her that people from different cultures have different ways to greet other people and that for me to be asked how I am in the hospital results in awkwardness. Do I simply answer, "Fine, thank you," or do I reveal in accurate detail how I really feel at the moment? My suspicion was verified when the nurse declared that "How are you?" was really no more than a polite greeting and that she didn't expect any answer more elaborate than simply "Fine." However, she told me that some patients do answer her by describing every last ache and pain from which they are suffering.

A significant question that comes to mind is whether the verbal pattern of greetings reflects any social relationship in American culture. The apparently warm and sincere greeting may initially suggest interest in the person, yet the intention and expectations are, to me, quite superficial. For example, most often the person greets you quickly and then walks by to attend to other business without even waiting for your response! This type of greeting is just like a package of American fast food! The person eats the food quickly without enjoying the taste. The convenience is like many other American accoutrements of living such as cars, household appliances, efficient telephones, or simple, systematic, and predictable arrangements of groceries in the supermarket. However, usually when this greeting is delivered, it seems to lack a personal touch and genuine feeling. It is little more than ritualized behavior.

I have noticed that most Americans keep to themselves even at social gatherings. Conversation may revolve around many topics, but little, if anything, is revealed about oneself. Without talking much about oneself and not knowing much about others, social relations seem to remain at an abbreviated superficial level. How could one know a person without knowing something about him or her? How much does one need to know about a person to really know that person?

After living in this culture for more than a decade, I have learned that there are many topics that should not be mentioned in conversations with American acquaintances or even close friends. One's personal life and one's income are considered to be very private and even taboo topics. Unlike my Thai culture, Americans do not show interest or curiosity by asking such personal questions, especially when one just meets the individual for the first time. Many times I have been embarrassed by my Thai acquaintances who recently arrived at the University of Hawaii and the East-West Center. For instance, one day I was walking on campus with an American friend when we met another Thai woman to whom I had been introduced a few days earlier. The Thai woman came to write her doctoral dissertation at the East-West Center where the American woman worked, so I introduced them to each other. The American woman greeted my Thai companion in Thai language, which so impressed her that she felt immediately at ease. At once, she asked the American woman numerous personal questions such as, How long did you live in Thailand? Why were you there? How long were you married to the Thai man? Why did you divorce him? How long have you been divorced? Are you going to marry a Thai again or an American? How long have you been working here? How much do you earn? The American was stunned. However, she was very patient and more or less answered all those questions as succinctly as she could. I was so uncomfortable that I had to interrupt whenever I could to get her out of the awkward situation in which she had been forced into talking about things she considered personal. For people in Thai society, such questions would be appropriate and not considered too personal, let alone taboo.

The way Americans value their individual privacy continues to impress me. Americans seem to be open and yet there is a contradiction because they are also aloof and secretive. This is reflected in many of their behavior patterns. By Thai standards, the relationship between friends in American society seems to be somewhat superficial. Many Thai students, as well as other Asians, have felt that they could not find genuine friendship with Americans. For example, I met many American classmates who were very helpful and friendly while we were in the same class. We went out, exchanged phone calls, and did the same things as would good friends in Thailand. But those activities stopped suddenly when the semester ended.

Privacy as a component of the American cultural value of individualism is nurtured in the home as children grow up. From birth they are given their own individual, private space, a bedroom separate from that of their parents. American children are taught to become progressively independent, both emotionally and economically, from their family. They learn to help themselves at an early age. In comparison, in Thailand, when parents bring a new baby home from the hospital, it shares the parents' bedroom for two to three years and then shares another bedroom with older siblings of the same sex. Most Thai children do not have their own private room until they finish high school, and some do not have their own room until another sibling moves out, usually when the sibling gets married. In Thailand, there are strong bonds within the extended family. Older siblings regularly help their parents to care for younger ones. In this and other ways, the Thai family emphasizes the interdependence of its members.

I was accustomed to helping Thai babies who fell down to stand up again. Thus, in America when I saw babies fall, it was natural for me to try to help them back on their feet. Once at a summer camp for East-West Center participants, one of the supervisors brought his wife and their ten-month-old son with him. The baby was so cute that many students were playing with him. At one point he was trying to walk and fell, so all the Asian students, males and females, rushed to help him up. Although the father and mother were nearby, they paid no attention to their fallen and crying baby. However, as the students were trying to help and comfort him, the parents told them to leave him alone; he would be all right on his own. The baby did get up and stopped crying without any assistance. Independence is yet another component of the American value of individualism.

Individualism is even reflected in the way Americans prepare, serve, and consume food. In a typical American meal, each person has a separate plate and is not supposed to share or taste food from other people's plates. My Thai friends and I are used to eating Thai style, in which you share food from a big serving dish in the middle of the table. Each person dishes a small amount from the serving dish onto his or her plate and finishes this portion before going on with the next portion of the same or a different serving dish. With the Thai pattern of eating, you regularly reach out to the serving dishes throughout the meal. But this way of eating is not considered appropriate in comparison to the common American practice where each person eats separately from his or her individual plate.

One time my American host, a divorcee who lived alone, invited a Thai girlfriend and myself to an American dinner at her home. When we were reaching out and eating a small portion of one thing at a time in Thai style, we were told to dish everything we wanted onto our plates at one time and that it was not considered polite to reach across the table. The proper American way was to have each kind of food piled up on your plate at once. If we were to eat in the same manner in Thailand, eyebrows would have been raised at the way we piled up food on our plates, and we would have been considered to be eating like pigs, greedy and inconsiderate of others who shared the meal at the table.

Individualism as a pivotal value in American culture is reflected in many other ways. Material wealth is not only a prime status marker in American society but also a guarantee and celebration of individualism—wealth allows the freedom to do almost anything, although usually within the limits of law. The pursuit of material wealth through individual achievement is instilled in Americans from the youngest age. For example, I was surprised to see an affluent American couple, who own a large ranch house and two BMW cars, send their nine-year-old son to deliver newspapers. He has to get up very early each morning to deliver the papers, even on Sunday! During summer vacation, the boy earns additional money by helping in his parents' gift shop from 10 A.M. to 5 P.M. His thirteen-year-old sister often earns money by babysitting, even at night.

In Thailand, only children from poorer families work to earn money to help the household. Middle- and high-income parents do not encourage their children to work until after they have finished their education. They provide economic support in order to free their children to concentrate on and excel in their studies. Beyond the regular schooling, families who can afford it pay for special tutoring as well as training in music, dance, or sports. However, children in low- and middle-income families help their parents with household chores and the care of younger children.

Many American children have been encouraged to get paid for their help around the house. They rarely get any gifts free of obligations. They even have to be good to get Santa's gifts at Christmas! As they grow up, they are conditioned to earn things they want; they learn that "there is no such thing as a free lunch." From an early age, children are taught to become progressively independent economically from their parents. Also, most young people are encouraged to leave home at college age to be on their own. From my viewpoint as a Thai, it seems that American family ties and closeness are not as strong as in Asian families whose children depend on family financial support until joining the workforce after college age. Thereafter, it is the children's turn to help support their parents financially.

Modern American society and economy emphasize individualism in other ways. The nuclear family is more common than the extended family, and newlyweds usually establish their own independent household rather than initially living with either the husband's or the wife's parents. Parents and children appear to be close only when the children are very young. Most American parents seem to "lose" their children by the teenage years. They don't seem to belong to each other as closely as do Thai families. Even though I have seen more explicit affectionate expression among American family members than among Asian ones, the close interpersonal spirit seems to be lacking. Grandparents have relatively little to do with the grandchildren on any regular basis, in contrast to the extended family, which is more common in Thailand. The family and society seem to be graded by age to the point that grandparents, parents, and children are separated by generational subcultures that are evidently alienated from one another. Each group "does its own thing." Help and support are usually limited to whatever does not interfere with one's own life. In America, the locus of responsibility is more on the individual than on the family.

In one case I know of, a financially affluent grandmother with Alzheimer's disease is taken care of twenty-four hours a day by hired help in her own home. Her daughter visits and relieves the helper occasionally. The mature granddaughter, who has her own family, rarely visits. Yet they all live in the same neighborhood. However, each lives in a different house, and each is very independent. Although the mother worries about the grandmother, she cannot do much. Her husband also needs her, and she divides her time between him, her daughters and their children, and the grandmother. When the mother needs to go on a trip with her husband, a second hired attendant is required to care for the grandmother temporarily. When I asked why the granddaughter doesn't temporarily care for the grandmother, the reply was that she has her own life, and it would not be fair for the granddaughter to take care of the grandmother, even for a short period of time. Yet I wonder if it is fair for the grandmother to be left out. It seems to me that the value of individualism and its associated independence account for these apparent gaps in family ties and support.

In contrast to American society, in Thailand older parents with a long-term illness are asked to move in with their children and grandchildren if they are not already living with them. The children and grandchildren take turns attending to the grandparent, sometimes with help from live-in maids. Living together in the same house reinforces moral support among the generations within an extended family. The older generation is respected because of the previous economic, social, and moral support for their children and grandchildren. Family relations provide one of the most important contexts for being a "morally good person," which is traditionally the principal concern in the Buddhist society of Thailand.

In America, being young, rich, and/or famous allows one greater freedom and independence and thus promotes the American value of individualism. This is reflected in the mass appeal of major annual television events like the Super Bowl and the Academy Awards. The goal of superachievement is also seen in more mundane ways. For example, many parents encourage their children to take special courses and to work hard to excel in sports as a short-cut to becoming rich and famous. I know one mother who has taken her two sons to tennis classes and tournaments since the boys were six years old, hoping that at least one of them will be a future tennis star like Ivan Lendl. Other parents focus their children on acting, dancing, or musical talent. The children have to devote much time and hard work as well as sacrifice the ordinary activities of youth in order to develop and perform their natural talents and skills in prestigious programs. But those who excel in the sports and entertainment industries can become rich and famous, even at an early age, as for example Madonna, Tom Cruise, and Michael Jackson. Television and other media publicize these celebrities and thereby reinforce the American value of individualism, including personal achievement and financial success.

Although the American cultural values of individualism and the aspiration to become rich and famous have had some influence in Thailand, there is also cultural and religious resistance to these values. Strong social bonds, particularly within the extended family, and the hierarchical structure of the kingdom run counter to individualism. Also, youth gain social recognition through their academic achievement. From the perspective of Theravada Buddhism, which strongly influences Thai culture, aspiring to be rich and famous would be an illustration of greed, and those who have achieved wealth and fame do not celebrate it publicly as much as in American society. Being a good, moral person is paramount, and ideally Buddhists emphasize restraint and moderation.

Beyond talent and skill in the sports and entertainment industries, there are many other ways that young Americans can pursue wealth. Investment is one route. One American friend who is only a sophomore in college has already invested heavily in the stock market to start accumulating wealth. She is just one example of the 1980s trend for youth to be more concerned with their individual finances than with social, political, and environmental issues. With less attention paid to public issues, the expression of individualism seems to be magnified through emphasis on lucrative careers, financial investment, and material consumption—the "Yuppie" phenomenon. This includes new trends in dress, eating, housing (condominiums), and cars (expensive European imports). Likewise, there appears to be less of a long-term commitment to marriage. More young couples are living together without either marriage or plans for future marriage. When such couples decide to get married, prenuptial agreements are made to protect their assets. Traditional values of marriage, family, and sharing appear to be on the decline.

Individualism as one of the dominant values in American culture is expressed in many ways. This value probably stems from the history of the society as a frontier colony of immigrants in search of a better life with independence, freedom, and the opportunity for advancement through personal achievement. However, in the beliefs and customs of any culture there are some disadvantages as well as advantages. Although Thais may admire the achievements and material wealth of American society, there are costs, especially in the value of individualism and associated social phenomena.

Study Questions

1. What are the social implications of the ways in which Americans greet each other? Is this a form of personal sincerity or is it, as the author suggests, to be viewed as similar to our fast-food habits—simply convenient and lacking sincerity?

2. How do American greeting practices and Thai greeting practices differ?

3. What are some American subjects that would be taboo in a public meeting with friends?

4. How are eating habits different in Thailand?

5. If you grew up in Thailand, what class distinctions would dictate your expectations as to whether or not you would work to earn money as a youngster?

6. In relation to American individualism, how do the family financial expectations differ from those in Thailand?

7. What might the effects of "doing your own thing" in American culture have on the nature of American family structure? How does this reflect on differences between how the elderly are treated in both cultures?

8. What are the cultural constraints in Thailand that prohibit one from seeking to attain wealth and fame?

16

Neighborly Strangers

HONGGANG YANG
NOVA SOUTHEASTERN UNIVERSITY

Dr. Yang spent two years doing fieldwork in a private cluster homes neighborhood in Florida. In this essay he focuses on how American homeowners both resist and come to terms with the ownership of common property by contrasting his experience in Florida to his experience in urban China. He clearly articulates the barriers that American individualism creates for the development of community among his neighbors in "Pondtrees."

Honggang Yang is Dean of the College of Arts, Humanities, and Social Sciences and is Professor of Interdisciplinary Studies at Nova Southeastern University. He worked as a research associate in Conflict Resolution Programs at the Carter Center of Emory University and taught at Antioch College. He did medical training in undergraduate education and studied social psychology in graduate school in China. Before coming to the United States in 1986, Honggang Yang was a faculty member in the Department of Sociology at Nankai University. He earned his PhD in Applied Anthropology at the University of South Florida in 1991. Dr. Yang's research interests are in the fields of legal anthropology, community organizations, reflective practice, and management of common property resources.

I spent almost two years doing fieldwork in an American neighborhood with a homeowners association. My ethnographic curiosity is about how American homeowners in a private cluster homes development share and manage common property resources, such as neighborhood fences, swimming pools, tennis courts, picnic sites, parking lots, entrance areas, playgrounds, and clubhouses. Like many anthropologists engaged in fieldwork overseas, I was often puzzled by the foreign patterns of social relations in this modern residential corporation in the United States, since I had grown up in China where communal life was quite different. At the beginning of my field endeavor, I could not see the "problems" in what were considered problems by my informants, and I could not understand why what I perceived as problems were not regarded as "problems" by the residents.

In my writings, I call my field site "Pondtrees"—a fictitious name. Pondtrees is located in a suburb of the Tampa Bay area. The development was started in the mid-1970s and completed in the early 1980s. There are now about five hundred homes in Pondtrees. As the place name indicates, there are several ponds and lakes and plenty of trees. The development has two kinds of homes: the single-family house or detached building and the townhome or contiguous unit. The larger lake in the area serves as a marker: All of the single-family homes are on the west side of the lake, whereas most of the townhomes are on the east shore. However, homeowners of both groups are mandatory members of the association. There are also a considerable number of absentee homeowners and renters in Pondtrees.

When I started fieldwork, I was first struck by the legalistic and commercial multiplicity of the residential organization. In Pondtrees, homeowners are obligated to pay dues to the association for maintaining the common facilities and common areas. Owners of townhomes pay more because they receive more services, such as pest control, mowing, roofing, siding, and repairing exterior parts of their property. The board of directors, consisting of five volunteers elected from among the homeowners, contracts a property manager to do the jobs. A set of documents are the legal basis for the operation and governance of the association. The highly specialized rules and regulations for Pondtrees are contained in documents entitled "Restated Articles of Incorporation; Bylaws; Restated Declaration of Easements, Covenants, Conditions, and Restrictions; Master Declarations; and Townhome Declarations." I was astonished by the complexity as well as the quantity of the collection. There are a multitude of signatures and stamps on the documents, imprints of approval and witness. In one of the documents, the Restated Declaration, there are at least twenty-three signatures and seven stamps.

Pondtrees is quiet. Residents are seldom well acquainted with one another, in sharp contrast to my residence in China where every neighbor knows each other. In the Chinese urban neighborhood where my parents still reside, the residential setting and communal atmosphere appear characteristic of *Gemeinschaft* (traditional community). Residents in such a community are often employed in the same work unit. There exists ongoing mutual aid among neighbors, which includes watching the stove, buying vegetables, helping move furniture, and taking care of children for each other. As a child, I customarily addressed my neighbors in senior generations by the kinship terms *uncle* or *aunt.*

Different from the American counterpart, urban houses in China are usually not privately owned but are provided by the government through work units. Migration into cities is restricted, unless one is recruited by the government. Urban residents are all legally required to register to gain jobs, housing, food, health care, school, and the like. The neighborhood is geographically bounded, consisting of several adjacent blocks with from one hundred to a few hundred households. There is a resident committee in each neighborhood, which is a semiautonomous multifunctional organization. I call it "semi" because of its political affiliation with the party and state and its folk ties with local residents. It is organizationally different from the board of directors of American homeowners associations in many ways. In China, the committee members are chosen or elected from among volunteers, most of whom are retired elders and housewives with charismatic authority carrying social respect, credit, and trust. They assist the local government in conducting household registration, inspecting block sanitation, supervising individual immunizations, family planning, handling minor criminal cases, mediating civil and domestic disputes, coordinating a neighborhood watch, and holding some social activities.

While my family and I were in Pondtrees, my wife often expressed to me her personal reactions to the neighborhood. She sometimes complained that our immediate neighbors never invited her over to chat, visit, or have supper together. I remember that last year when we were moving from one house to another within Pondtrees, my wife intended to look for help from the neighbors and wished that someone had given us a hand.

Undoubtedly, the prevalence of high residential mobility in U.S. society is a factor contributing to the existing lack of communal sentiment. Around my house in the townhome section, there are several adjacent buildings with four units each. My neighbors change almost constantly, moving in and out. There are quite a few vacant units, and on several are signs of "For Sale" or "Assumable Owner." I found that residents rarely get to know each other. One of my informants in the single-family section told me that his next-door neighbors have changed three times in the past two years. But my fieldwork experience also taught me that most of the residents do not have intentions or expectations to know each other beyond saying hello in the street. Some of them believe that Pondtrees is simply a place to live; others consider it an investment; still, a few of them refer to it as a "community." Despite the cognitive differences, they always seem ready to move.

I describe the residents in Pondtrees as "neighborly strangers." "Neighborly" used here has two meanings, one referring to the physical vicinity or the spatial contiguity of their residence and another connoting a routine presentation of self as "nice." A good neighbor in this context is expected to be "friendly" with others, rather than a friend. "Strangers" implies the remote interpersonal distances among the neighbors, as distinct from my neighbors in China, who not only know each other's ages, occupations, ranks, economic conditions, family histories, relatives, and personal hobbies but also often offer help. My neighbors in Pondtrees, on the other hand, seldom have that kind of knowledge and trust, since such knowledge may entail a sort of invasion of privacy. Their shelters are too close to allow them to be friends in such a living domain, perhaps due to what I term "privacy considerations." My wife once commented that maintaining surface interaction without a greater sense of community was almost meaningless, and it would lead to feelings of uncertainty and indifference among neighbors. Not having neighbors as friends doesn't mean that the residents have no friends but that they make friends somewhere else. When I approached the residents, asking questions about neighborhood concerns, they often responded very briefly with common expressions of "You know what I mean" or "You know what I am saying." They seemed reluctant to talk more and were politely on guard. There seems to exist an invisible interpersonal boundary that is almost impossible for "nonfriends" to penetrate.

The mobile and anonymous conditions of life in Pondtrees significantly affect the harmony of communal life. The neighborhood atmosphere is sometimes marred by the prevalent apathetic attitudes and frequent complaints about the commons shared and managed by residents themselves. One informant, who had been vice president of the board, told me his experience: "No matter what you do, everybody hates you." While I was in the field, I attended every monthly board meeting, and there were only about one dozen participants. I was surprised at the beginning because I expected more residents to be active in their neighborhood. One of my informants told me that low attendance is a good sign that means fewer complaints and less trouble. Later, I found that my informant was right about those who came to the meetings. Most of the participants usually have ideas, concerns, confusions, problems, or issues on the maintenance and services. For example, some of the common complaints were about the inconsistent decorative colors of homes, curtains, windows, and fences, which in my eyes could have been ignored. Typically, there are more complaints than constructive suggestions about the commons in the neighborhood, and there are fewer residents willing to volunteer for the board or committees than critics. For several consecutive years, the annual meeting, the most important activity of the association (election, budgets, and finance), could not reach a quorum and had to hold a second meeting with a lower quorum.

In Pondtrees, I presented myself as a resident as well as a student, and I volunteered in quite a few ways to get more involved. For example, I served as a clubhouse coordinator. One day when I was on duty at the clubhouse, I found an interesting newspaper clipping titled "Motto":

> Stay away from meetings. If you come, find fault and never offer an alternative. Decline office or appointment to a committee. Get sore if you aren't nominated.
>
> After you are nominated, don't attend board or committee meetings. If you get to one, despite your better judgment, clam up until you get outside, then sound off on how things should have been done.
>
> Don't work if you can avoid it. When the old reliables pitch in, accuse them of being a clique.
>
> Oppose all banquets, parties, seminars, conferences, and trade missions as being a waste of the attendees' money. If everything is strictly business, then complain that the meetings are dull and officers belong to the old guard.
>
> Never accept a place at the head table. If you aren't asked to sit there, threaten to resign because you aren't appreciated.
>
> Don't rush to pay your dues; let the directors sweat—after all, they wrote the budget. Read the mail from the association only now and then; never reply if you can help it, and then ask why you were not informed.

This "motto" is an exaggerated depiction of some common dilemmas involving sharing in such an environment. It reflects, in a dramatic way, an embedded contradiction between the individual and the commons. The essence of the commons is to provide resources that are needed but are difficult or impossible to provide individually. I asked some of my informants for their comments on the "motto." They told me that it was true but varied per particular individual, for a particular period of time, on a particular issue, and in a particular context. The cynical attitudes in the "motto" expressed implicit tension and disharmony, and these attitudes were, in fact, not less influential in neighborhood life than apathy. Neither the cynicism nor the apathy, in my opinion, is constructive or healthy.

There were also occasional legal battles that reflected another aspect of the neighborhood—communal politics and interpersonal tension in Pondtrees. About two years ago, a number of the homeowners found that a board member was delinquent in his monthly dues but was somehow permitted to take part in the association election at the annual meeting. This incident happened at the time when a controversial, extraordinary assessment was proposed by the board. The dissatisfied homeowners decided to hire an attorney to sue the board of directors for permitting the board member to vote. According to the bylaws, homeowners failing to pay assessments prior to the meeting are not entitled to enjoy the benefit of association membership, including electing and getting elected. But the tricky part of the dispute centered around the fact that the delinquent board member submitted a check for payment just before the meeting and then requested that the check be returned to him the following day because he was not financially able to meet his obligation. To defend the stand taken, the board also sought legal counsel from the association attorney. The association attorney held that the board's permission was legally legitimate and did not influence the voting.

Facing such legal threats and possible court action, the board of directors decided to indemnify its members, which meant spending additional money on buying insurance—a guarantee against personal liability in conjunction with board service in the nonprofit corporation. This episode illustrates a painful and complex aspect of the usually quiet situation in Pondtrees. It reveals that going to court more or less becomes one of the standard facts of communal life in a neighborhood like Pondtrees. This whole issue perplexed me. I thought that life in an American suburban common property development would be peaceful and economical. To achieve harmony, however, the residents need to work to solve their problems while maintaining communal unity.

In China, neighborhood mediation is one of the distinctive functions of the resident committee, and it is characterized by an informal, decentralized, self-governing approach on a face-to-face basis at the grassroots level. Under the state ownership of housing and with the dominance of the cultural value of kinship, not many residents concern themselves with the maintenance of the common resources they share or other nonkinship, public matters. These are the recurrent problems and issues in such scenes. The inside of individual homes may be tidy and in good order, but the shared areas like corridors and entrances are sometimes messy and vandalized. In such cases, the committee members will approach the responsible residents directly, explain the problem, and persuade them to correct it. Conflict resolution within the neighborhood remains relatively undifferentiated between communal matters and family affairs. For example, if a couple has a big quarrel and one of them seeks a divorce, the neighbors who hear it may tell the committee members and then the committee members may mediate between the two sides, reminding them of the happiness of their marriage and helping them understand each other in that emotional situation. This pattern of neighborhood dispute resolution correlates with the emphasis on "harmony of life" in Chinese culture as well as with the socioeconomic context where urban mobility is low.

Even in Pondtrees, against the background of apathy and cynicism, there has been a successful community organization operating without interruption—the garden club. It came into being on the partial completion of the development and is still running. It demonstrates the convergence of individual interests and communal benefits. Every home has a courtyard, and greenery is found throughout Pondtrees. Either the individual or the association must take care of the gardens, yards, and common areas one way or another. Also, the increasing environmental awareness in society reinforces the positive perceptions of the role of this organization.

Basically, the garden club is autonomously organized for the informal exchange of ideas, information, and help in the maintenance and beautification of the surroundings within individual courtyards or in front of homes. Starting with some individual horticultural hobbies, the club extended its activities to natural preservation and neighborhood landscaping in Pondtrees. It was loosely organized, so there was little pressure. It served as a popular arena for residents' interests and provided some enjoyable labor for members in their leisure time. The club activists responded to my curiosity about its success with "We just love doing it." The club introduced plants and shrubbery suitable for the soil and seasons and managed to get a good deal for the plants. They also offered their expertise and made recommendations to the association and individual residents for the selection of plants both in the common areas and in individual backyards. The club also invited local speakers for water, land, and other natural conservation campaigns and helped distribute the information.

Although there is a separate committee in charge of landscaping in Pondtrees, the tasks are sometimes closely combined with those of the club. In the last two years, the garden club has selected four "Yard-of-the-Month" designations. The award is based on overall attractiveness and improvement and is intended to recognize and honor those promoting natural beautification on their property and in Pondtrees. The selection goes on smoothly except that two of the honorary signs were once stolen. These special efforts improve the communal atmosphere while contributing to community formation, and some of the residents even purchase plants for the common areas. Quite a few of the club members volunteered for other neighborhood committees and later got elected to the board of directors. To my surprise the other day, I saw one of my neighbors (renting in the building next to mine) taking care of the plants in the common area the day before he moved out of Pondtrees.

The homeowners association in Pondtrees is a fascinating sociocultural and economic construct. I find that the management of common property by the residents themselves shows a convergence of individualism and volunteerism, although there exist ambiguities concerning the commons, leading to a variety of disharmonies and conflicts. Individualism is a way that people look at and are adapted to their world. An individualistic worldview considers the individual as the elementary unit of primary order, whereas society is viewed as a secondary or artificial construct.

Like any other cultural value, individualism is effective only in some contexts. In some ways it is liable to produce alienation. I see individualism as a reaction to the constraints of society and nature that tries to solve the contradictions between self and the outside world by assigning primary importance to the individual. Residing in a neighborhood with a homeowners association entails cooperating and sharing, which is sometimes incongruent with American ideals of individuality and independence. American individualism is quite like a two-edged sword: on the one edge, trying to gain something always pursued, such as individual freedom and happiness; on the other, taking a risk of losing something still needed, such as a trusting human community and togetherness.

Compared with the community life in my Chinese neighborhood, interpersonal relations among neighbors in Pondtrees were aloof, cold, and lacking of an expectation for future interaction. However, human problems and issues are ubiquitous and embedded in sociocultural institutions. Furthermore, communal life indeed varies in different societal structures. Both Chinese and American cultures have their weaknesses and shortcomings as well as their strengths and advantages. The headaches suffered by my Chinese neighbors were different from the complaints expressed by my American neighbors in Pondtrees. I believe that the neighborly strangers in my neighborhood could benefit by becoming more aware of their common ground and communal needs, while the quality of life in my Chinese community could be enhanced by overcoming institutionalized political and economic barriers and sociocultural weak points. After all, we are transients, as Chinese-American anthropologist F. L. K. Hsu points out, and what we need is a pleasant journey through this world. We should try our best to gain benefits from cross-cultural knowledge and to be free from those physical and psychological sufferings existent in both of our cultures.

Study Questions

1. What are some of the residential differences between rural lifestyles in China and Dr. Yang's Florida research site?
2. What is intended in the description "neighborly strangers"?
3. What are the social and personal reasons for the residents of Pondtrees being "strangers" to each other?
4. Contrast communal conflict resolution practices between Pondtrees and residential communities in China.
5. In which way is the American value of individualism incongruent with the neighborhood requirements of Pondtrees?

Acknowledgments

I am grateful to Professors A. W. Wolfe, M. V. Angrosino, S. D. Greenbaum, J. E. Jreisat, and E. G. Nesman for their direction and comments during my studying and writing at the University of South Florida. I am also thankful to Ron Habin for his editorial assistance.

17

Learning to Hug
An English Anthropologist's Experiences in North America

GEOFFREY HUNT
INSTITUTE FOR SCIENTIFIC ANALYSIS

Expecting to make an easy adjustment to American life, the author is shocked by the differences between English and American cultures. He analyzes alcohol and drug addiction treatment, exploring the beliefs and practices of the therapeutic bureaucracy as reflections of American culture.

Geoffrey Hunt grew up in England. He studied anthropology at London University, doing fieldwork with a West African religious group in urban South London. He came to the United States in 1989, and after twenty years of academic work, he began a new career as an applied anthropologist working on drug and alcohol addiction.

Anthropology today is in deep turmoil. Starting in the late 1960s and the early 1970s, anthropologists have been involved in questioning the very foundations of their chosen discipline. Initially, the questioning concentrated on their geographical focus: Third World societies. As liberation movements in these countries ripened, and intellectuals within these countries began to analyze the intellectual dominance of the West, so anthropologists found themselves identified unfavorably with forces of oppression, colonialism, and imperialism, and even highly respected "founding fathers" were discovered to have collaborated with the colonial powers. As the anthropological research terrain shrank and anthropologists became persona non gratae, so also did the basis of anthropological thought come increasingly under scrutiny. Marxist and more radical anthropologists laid siege to the functionalist paradigm developed by Radcliffe-Brown and Malinowski.

Today, attention has shifted, and the discipline is involved in examining the holy grail of anthropology, the ethnographic text. These texts on which anthropology teaching was based have become the focal point of some very deep divisions. Partly as a result of critical thinking in all the social sciences, the motives of anthropologists and their writings have been questioned. Instead of accepting the text at face value, contemporary anthropologists have begun to reexamine the motives and the cultural assumptions of Malinowski, Evans-Pritchard, Firth, and Benedict. Such intensive questioning of the ways in which anthropologists construct the text is clearly a double-edged sword, for although on the one hand it has produced important and, in some cases, liberating assessments of possible ways of producing the ethnographic text, it has at the same time had the effect of making both neophyte and experienced anthropologists nervous about how they present their material. Today, authors can no longer remain hidden behind the narrative, but instead must reveal themselves in all their cultural nakedness.

Although some still decry such a development, anthropologists no longer need to have their personalized accounts published posthumously, as in Malinowski's case, or hide behind a pseudonym, as Laura Bohannan did.[1] Although trained in the ways of traditional anthropology, I have always found a "confessional" style of narrative more appealing, and hence the current debate has provided greater legitimacy for me to discuss fieldwork experiences. Such a discussion, however, should not be viewed as merely an example of personal indulgence or, as Llobera (1987) has called it, "navel gazing," but instead as a serious attempt to examine important current anthropological issues.

Anthropology Training in England

Anthropologists have always involved themselves in somewhat ludicrous tasks, especially seen through the eyes of their fellow social scientists. Unlike other researchers, who are perfectly satisfied to conduct controlled experimental tests or design questionnaire surveys, anthropologists have been keen to explore far-off cultures and isolate themselves in relatively hazardous fieldwork circumstances. Until very recently, especially in England, which has a long tradition of Malinowskian fieldwork, a trainee anthropologist would never gain acceptance into the discipline unless he or she had gone through the traditional "rite de passage" of extended fieldwork in an "exotic" and often isolated society. This designated route of anthropological apprenticeship was not for me. Although Third World societies and their respective cultures were of interest, my chosen research focus lay within my own society. I had always been intrigued by cultural frameworks, but unlike others who sought to study them within distant societies, I wanted to look at them within my own. A West African religious immigrant group in South London was my chosen topic. Such a choice, however, was not received altogether enthusiastically by my teachers in a very traditional anthropology department at London University. The department was the home of Mary Douglas and also of Phyllis Kaberry, a student of Malinowski; Edmund Leach and Evans-Pritchard were regular visitors. On first learning that Camberwell in South London, and not India or Africa, was to be my fieldwork destination, my Professor informed me that Camberwell was neither exotic nor strange enough for fieldwork and that I was clearly playing at being an anthropologist. In spite of my efforts to emphasize the extent to which a syncretist West African religious group was culturally distant from my own white middle-class culture, he was not impressed and told me that to be taken seriously in anthropology I must remove myself completely from my own culture and conduct fieldwork in a far-off place. Promptly ignoring this advice, I set off, without their approval, for the uncharted urban terrain of South London. So began a checkered anthropological career.

My abiding interest in culture led me from immigrant religious groups to socially diverse drinking groups. In pursuing this latter topic, I began to confront the difficulties of attempting to decipher the culture of drinking among the middle class. For the first time, I encountered rituals, symbols, and meanings that I knew well. Nevertheless, sharing a common culture with people whose practices I wished to understand created new difficulties. Rarely had I given much thought to my own rituals of drinking and entertaining, and I had never conceptualized these practices as symbolic arenas.[2] Moreover, little of the anthropology literature discussed how to examine one's own culture, or engage in self-reflexivity. Although anthropology had indeed begun the process of "coming home," much of its attention, at least within England and Europe, still focused on "peripheral" groups, and few anthropologists studied mainstream middle-class culture. Most academic anthropologists and sociologists, socialized within the middle class, saw their own culture as normal and natural, with little implicit anthropological interest. To understand middle-class meanings and values, I was obliged to become self-reflexive, suspend my preconceptions, and imagine myself to be an alien researcher come "to study the culture of the English natives." Culture, through such a process, would become anthropologically strange, and what had previously been taken for granted would become culturally alien. Learning such a process of self-reflexivity and enforced cultural strangeness would become even more important as my career in anthropology suddenly took an unexpected change in direction.

Moving Countries

In 1989, after nearly twenty years of academic research, I decided to leave England and start a career in the United States. I saw my decision to move as relatively straightforward and thought only of the many possibilities that would open up for me. Because of an increasing specialization in research on alcohol issues, the prospect of continuing in this area in the United States seemed favorable. The United States federal government was well-known for its extensive research funding in both the alcohol and drug fields, and a number of specialist research institutes existed. Furthermore, the recent start of the "drug war" seemed to point to a political climate that saw both drug and alcohol issues of some importance. Moreover, having never shown any flare for mastering foreign languages, moving to the United States seemed a sensible transfer, and integration into the society seemed easy. It was not that I underestimated the possible differences between England and the United States, but I saw those differences as resulting from different levels of economic development and mass consumption, and not arising from deep cultural divides. Aside from minor readjustments, I assumed that my moving to the United States would be culturally straightforward. Such a belief stemmed in part, from the existence of a common language, and a three-hundred-year history, in which the two countries were inextricably linked. But whatever the origins of my naivete, I soon found myself facing a system of different cultural values and expectations. From day one, seemingly simple everyday occurrences shocked me. For example, I would become confused when a shop assistant greeted my American partner with such a warm and personal welcome that I assumed they must be close friends, only to discover later that they had never met. I also reacted with surprise when telephone sales staff called me by my Christian name, a custom rarely practiced in England. Such simple cultural differences exasperated me, not merely because I was unprepared, but also because the very existence of the shared language had an effect of lulling me into assuming a false sense of cultural familiarity. If I had moved to France or Italy, the necessity to talk in an alien language would have been a constant reminder of cultural differences. In the United States, the shared language created a false sense of cultural security that, suddenly and unexpectedly, would be disturbed by minor cultural misunderstandings. For an anthropologist who had studied cultural frameworks for nearly twenty years, such experiences seemed ironic. Yet, whereas in England my attempts to make sense of alternative cultural systems had been contained and compartmentalized under the heading of research, here in the United States they pervaded my day-to-day existence. Such cultural conflicts soon became heightened in my professional work.

The Anthropologist as Local Government Bureaucrat

Initially, unable to obtain an academic research position, I began working for a county government alcohol treatment bureau that administered local residential and day care services for alcoholics. My rationale for working for local government was that it would teach me how to tailor my theoretical research interests to the needs of social policy. I anticipated an environment within which a fruitful interchange of ideas would take place. A world where, on the one hand, I would lay out the academic and theoretical parameters of a particular issue, and on the other hand bureau officials would point out important practical modifications. No such interchange occurred. Instead, I found myself confronting a belief system in which the official ideology had to be followed despite personal or professional beliefs. Within this setting it was not surprising that my detached and analytical training and perspective was not well received. The director and approximately 99 percent of the staff believed that the society was riddled with alcohol problems and alcoholics, and that if only alcohol could be removed from the society, many of its major problems would vanish. The staff, whether they were "in recovery" or just abstinent, believed that working in the alcohol bureau was not merely a job but a calling. They were there to pursue a mission to improve the society. This closed belief system viewed alcohol issues in a one-dimensional manner and allowed no discussion of alternatives.

This was my first encounter in the United States with the recovery movement, a mass movement that, although emanating from Alcoholics Anonymous, was no longer confined to providing solutions to alcohol problems. Today, as many writers have noted, the recovery movement offers panaceas for a whole host of personal and social problems. The near universality of this movement in the United States, propagated through individual groups, self-help books, criminal justice referral programs, television talk shows, docudramas, and seminars, is in marked contrast to its influence in England and other Western European countries, where its impact has been much less pronounced.

Into this environment, I arrived with views about alcohol diametrically opposed to both the personal beliefs of the staff and the official ideology of the bureau. Instead of an unquestioning belief in the idea of alcoholism, I held a cultural relativist position on alcohol problems and believed the Durkheimian principle that research on "normal" drinking was an essential prerequisite for understanding "abnormal" drinking. The disease notion of alcoholism seemed at best a very shaky concept, and the efficacy of the abstinent model of treatment seemed doubtful. A three-year study of alcohol treatment agencies in England had convinced me that "controlled drinking methods" were just as effective as those based on abstinence and the twelve-step movement.

Given the views of the bureau on the one hand and my own on the other, it was not surprising that a frosty atmosphere soon developed between myself, the director, and the staff. My brief stay at the bureau involved painful sparring matches. Although I tried to remain vague and noncommittal about my "heretical" views on such matters as the disease concept, controlled drinking, and alcohol use messages, the director became exasperated with my failure to become one of the team and was increasingly concerned that I might make an embarrassing public announcement on the disease concept. On one occasion, however, it was my *behavior* rather than my ideas that provided proof of my unwillingness to fit in.

The director, an ex-nun, who ran the bureau as a religious institution and administered large doses of moral guilt to her subordinates, decided to arrange an executive staff retreat to increase "team spirit." She believed that working in the bureau should not be just a job but that all members, and especially the executive staff, should be deeply committed to the philosophy of the bureau. The retreat, which lasted two days, took place at an expensive and secluded hotel and commenced late in the afternoon on the first day. During the first session, which, according to the agenda, was to be on the philosophy of the bureau, I realized that I would need to be especially diplomatic about my views. Fortunately, instead of a deep discussion of the bureau's philosophy, individual executive staff members took the opportunity to share with the group favorite poems, passages from novels, pieces of music, and even a short video of a balletic juggler. After the session, the staff met for dinner and as we sat around deciding what to order, the waitress asked if we wished to have something to drink. While the rest ordered iced tea, I chose a glass of red wine. Although I suspected that this gesture could be provocative, I felt that because this was now my free time, not bureau time, I should be allowed to drink wine at dinner as I normally did. My behavior disturbed the director, who, I later discovered, had wished to reprimand me. However, she decided that because I was European she should excuse my behavior. Nevertheless, she considered my openly drinking alcohol in front of two staff members who were "in recovery" to be "a failure of good conduct," and because of my unacceptable beliefs she sent me a sharp memo questioning my "organizational fit." Fortunately, soon afterward, having found alternative work, I left the bureau. But though the difficulties of matching my professional and personal views with the requirements of a local government department had been removed, new cultural conflicts soon arose.

The Anthropologist as Evaluator

I began a new "career" as an evaluator for a local nonprofit research company, hired to assess a federally funded substance abuse community prevention program. In England, I had little contact with evaluation or evaluators, and it was not until I commenced work in the United States that I encountered representatives of this new profession and realized that evaluation was a burgeoning career for unattached and out-of-work social scientists, and even anthropologists.

As the number of qualified anthropologists has increased and the number of teaching positions has declined, would-be researchers have found work in the field of applied anthropology. Here anthropologists are expected to apply their training and expertise to solving social difficulties or assessing the possible impact of social change. For these anthropologists, postmodern debates about anthropological writing may seem a theoretical fad that has relevance only in ivory towers. Such debates hardly concern applied anthropologists toiling in the trenches. Nevertheless, working as an applied anthropologist involves new problems and new conflicts. Forced to survive outside the academy, anthropologists have sought to balance their assessment of what is required, given their perspective as professional anthropologists, with the needs of the people who hired them. In these new environments and under these new pressures, they have learned to accept that researcher-centered research has to give way to client- or community-centered research and evaluation.

Following this new career path, I convinced myself that surely twenty years of academic research would enable me to take on this new role.[3] Once "on board," I would easily learn new techniques and acquire the appropriate terminology and jargon. Unfortunately, I was mistaken, for although the technical part of being an evaluator was straightforward and I quickly learned to use all the key terms such as *process evaluation, formative evaluation,* and *outcome measures* in all the appropriate places, I failed to comprehend clearly the requirements of being an evaluator within the drug and alcohol arena. It was not my inexperience of evaluation technique that created the difficulties; it was instead my total inability to understand and fulfill the cultural expectations of being an evaluator in the United States.

Evaluating a Federally Funded Program

My task was to evaluate the impact of a federally funded community substance abuse program. In 1990, the Office for Substance Abuse Prevention (OSAP)[4] created by the Anti-Drug Act of 1986 began funding a series of community prevention projects. The projects, known as the Community Partnership Program, eventually totaled 251 nationwide. Broadly defined, the purpose of this grant was to encourage the formation, development, and, thereafter, the ongoing existence and vitality of grassroots, community-level organizations and initiatives aimed at preventing alcohol and other drug-related (AOD) problems within local communities. The basic premise of the Partnership program was that meaningful, long-term reductions in alcohol and other drug problems would be won only when the concerns, energies, and commitments of local communities are focused on this problem territory.

One requirement of this program was that a local evaluator should evaluate each individual partnership. This was my task, and I began to attend a series of local prevention meetings that took place at county health departments, government offices, and community-based organizations. I also attended a series of prevention trainings held both locally and nationally and a series of national conferences. In attending the various meetings, I began to realize that, besides any technical expertise, they expected that I do three things: (1) join in, (2) be intimate, and (3) believe.

Joining In

In previous research settings, I had been expected to participate in many diverse activities and situations. Some had been easy to fulfill, others not. For example, rolling across the floor while chanting religious slogans and pretending to fly was not easy, but my fellow West African church members had been impressed by my attempt, especially knowing that I was not a believer. They secretly hoped that through the process I would learn to believe. Drinking with the "lads" in a village pub as part of my "culture of drinking" research was much easier, except that I did not like beer. For my new drinking friends, this raised doubts about my masculinity and my character as a serious drinker. Nevertheless, as long as on occasion I drank distilled alcohol, they accepted me in their company. Such fieldwork activities taught me how to become involved while remaining detached enough, or occasionally sober enough, to be able to record what was going on. But these techniques of remaining detached were, I soon discovered, unacceptable in community prevention evaluation. There the participants wanted me, despite my evaluation status, to be a believing member of the team.

Being Intimate

A key feature of joining in was being intimate. This was done in two ways. First, participants believed that joining in meant shedding any sense of formality or social distance and revealing both some personal information about oneself and one's harmful experiences with alcohol or other illicit drugs. This created serious dilemmas for me. Although willing to share personal information with friends over a long and indulgent dinner, I was extremely unwilling to confide any confidential information to a group of strangers. Furthermore, my experiences with illicit drugs were virtually nonexistent, and in relation to alcohol I often described myself as a "wino," consuming wine at every meal except breakfast. My love of alcohol meant that I was clearly different from the prevention practitioners who sought to increase societal restrictions on alcohol use. Far from seeing alcohol as an evil substance, I viewed it with a benevolence verging on deep affection. Having been raised within the environment of a large hotel, where drinking was a central feature, alcohol occupied a central symbolic and ritualistic position in entertaining and in the art of being sociable. Not only had my experiences with alcohol been entirely positive, so also had the experiences of my family. Therefore, whenever an exercise at a prevention meeting was called for that entailed revealing personal and painful information about myself and my relationship to alcohol and drugs, I would begin to feel terrified and extremely self-conscious and would desperately try to think of something I could say that would reveal little about myself while not offending the other participants. Although I believe that anthropologists should be honest in doing fieldwork, I do not think that the official evaluator should openly declare his doubts about the program at public prevention meetings. Therefore, if asked by the group why I was attending the meetings or what I needed from the group, I would avoid all references to personal details, adopt a businesslike attitude, and reply that my aim was to encourage better collaboration and coordination among prevention activities. Such terms were frequently used in local government parlance, and the participants accepted them. Thus, I survived another day as evaluator.

Second, being intimate required physical contact with fellow participants. At these prevention meetings participants expected that I would hug people I hardly knew, hold hands with perfect strangers, and even, once, fall limp into the arms of people I knew only superficially. For example, early in the project, at the end of one meeting, the leaders asked the group to stand in a circle, hold hands, and close our eyes. Then, one at a time they instructed us to squeeze our left hand when we felt our right hand being squeezed. The group facilitator started the exercise and told us that it would circulate around the group and eventually return to him. So there I stood with nineteen other leading and committed local prevention practitioners, supported by federal dollars, holding hands in a circle with my eyes closed and waiting for my right hand to be squeezed. As I waited, I truly wondered why I had moved to the United States. Would I have come if I had known that my lofty training as an anthropologist would have led me to this exercise of holding hands with strangers? On another occasion, at a team-building event in the redwood forests, to learn more about "risk taking," I and another seven participants were instructed to arrange ourselves in a circle. Each of us, in turn, was chosen to stand in the middle, with our feet together, hands across our chest, and fall back limply against the circle. The rest of us were told to catch the falling person and gently push him or her toward another part of the circle. This exercise, the instructor informed us, would help build a sense of trust and develop team spirit.

Such behavior meant that any formal or aloof stance was clearly unacceptable. As the child of a middle-class family raised within the formal confines of an English hotel and the enforced male bonding of a Catholic boys' boarding school, notions of propriety were clearly embedded in my psyche. Physical contact between boys at school was clearly frowned upon, in spite of all the jokes about English homosexuality. Because of these childhood experiences, I had developed a keen sense of dread of physical contact except with people with whom I had deep personal relationships, and even with these people, physical contact was limited. In fact, I believe my mother once said words to the effect of "Don't touch people, because you don't know where they have been." Yet here I was expected not only to touch people but to fall into their arms. As I stood looking at the trees, wondering how to avoid the exercise, I pondered ruefully why it was that the anthropological methodology books I had read as a postgraduate had not mentioned such fieldwork activities.

Believing

A basic assumption of all those involved in the program was that they believed in the need for such a substance abuse community prevention program, and by definition they assumed that the evaluator would also believe in the program. Yet for myself believing raised many problems. First, I was skeptical as to the need for such a program. Notions of drug and alcohol problems are socially constructed and socially amplified. This is not to imply that drug and alcohol problems do not exist, but instead to assert that social and cultural factors determine the way that the problems and their solutions are conceptualized. Thus, I wondered to what extent this emphasis on alcohol and drug problems allowed federal sponsors, local government supporters, and local participants to avoid concerning themselves with other, more intractable structurally based social problems. This skepticism, which created difficulties, could have been overcome by adopting a detached professional position. But there existed other, more serious problems. To believe wholeheartedly in any program raises the danger of either falling into what House (1993) has called "clientism"—doing whatever the client wants—or failing to maintain any sense of objectivity. Although doubts have been raised about the researcher's privileged position of objectivity, having a detached outsider examine and assess a program is still beneficial. Such a position requires remaining at least intellectually distant from the program. This, in itself, did not mean that I should remain totally aloof from the participants, but did mean that I should refrain from believing in the program so completely that I failed to retain a sense of critical awareness. Only by being detached could I assess the extent to which the program fulfilled its own requirements, whether they be those of the local participants, the federal government, or the local government that financially administered the program. Evaluators and researchers who champion participatory research often underestimate the difficulties of assessing a program objectively, while being part of the team. Finally, I found the pressure to believe in the program to be culturally disturbing. Why was it that the participants felt I should believe? Was it, as in the recovery movement, that they refused to contemplate alternative beliefs? Such questions reminded me of my research on the West African church. Unlike the prevention activists, the church members were willing to accept my not believing, and never did they exert pressure on me to believe. Why then was there this difference?

In the initial months of the project, although unable to find satisfactory answers, I came to understand that the culture of the program and the participants' expectations of the evaluator were connected in some way or another to the society's belief that team and community building were the way to solve society's problems. In my desire to find answers, I eagerly awaited my first national Community Partnership meeting in Washington, where I would meet other local evaluators who, I was convinced, would supply me with answers.

Meeting the Evaluators

The start of the meeting in Washington did not bode well. The organizers gave each attendee a name tag on which his or her Christian name appeared three times larger than the surname—a clear indicator of future enforced familiarity. To those who were to present papers, name tags with bright green ribbons were provided, which made the presenters look like prize cattle at the local agricultural show. In addition, all participants were given a black plastic conference bag on which was emblazoned the slogan "Prevention Works." The slogan seemed a little premature since the prevention program had only just begun and its effects only recently monitored. Having received our gifts, all one thousand of us trooped into the hotel's main ballroom. The opening speaker, the director of the federal agency, began by telling the participants to stand and say to each person on either side of them, "Hello, neighbor." She then informed the assembled group that they "were truly a beautiful audience and part of a changing landscape," and because of that we should applaud ourselves. The audience, acting like a group of well-trained seals, proceeded to clap enthusiastically. After her speech, in which she praised the audience for their prevention work and told them they were clearly developing a bonding with each other, she introduced the next speaker, an African-American pastor. He also made the audience stand, but this time instead of acknowledging their neighbors, he instructed the participants to give thanks to God. Again, the audience obeyed with enthusiasm, ending their praise of God with a resounding "Amen." What followed was in essence a revivalist sermon, in which the pastor attributed drug and alcohol problems to a decline in moral and spiritual values. Toward the end of his talk, he instructed the audience that before leaving the conference each of them should bond with someone. When he had finished, the audience spontaneously stood and rapturously applauded. As I looked around, few in the audience seemed in any way surprised at receiving a religious sermon at a federally sponsored conference. I assumed that the event had been provided primarily for the local activists, and I was sure that once the evaluators met on their own, many would voice their surprise and concern at the appropriateness of such an event.

This, however, did not occur. When the evaluators met, most of them noted that they had enjoyed the speech. Their response, and the extent to which it differed from my own, made me feel confused and isolated. I wondered how these social scientists could have been anything but amazed at the tenor and message of the talk, which seemed contrary to much of the social science thinking on drug and alcohol abuse. A growing sense of cultural isolation overtook me as I observed them and listened to their responses to the opening evaluation session. The head of the prevention program and the chief evaluator outlined their vision of the role of evaluation and the work of the local evaluators. After informing us that we were "on the cutting edge" of prevention work, they told us that our primary task was to work closely with the program managers to ensure "program plausibility and, whenever possible, act as advisers to the program." According to them, evaluation was to be an integral part of program planning, and the evaluator must see himself or herself as part of the program team. In emphasizing this perspective, they showed that their view of evaluation inclined more to program guidance than to critical research. Being told to work closely with the program participants and staff was not a problem in itself nor was it a problem for evaluators like myself, trained within anthropology, who, unlike other researchers, always worked in close contact with the people. However, what was troubling was the impression that critical assessment was not welcome.

During the session, my colleagues sat, listened, took notes, and asked only technical questions. Never did any of the approximately ninety evaluators question the perspective of evaluation. Never before had I experienced a meeting between government officials and social scientists where the latter not only accepted the government view but in fact welcomed it. Where, I asked myself, were the critical thinkers, the skeptics, or even just the suspicious ones? Not only was there no critical questioning of the philosophy of the program, but also a great deal of enthusiasm was expressed. As a group, the evaluators celebrated the program, seemed honored to have been chosen, voiced their belief in its efficacy, and stated how important it was that the program be a success.

Even after the meeting, in private conversations, where one might have expected some dissension, little was expressed. Whenever I communicated my own reservations about the program and its rationale, my colleagues viewed me with some surprise, and I began to feel as though I possessed a contagious disease. On occasion, their looks conveyed a sense that they thought I was a troublemaker. Some, having discerned my nationality, would

listen patronizingly with a bemused look to the theories of the misguided foreigner who clearly did not understand the purpose of the program. One evaluator, having overheard my questioning of the program, even invited me to
lunch to hear more. He was very pleasant, listened with respect, and assured
me that I had a very "interesting" perspective.

As I sat in my hotel room and thought about the day, I realized that of
course they were right; I was indeed a foreigner and a stranger in my newly
adopted country. I also began to understand that by suggesting that social scientists, whether in the guise of federally designated evaluators or not, were
there to ask critical questions, I had naively assumed that having a shared professional designation inferred similar cultural and professional values. In
making such a cultural assumption, I was behaving like many other anthropologists, who on first encountering the "natives," committed a series of cultural faux pas. Just as my experiences with the program participants had
illustrated the cultural divide, so also did my interactions with the evaluators.

Through these encounters and my continuing involvement with the program, I began very slowly to perceive a common thread in my experiences
since I had arrived in the United States. Just as in the alcohol bureau I had
failed to comprehend the strength and rigidity of the belief system, which
brooked no questions, doubts, or alternatives, so now I realized the compre-
hensiveness of a belief system that saw the whole society gripped by an epi-
demic. Illicit drugs, alcohol, and, later, tobacco had become the evil substances
that were undermining the community and gnawing at the society's moral
fiber. Into this crisis I had arrived, and instead of believing, or at least remaining silent, I had expressed disbelief.

Nevertheless, more than just failing to comprehend the extent to which the
society had become gripped by the rhetoric of the drug war, I also began to
realize the extent to which I, a cultural anthropologist, had failed to think like
one. Instead of examining both the latent and manifest functions of the community prevention program, I had chosen to consider only the latter. I had
completely failed to see the program and the role of evaluation as part of a cultural and "symbolic universe" (Berger 1967). The Community Partnership
Program had been developed within a social climate that believed that the
social and moral fabric of the society was under threat. The reasons for the
malaise were identified as drug and alcohol problems. The period that began in
the sixties and continued into the seventies had led to an indulgence in the personal use of drugs. This indulgence had now got out of hand and led to a situation of disorder. Social order had now to be re-created and reestablished. The

Community Partnership Program had been given the task, and through a therapeutic process and a series of ritualistic practices, each local program was to regain a sense of permanence and a sense of order and reaffirm community.

Unlike previous social problem programs, for example the War on Poverty, the Community Partnership Program reaffirms community not necessarily by doing any real community building, but instead by creating community as a psychological phenomenon. As Sennett has argued, community can be built not by any physical activity but by developing a sense of shared "imagery and feeling." "What matters is not what you've done but how you feel about it" (quoted in Rapping 1996: 124). A therapeutic belief in a "change of heart" had been transplanted to the community level. No longer were the participants expected to change society, they only had to change themselves. In other words, social change was no longer structural change; it was instead "establishing relationships with people." Within this framework, it is therefore not surprising that "hugging" had become such a crucial element.

This view that sees social change as resulting from a "change of heart" is not specific to the partnership but can be traced to more general themes within U.S. culture. For example, Skolnick argues that these ideas result from a strong sense of religiosity that "promises that we can solve our problems through changes of heart rather than through the difficult and divisive route of political and social change" (1991: 203). Other writers have noted the importance of this view within the recovery movement. For example, Kaminer, in her particularly caustic and insightful analysis, shows how the movement sees the process of reforming ourselves and our families as the way to reforming society. According to Kaminer, this view is the "movement's party line," a point neatly captured in the quotation from Bradshaw, one of the gurus of the codependency and recovery movement, who suggests that "recovery will save us as a society . . . you have only to recover and the world recovers with you" (Kaminer 1992: 94).

When seen from such a perspective, activities that had appeared strange if not bizarre seemed now to make sense. The local participants' desire to have me join in, be part of the team, hold hands, hug, and fall into waiting arms were all understandable when seen as part of a process of therapeutic community building. Sharing experiences on the evils of alcohol and drugs were necessary if individual members and newcomers were to become bonded. Even religious sermons at federal conferences no longer seemed out of place when viewed from the perspective of a reaffirming ritual intended to galvanize the audience into feeling special and part of a nationwide team.

From such a vantage point, it also became more clear why CSAP should promote a view of evaluation that was inherently uncritical. If the underlying purpose was to develop a psychological community, then the official monitors must also be part of the team. No longer were they to play the role of "critical observers"; instead, evaluators were there to be "facilitative participants" within the collaborative model. As one evaluator noted, evaluators should become more like therapists. If evaluators are to be highly collaborative and part of the team, then they must also join in and believe, both in the program and its activities, and, like the program participants, proudly display the conference slogan "Prevention Works." Given such a viewpoint, uncritical evaluators appeared less reprehensible when viewed as believers in the pursuit of building community.

In part, some of my inability to think like a cultural anthropologist lay in the difficulties I faced since my arrival in the United States, and especially in relation to cultural differences around drinking and the use of alcohol. As a European, I am still struck by the way in which alcohol and the influence of Alcoholics Anonymous pervade day-to-day life. Why is it, as Peele (1989) has noted, that approximately 90 percent of Americans believe that alcohol use—an accepted part of social life in most European countries—is a disease over which millions of people have no control unless absolute abstinence is adhered to? This cultural belief in the inherent dangers of a substance is significantly different from views about alcohol in England and parts of Europe, where in general the problem is regarded as inherent in the drinker, not in the alcohol. For example, an alcohol ban in Italy during the 1990 World Cup competition was acceptable because "fans" or "supporters" were already regarded as potentially disreputable and, admittedly, alcohol makes bad behavior worse. However, the average citizen can distance himself or herself from the kind of person to whom such restrictions must be applied, their views about alcohol remaining unaffected.

In spite of the seeming "sameness" of the cultures, different sets of cultural values and meanings surround alcohol and drinking behaviors. In the United States, people scrutinize an individual's drinking behavior for signs of problematic social and health developments. In my own situation, I soon discovered that my social drinking practices, considered perfectly normal within England, had become a point of issue. Levels of consumption defined as acceptable by the British Ministry of Health's "Sensible Drinking" guidelines became, in the United States, indicators of problem drinking. Even innocent statements such as "I need a drink" (which often expressed my feelings after having attended yet another prevention meeting) were judged by some as signs of alcohol dependency. No longer did I live in a society where alcohol occupied a generally positive position; instead I lived in a culture where it possessed increasingly negative characteristics. The harmful effects of alcohol are seen everywhere, and the club of recovering individuals grows larger every day. In fact, to be in recovery or to be an ACOA (adult child of an alcoholic) confers status and bonds the individual with others who have been through a similar experience. In casual conversations or even chance meetings, it is often one of the first pieces of information supplied. Supplying this information, individuals make public their position regarding the alcohol issue and pledge their allegiance. In so doing, they resolve any issues of ambiguity, a trait that Wasserfall (1993) has suggested is seen within America as untrustworthy.

Rather than submit to the societal pressures to conform, I decided instead to assert my cultural differences. As I began work in the United States, first at the alcohol bureau and then as an evaluator, I became increasingly defiant about my own views about alcohol and my drinking practices. But my personal reaction interfered with my professional perspective. Rather than adopting a position of intellectual detachment on issues of alcohol and alcohol problems, I took sides, and in so doing failed to be self-reflective. Instead of examining those times or occasions when I felt "uncomfortable" or "out of place," in order "to map the dark side of others' worlds" (Willis 1978), I merely bristled. Instead of attempting to understand the meanings that the society attributed to alcohol, and hence the symbolic purpose of the program, I saw only differences between the cultural position of alcohol in England and the United States. Fortunately, in using ethnographic techniques to evaluate the program, and especially in producing extensive fieldnotes, I gradually regained a position of detachment from which I could analyze the underlying purpose of the prevention program and the sociocultural context of alcohol and drug problems.

Conclusion

In hindsight, the experience has taught me the difficulties of retaining a professional anthropological stance while attempting to settle in a new country. Unlike anthropologists who begin fieldwork and are warned of "going native," I had chosen to move to a new country not to study the "natives" but to create a new life with a new partner. Soon after arriving, I began to realize just how culturally dissimilar England and the United States are, and to recognize the informal pressures placed on immigrants to conform to the dominant culture. The process of dealing with those pressures and maintaining my own identity emphasized my cultural isolation. In fact, whenever a visitor from Europe arrived at our house, we spent considerable time comparing notes and discussing what we saw as strange U.S. customs or activities. The sense of cultural isolation was exacerbated by working in a culturally alien nonacademic work environment, whose ideology seemed diametrically opposed to my own. Taken together, these factors contributed to my inability and unwillingness to accept a series of cultural practices that irritated me and against which I reacted. In so doing, I became unable to make sense of the culture into which I had arrived, even when as an anthropologist I was assigned the task of evaluating a prevention program.

Today, though still reacting negatively to such everyday forms of familiarity as "Have a nice day" or "My name is Joseph, and I'll be your waiter," I see more clearly some of the threads that weave together the cultural fabric and that help explain the connections between notions of individual and community identification, substance abuse problems, perceptions of societal malaise, and federally funded prevention programs.

Study Questions

1. Whether an anthropologist, sociologist, or student of American culture, what problems can you imagine you would face in attempting to conduct research in your own culture?

2. What is meant by "self-reflexivity" and "enforced cultural strangeness" as research requirements in one's own culture?

3. In Dr. Hunt's first encounter with an American alcohol treatment bureau, how did his views and those of the program differ? What are your own feelings on these operational and philosophical differences?

4. What personal and cultural experiences and beliefs posed problems with the requirement that the author become intimate within the prevention program?

5. What were the author's practical and objective concerns about uncritically "believing" in a program that he was hired to evaluate?

6. The author portrays the meeting of the evaluators as a comic opera. How conscientiously did this federally funded agency concern itself with issues of critical social research?

7. In what important ways did the author reassess the symbolic structure of the therapeutic communities? What were the cultural value differences toward drugs and alcohol between England and the United States that had to be reconciled?

Notes

[1] See Smith Bowen 1964.

[2] See Hunt 1991 and Hunt et al. 1988.

[3] Although relatively few anthropologists can be found working as evaluators in the drug and alcohol fields, ethnographic evaluation has made a significant impact, especially in the field of educational evaluation (Wolcott 1987; Fetterman 1986).

[4] The name of the agency was subsequently altered to the Center for Substance Abuse Prevention (CSAP).

References

Berger, P. 1967. The *Sacred Canopy*. Garden City: Doubleday.

Fetterman, D. M., and M. A. Pitman. 1986. *Educational Evaluation: Ethnography in Theory, Practice and Politics*. Thousand Oaks, CA: Sage.

House, E. R. 1993. *Professional Evaluation*. Thousand Oaks, CA: Sage.

Hunt, G. 1991. The Middle Class Revisited: Eating and Drinking in an English Village. *Western Folklore* 50: 401–420.

Hunt, G., J. Mellor, S. Satterlee, and J. Turner. 1988. Thinking about Drinking. *Surveyor* 22: 20–32.

Kaminer, W. 1991. *I'm Dysfunctional, You're Dysfunctional: The Recovery Movement and Other Self-Help Fashions*. Reading, MA: Addison-Wesley.

Llobera, J. 1987. Reply to Critics. *Critique of Anthropology* 7(2): 88–90.

Peele, S. 1989. *Diseasing of America: Addiction Treatment Out of Control*. Lexington, KY: Lexington Books.

Rapping, E. 1996. *The Culture of Recovery: Making Sense of the Self-Help Movement in Women's Lives*. Boston: Beacon Press.

Smith Bowen, E. 1964. *Return to Laughter*. New York: Doubleday Anchor.

Wasserfall, R. 1998. Gender Encounters in America: An Outsider's View of Continuity and Ambivalence. In P. DeVita and J. D. Armstrong (eds.), *Distant Mirrors: America as a Foreign Culture* (2nd ed.). Belmont, CA: Wadsworth.

Willis, P. 1978. *Profane Culture*. London: Routledge.

Wolcott, H. F. 1987. On Ethnographic Intent. In G. Spindler and L. Spindler (eds.), *Interpretive Ethnography of Education: At Home and Abroad*. London: Lawrence Erlbaum Associates.

18

Giving, Withholding, and Meeting Midway
A Poet's Ethnography

SALEEM PEERADINA
SIENA HEIGHTS UNIVERSITY

A Westernized Indian, stubbornly resistant American, poet, teacher, and participant observer compares the customs of his native Bombay with those he experiences while coming to terms with American life. Values associated with hospitality, social reciprocity, the concept of neighborhood, and higher education are critically and lyrically evaluated.

Saleem Peeradina is a poet who grew up in Bombay, India. He came to the United States as a student in the 1970s, living for three years in the South. He returned again in the 1980s to teach writing at Siena Heights University in Adrian, Michigan.

Before I lead the reader into my chosen landscape, let me offer a wide-angle view of the terrain so that my antecedents become clear and my intent and direction are laid bare.

What will become immediately apparent is that I speak out of a double consciousness: a Westernized Indian, a stubbornly resistant American, a poet-teacher, a migrant-expatriate looking over his shoulder, a participant-observer. Even bureaucratese offers a gem: resident alien! My thesis is that this is the contemporary condition, even without the fact of migration; that the clash of multiple choices complicates but also enriches our life. And what we work toward is a balance, a synthesis.

200

I hope the reader will bear with me if the opening section of this essay feels like a bumpy ride in a crammed vehicle. I can assure you the voyage will be smooth once we settle down.

Moving in 1988 from Bombay's congested, noisy, vibrant metropolis of ten million (the 1995 figure is fifteen million) to a small Midwestern town of twenty-two thousand people can set the stage for multiple layers of dislocation. Subjectively speaking, the levels of contrast fall into the following categories: the massive scale, fast tempo, stimulus and stress of big city life versus the diminished size, peacefulness, and dull pace of small town living; the year-round heat and humidity of Bombay versus the temperate and freezing temperatures of the lake region; the hard, daily struggle for survival under deteriorating sociopolitical conditions in modern India versus the comfort and ease of a stable, new professional and domestic environment; the exchanging of family ties, connectedness with the community, and abiding friendships in the homeland for the alienation and isolation of the adopted country; the escape from oppressive cultural dictates of a tradition-bound society to a more liberating social framework. And so forth.

The pluses and minuses fall on both sides, even vary with the passage of time, changing circumstances, past histories, and modulations of desire. In the case of my family, individual responses and equations running the gamut of gender and generational differences were balanced by a collective wish for a "new" life.

In my own particular instance, a previous stay of three years in the American South, as a student in the early 1970s, propelled by a lifelong aspiration to cross the bright waters, made my earlier quest (as it does my present one) an adventure. Through this mind-set, what could be potential "dislocations" were really altered states of being in different geographical and cultural locales. I was ready to encounter and eager to participate in the new ethos.

I offer this as a preamble to establish the backdrop against which I will make my pitch. As a poet and social commentator I am always in the field. The gestures, products, and the systems of culture are my raw material, the vital signs of life. Cultural jousting is work, play, and a fine art. Every setting presents itself as a watering hole, an arena; every encounter becomes an enactment in which articulate informants vocalize, whether they realize it or not, a script. I am simultaneously witness, participant, and scribe. I am never off duty.

The mix and rush of metaphor in the foregoing paragraph is intentional. It attests to the dramatic possibilities residing in cultural scenarios.

From the global to the local everything flows into my funnel. (As an East-erner, my metaphors are still pretechnological; an American poet would say, "Everything beams into my screen!") My sources include international poli-tics, big business and service industries, the consumer marketplace; televi-sion, movies, advertising, and other media; literary, artistic, and intellectual endeavors; and, finally, street-level activity, neighborhood existence, and the realm of the domestic and personal. Because it is the last I observe most closely on a daily basis, and whose immediacy forces radical adjustments of lenses in my own cultural biases, I will develop some themes that grow out of this. Besides, I am a hands-on kind of writer, preferring the concrete and par-ticular to toying with abstractions. I work from the ground up, allowing the experiential to lead to the conceptual. So I will peer into the pond and hope to find in the teeming life there the distant sky intertwined in it.

Although all this may approach the methodology practiced by anthro-pologists—and I am aware the field is rife with contending ideologies—I must disclaim any intent of making my viewpoint carry the weight of researched and scholarly accounts. Still, while operating firsthand, I have constantly applied checks and references from a wider set of testimonies not necessarily limited to the experiences of other foreign culturalists. My jottings find analogues and parallels and therefore the backing of numerous and diverse "authorities."

To put it another way, the poet's speculations, arrived at from a different angle of perception, complement the "scientific" and other angles. In the poet's way of seeing, there occur certain revelations and disclosures from the world that, in their particularity, offer themselves as epiphanies. Perhaps it would be more correct to say that although the poet revels in the unique, the idiosyncratic, the strikingly new or the strangely different, his poetic creed nudges him toward a double consciousness of the universal-in-the-local. Often there is no overt or visible separation between the center and the mar-gin: It is one encompassing moment, one encapsulated value striving for poetic validity.

One final disclaimer: From the very nature of the historical "position" and the local "presence" that informs my ethnography, what results is an inevitable comparative approach between the subject (that is, myself) and two cultures (that is, American and Indian). This can be perceived as circum-scribing locational boundaries, or simply as defining those boundaries: a point of origin and subsequent shifts. I see it as relational rather than binary, a connection that catalyzes the interplay of two mirrors. The use of contrast between cultural forms and practices, between disparate geographies and belief systems, allows both writer and reader to construct several additional layers of significances beyond the ones unfolded.

This stance, however, is not as clear-cut as it appears. In India, the place of origin, my view of the home culture is far less partisan, much more critical, influenced by the ideologies of the West. Once that self is replanted in the West, the cultural winds and temperature strike at an angle more oblique than the one imagined, inviting a more critical stance. Simultaneously the place of origin and the past does not remain static. It turns fluid, then reassembles to other shapes and colors. Another paradox emerges: Subject and place share an extra physical and extra temporal space. The culture is out there and embedded in me; I carry its imprint wherever I go. It fades, flames, or erupts like a chronic skin condition. In the face of local imperatives, it subsides, like water seeking its level.

The whole point of laying open my antecedents, the unmasking of my proclivities and vulnerabilities, is to let the reader in, to reveal the persona, to clear roadblocks, and leave a trail. The reader can then see not only the conclusions, but also how they were arrived at.

If the general tone of this article tends to be critical of American culture, it is a result of the choice of themes. It does not define or exhaust my view or appreciation of the culture's many attractive features—features that continue to draw a cast of thousands to the ongoing show.

After one has flown in and found a spot to set up camp, the sizing up begins almost immediately. So, this is America. Or is it? The distant rumblings of America speak in the superlative accents of history, myth, and media images: unrestricted freedom, unlimited opportunity, constant mobility and rush, crime figures, fast food, casual sex, and AIDS. A 360-degree tour of the local habitat reveals a small, quiet campus, friendly people, and a somewhat run-down town that boasts of a symphony orchestra but no bus station.

The rumblings soon fade as more pressing daily concerns surface: how to make oneself at home, how to belong to the campus community, how to get to like the food, how to find one's bearings in the supermarket, how to conduct oneself with students, colleagues, friends. The small but friendly and supportive Indian community eases the transition in many ways, providing kitchen stuff, transportation, and welcoming us into their homes.

In one year we make three changes of location and four changes of residence (contributing our share to raising the national average), creating corresponding degrees of instability for the children and the household economy. It is easier for me since the job is the driving impulse, while the family has to cope with its dislocating rhythms.

Settling down, acquiring the accoutrements of American living—a used car, television, microwave, yard sale odds and ends—prepares us for the real business of living: understanding American ways, finding acceptance for Indian ways, investing in friendships, giving meaning to our lives, figuring out the stacked aisles in the supermarket!

No matter what the material gains manifested or how the external changes shaped our lives, the satisfactions or the lack thereof, the heartaches and the spiritual disquiet always centered on the following clusters: notions of generosity and reciprocity; interpretations of what constitutes hospitable gesture, selfless action, helping behavior, and "the deal"; issues of independence and interdependence; intolerance of ambiguity and mistrust of those attributes of personality that tend toward the indeterminate or the inscrutable; surrender of the subtle and the complex in the public sphere to the onslaught of the crass, the simplistic, and reductionist.

Let me jot down a set of "quick and dirty" impressions harvested from a site that might be considered a natural starting point for my inquiry: the home.

To an Indian, Asian, or Easterner (henceforth, each term will be used inclusively), home is a shelter with open doors, privileged space for communal use. Hospitality not assumed or turned down by the visitor is cause for offense. The guest is an honored figure, be it a relation, friend, or stranger.

For most white, middle-class Americans (and those who have been assimilated into that group's value system), home, as the prime embodiment of private property, is a protected area, an armor against intrusion into personal space. The business of hospitality is often deflected into public places— in restaurants and at park picnics. Stayovers are to be accepted only when offered and are time-bound. Even then, Americans grumble incessantly about putting up with family relations visiting during the traditional holidays.

Within the Indian house, all spaces are accessible. In our small apartment in Bombay, we often sat company on the bed; our small living room was too small for furniture. Even when the conveniences are limited, the best is placed at the guest's disposal. If company stays over, the hosts will sleep on the floor, insisting that visiting guests take the bed. Even a poor family will share its food and order or make special items that are normally beyond its means to buy or consume. Sharing is a given. Two of my colleagues and several students who have visited poor communities in Mexico and Central America attest to identical notions of hospitality among the people there. For instance, guests had first dibs on scarce resources like bathwater.

In the American home, the bedroom is always off-limits; even within the family, territorial markings are explicit though not rigid. No great fuss is made over food; self-help is encouraged. Visiting relations are clearly directed to neighborhood motels.

According to Indian protocol, invitation to a home is the first of a series of renewable gestures toward establishing ties of friendship and better mutual understanding. It is also a statement of acceptance and dependability. Walking in and out of each other's home ground is the outward sign of easy exchange of confidences and support in times of need.

An early, now almost archetypal portrayal of this relationship occurs in E. M. Forster's *A Passage to India*. For Aziz, to open his heart to Fielding comes naturally after he has befriended him; it proves somewhat of an embarrassment to the Englishman to be the recipient of such confidences. On his own part, Fielding finds it difficult to return the familiarity that Aziz assumes will flow as a logical outcome of the equation of hospitality he has established with the guest. Among other things, the novel is a classic statement of cultural misunderstandings and the cross-purposes under which individual and political relationships labor.

In the American view, the home visit is a single event entailing no obligation to reciprocity. Our American friends are often flattered, touched, and sometimes leery of undeserved (in their eyes) invitations to our house. We do this routinely, but our expectations are often frustrated because we see ourselves trying too hard to extend warmth and receiving no such gesture in return. Evidently, we are being unreasonable given that we are not singing out of the same hymn book.

Under Indian auspices, the gifts that friends bring are usually for the host family's use, not for serving up to company. Similarly, the spread that the host provides is ample, thoughtful, and an expression of genuine sharing to delight the guest.

Americans usually carry gifts (other than flowers) of which they will be co-consumers. Not only that, they will take back what is left! The menu is most often spare and functional unless it is that glorious American invention, the potluck, or the annual Thanksgiving meal. Oftentimes, items like steak will be counted one to a person—no seconds available. At first we were outraged at what appeared to us to be small-heartedness; now we laugh it off.

In India, dropping in is celebrated, taken for granted, existing as it does in a culture that thrives on contact, that generously devotes its time to serving the needs of others. Besides, the absence of telephones in most middle-class homes in India rules out calling ahead: You assume the party at your destination will greet you with smiles when you show up at the door. Because you have trudged halfway across town to accomplish this, the host is in fact delighted. Improvisation is the rule, for the welcome you are given. I can vouch for the wide application and validity of this practice.

In America, dropping in is taboo, violating codes of etiquette connected with privacy, personal time, and planning; thus, springing of social surprises is not welcome, not even at short notice.

For years, we lived without a telephone in the distant suburbs of Bombay. We woke up on Sundays playing the guessing game of anticipating visitors during the day: It could be parents, cousins, brothers, sisters, or friends. On days when no one appeared at our door, we went to bed feeling let down.

It is not as if the codes for privacy or personal space are not recognized or not valued by Asians; they are simply set aside voluntarily to honor more sacred obligations. From the domestic sphere to the larger social framework, what makes for the greater interdependence between individuals and the group is a higher degree of tolerance, accommodation, and sacrifice, which balances out individual claims against community goals.

In the American family and social network, support is limited to whatever does not interfere with individual space, time, and freedom of choice. When these lines are overstepped, the vote cast is always on the side of individual rights, the pursuit of personal fulfillment and profit, defined from a peculiarly self-driven standpoint.

So lost are some self-evident truths that researchers actually have to conduct studies to demonstrate that service toward others, devoting oneself to another's well-being, can be good for one's own psychic welfare! So unfashionable is conventional wisdom that the bringing together of the elderly and very young children in a supervised setting is seen to be a revolutionary idea. So misplaced are family memories that stories of sons and daughters taking in sick or disabled parents actually make news! Americans *en masse* tend to abdicate common sense and intuition in their reliance on "scientific data" and "experts" to help them monitor their personal lives. The diet industry's periodic "findings" (usually backed by drug-industry-funded "research" and bandwagoned by other ancillary enterprises) is another example of this mindless conformity. For a culture that prides itself on individuality, this conformity is shockingly routine in many areas of life.

Language is the first casualty in this broadside of jargon and rhetoric, the leveling of conceptual thought. For a country with a flair for developing the most colorful Americanisms out of the English language, there is the flip side in which language is constantly under assault and subject to trivialization. Words like *stress, disorder,* and *abuse,* for instance, are currently the most abused words in the language. They are applied loosely and across the board, and they infect and distort discussion leading to abbreviated thinking. Everywhere, labeling is handy, a quick way of slotting opponents, polarizing issues, and preempting any complex examination of gray areas. Look at the battle lines drawn between pro-lifers and pro-choicers.

In schools, the condition of "disorder" runs rampant, an assumption that underlies the representation of students' abilities and deficiencies, their diagnoses and prescriptions for cure.

Often I enjoy the use of sports terminology in the forecasts on the Weather Channel. The use of athletic metaphors, which is pervasive in all walks of American life, from boardrooms to bars, became quite offensive and dehumanizing when applied thoughtlessly—"kicking butt"—to the "enemy" in the Gulf War.

Reliance on learning tools such as the calculator and spell checking function on computers has virtually dried up mental arithmetic and versatility with language. I have seen friends incapacitated without a tape measure when rough-and-ready estimates of size and fit are called for. The indiscriminate use of words like *pretty* and the generic verb *bug,* for example, grates monotonously on my sense of proper usage as it strikes me as a teacher and writer. Definitely not "cool" in my book.

But I am not yet done with the domestic. Having children sleep over, which they do all the time in the homes of classmates, is a good way of infiltrating into the domestic stronghold. The vantage point that invisible informants have is priceless. The same applies to our children's friends who sleep over at our house—we have the benefit of examining ourselves from their insider viewpoints. Some revelations: As parents we rated easygoing, liberal, unfussy. So there is some truth to the suspicion that this is a conservative town! The other possibility is that this particular set of families makes up rules that are stricter than ours.

I must confess that my score as a husband fell a lot lower than the American standard set by my wife's peers and coworkers in relation to decision making and independence in financial matters enjoyed by them. *Mea culpa.* On the other hand, my wife's friends inquire if she will rent me out for my domestic reputation as a cook and babysitter. They are also somewhat astonished that we give each other permission to go out for dinner/movies with friends of the opposite sex. We also did this in Bombay, totally horrifying our respective parents.

Food cropped up again on the children's list of noticeable differences—specifically, a reluctance to share. The father of one of my daughter's friends will say within my daughter's hearing when she comes over unannounced to do homework: "What is she going to eat? We didn't make enough." The two parents work five jobs between them, carry their badges of affluence, and, reports my daughter, their kitchen shelves and freezer are stacked with food.

When my daughters' friends drop in unannounced after school and there isn't enough food or nothing to their taste, we generally concoct something without any fuss. In our house, our children's friends enjoy the same status as other guests with the attendant services due to them. Most of them, to our delight, have become connoisseurs of curry and Indian *chai* (a strong concoction brewed with tea leaves, to which is added sugar and milk).

Reluctance to share food: two more images vie for attention. People solemnly munch brown bag lunches in company without the least bit of self-consciousness. Same scenario among Indians—an impromptu and jovial division of the spoils from bags and tiffin boxes to everyone present is undertaken, especially for those who haven't brought their own.

There is the example of a good friend of ours for whom our doors have always been open and a meal guaranteed, and who has regularly partaken of our hospitality. Once, when my wife dropped in on her at noon, she was lunching on fast food but showed not the least bit of courtesy by sharing even a french fry. I am not offended, simply amused to see such narcissism with respect to food. Of course, our friend, in her own way, has been generous to us on plenty of occasions. The modes have varied; the terms have differed.

Before moving from the present locale to the classroom, let me, by way of transition, make a quick stop in the neighborhood.

Having spent between two months to four years in five different residential areas, having seen a pattern replicated in the lives of friends across the country, my impression about small town, suburban living is one of overwhelming desolation. While appreciating the logic behind the rapid growth of suburban living as a retreat from the busier, centralized, and faster-paced pattern of urban planning; while enjoying the benefits of space, quiet vistas, clean air, safety, and other perks that I would never give up; while empathizing with the American desire to shut in the self and shut out the world, I am still left with missing pieces.

To start with, the suburban neighborhood hardly qualifies as "user-friendly," to borrow another one of those cryptic American terms. "Neighborliness" as a concept has all but been erased from what used to be understood as community life. There is only mild concern or interest in who lives next door; there is hardly any at all in who lives down the block. Greetings in passing and a quick wave of the hand are the standard modes of communication; carpools are the common mode of interaction. The appearance of utility vans in the driveway or the arrival of ambulances is the only spark generating curiosity. In warm weather, more faces and bodies become visible, but exchanges remain superficial or ritualized over the drone of the mower. Many properties have no fences—an attractive feature, despite Robert Frost's ambivalence in "Mending Wall": "Good fences make good neighbors." But appearance belies the reality: The walls between neighbors are impenetrable, unscalable. Sometimes, I think Americans have succeeded only too well in realizing their dream of living in private paradises that resemble solitary confinement cells.

It is true that ties with the broader community, not the immediate one, continue to be maintained. But it is often from a consumer orientation that these exercises are conducted: out of the security of home and into the comfort of the car to make a trip to the store, the mall, the sports stadium, the aerobics class, the vacation, the fast-food stop, and back to the nest. To be fair, the real moments of America at leisure not dictated by everyday exigencies or the enticements of the leisure industry take place in restaurants, bars, bookstores, theaters, music and movie halls, parks, pools, beaches, nature trails, and above all, in front of the television set. Americans love "the good life" and work hard at having fun.

It might also be a truism that the whole point of domestic striving is to shut in and to keep out. I enjoy my share of it, and indeed, it is a change from the traditionally intrusive mode of neighborhood living in Indian cities and suburbs. Apartment and condo building in big cities has somewhat discouraged the old-style, open, in-your-face living arrangements, sometimes with traumatic consequences for tenants used to more informal and cluttered lifestyles. A recent study undertaken in Calcutta describes the depression experienced by women living in skyscrapers whose contact with ground-level existence and joint family dynamics is cut off for prolonged periods because of the husband's upward mobility, and migration into a nuclear family setup.

It is this deep conditioning that, in time, makes the Asian-American long for the vitality of a neighborhood alive with children, vendors, cyclists, shops, surprise, drama. Some of this is on vivid display in ethnic enclaves in New York, San Francisco, and other big cities—Dearborn, near Detroit, and Devon

Street in Chicago are sights familiar to me. Not so long ago in American memory, Jane Jacobs in *The Death and Life of Great American Cities* described the texture and tone of sidewalk contacts as the "small change" out of which grew the community's wealth of public life. The props and paraphernalia of city property are designed to stimulate this growth. When this high-pitched vitality degenerates into an environment of noise, dirt, congestion, and crime, suburbia offers a welcome alternative.

But suburban subdivisions and layouts are designed as closed, static systems. With all of their attractions, conveniences, and gratifications, they seal the American soul in an ingrown, selfishly guarded, dead-bolted cell, insulated and detached from the principle of a shared community life. Where this principle comes into effect, it is through the structured network of church, club, bingo group, or work-related interests, with established and limited goals.

In good weather, when children spill out on the lawn, an exchange of sorts takes place. In one of our former settings, where two houses in the same yard were rented out to two families, stay-at-home mothers and children provided the glue for interfamily contact, exchange of recipes and food items. The relationship between these families continues—now that one family has moved to the Upper Peninsula—through mail and telephone, gift exchanges, and summer visits. In our present neighborhood, however, our friendly overtures have worked with only two out of twenty households. Superficiality reigns; anonymity is the norm.

Let me see if the shift to the third locale will help me round out and culminate the themes I have unfolded.

Having begun by identifying the context from which I speak, I went on to examine the notion of hospitality, reciprocity and related behaviors, and the withholding of these gestures. I tried to link these with wider historical and cultural patterns. From there I looked at the idea of "neighborhood" to find out if there was a cause-effect relation between designs and systems of living and social interaction. Now I intend to focus on how some of these manifestations affect the educational system and the lives of students, and what lessons we may learn from a renegotiation of current realities.

For me, the impulse to write comes out of the same source as the desire to teach—giving voice to a shaping spirit. In one, the speaking self constructs a text and in the other, the self lends its voice to give life to other texts. Both are inner-driven and outer-directed: They presume an attentive consciousness, a longing, and an active intent at both ends of the process.

I picture the classroom as a crossroads, the place where worlds collide; where, along with the dismantling and rupture of theories and practices, a fusion is also taking place in a series of continuous, dynamic moments in the act of reading, writing, and conversation. The ruling principle here is *connectedness*—a network of links between teacher, learner, materials; worlds occupied, abandoned, yet to be born; ideas, stories, dreams.

Here, again, I find myself in a place of dissonance. Although theoretically as well as in practice, American higher education functions in a more stimulating, liberal atmosphere than comparable systems elsewhere, its pedagogical bent militates against any deep-rooted, sustained *engagement* between teacher and learner. Textual learning is elevated above everything else, performance and scoring are the highest rated values, development of "skills" the ultimate goal. Individual success, which is evidenced through completed assignments and secured grades, is emphasized more than the quest for meaning. The idea of personal growth is touted loudly and ritually, but often revolves around the notion of self-acceptance and "feeling good"—almost totally denuded of the refining edge of critical self-scrutiny.

Although the educational system is differentiated enough in terms of programs, value orientation, and choice of schools to allow for a more humane scale of interaction (a focus on intellectual and humanitarian pursuits), the attempt is effectively undermined by the habits and structures of American mass culture. The grain of American life, its temper and tempo, its headlong rush into short-term, goal-centered styles of living, the dependence on products of technology and the agendas set by it, the media's subversion of sacred and rational discourse, and any number of related phenomena ensure that intellectual and humane concerns always get the short end in a culture driven by innovation, consumption, profit, and self-serving motives.

In this climate, to define one's calling as a teacher as that of a friend, guide, and philosopher raises eyebrows, arouses suspicion, and generates disbelief. Coming from an ancient "guru" culture, I am branded by that tradition that still thrives in the spheres of music, theater, dance, and religious training. Admittedly, even in India, higher education has become mechanized to the point where any possibility of negotiated relationships between student and teacher has been virtually eliminated.

Over here, although my commitment as a teacher and the energy I invest in the life of students is appreciated, my attempt to invite partnerships, to offer apprenticeships, appears like a sad and touching anachronism. There are few takers. Any arrangement showing any sign of mutual dependence produces distinct discomfort in the American ego. On the part of the younger generation, this fear is often based on a general distrust of teachers and of the adult population. Because I am forced to deal with this every day, I have struggled with trying to come to terms with this resistance.

Some observations: Helping behavior, especially of the unsolicited voluntary kind, is regarded as presumptuous, almost a judgment of another's ability; in the eyes of some, it amounts to an insult. Since independence is such a prized virtue, looking out for oneself is the prime value.

Because, in the American rule book, selfless behavior is suspect, actions are viewed as always having a motive. Similarly, if help is acknowledged or accepted, the recipient assumes that an unspoken obligation or demand may ensue. Because this will impinge on the freedom to make up his or her own mind, the helpful action is declined. When a "favor" is accepted, it is sought to be quickly squared off through payment. Nothing is as easy and business-like in personal dealings between Americans—even in marital and intimate family transactions—as settlements worked out in dollar amounts for specific help or gain. Money is the great leveler.

Nothing is as touchy to Asian-Americans as the equating of acts of friend-ship and gestures of goodwill with monetary value. An act of generosity is meant to be accepted as a gift, a token of affection and esteem for the one on whom it is conferred. The receiver waits for the right occasion to show appre-ciation in return. When the smell of money intrudes, the deed is paid for, bought, and concluded. The future of giving is nipped.

For Americans, the most universally understood metaphor for transac-tional behavior is "the deal." Although this originates in the dominant, male, competitive culture, women get drawn into it easily. You get fair exchange, or you get the better of the other. In competitive relationships, you work toward gaining an advantage. In unsavory situations, you screw someone; in outright exploitative ones, you do worse. No wonder my wish to function outside these tried and tested parameters invites suspicion and mistrust.

Students, as well as colleagues, prefer an up-front accounting, a visible contractual relationship rather than one with latitude that may have a hidden agenda. I suspect issues of autonomy, control, trust, and vulnerability have a lot to do with this holding back. In today's climate, the legality of roles and functions and the status of what is "appropriate"—another one of those words running loose—also probably inhibit the following of one's own drumbeat.

If giving, generosity, bestowing on others the gifts that arise out of doing one's duty or out of one's temperament is frowned upon, what is propelling the spreading cult of "random acts of kindness"? Why is there such a yearning for groupism? Wherever you turn, whatever you tune into, the language is saturated with "support," "caring," "self-worth," "growing." But this is a halfhearted yearning, an artificially contrived cure played out in the atmosphere of a hothouse. It evades the bedrock ideology of American individualism: An assumption, though vaguely questioned from time to time, has not quite become problematic enough for a radical reappraisal. Indeed, support groups subvert their own logic by offering a ritualized, rehashed kind of community (shades of the encounter group from an earlier era?) that makes no onerous demands but panders to individual-focused agendas that suit perfectly the self-centered habits and aims of its followers. As such, these genuine but misplaced attempts are doomed to failure—the residue of another lost art.

The need for periodic reviews of values, attitudes, and behaviors seems to be ongoing—clearly, a sign of health—in the life of the culture. But it invariably takes place through the agency of a passing fashion or fad, only to be replaced by the next one.

Limitations of space have constrained me from a fuller examination of the excursions I've made. My hope is that readers will be motivated to look more deeply into the psychological and cultural ground on which these sightings have been made. In wrapping up this narrative, I'd like to linger awhile in the inviting space between giving and withholding.

The solid core of American values—the good old standbys of self-reliance, industry, profit and pleasure, good humor, an incurable optimism, and the need to move on—remains unshaken.

Despite the frictions and misunderstandings—it is unrealistic after all, to expect complete harmony or thorough understanding among diverse groups, classes, genders, and national cultures—there is a drive and a level of coherence that makes this society run.

Signals and prophecies of doom are announced at regular intervals. But if history is any comfort, this tendency is a well-established cultural trait. Except that at this historic moment, the culture will have to invent a more active ingredient than the stale formula of "tolerance" in order to accommodate current and developing realities. Tolerance is easy when it issues from a privileged source. Tolerance distances and separates because it is patronizing and benevolent; it is the gruel dished out to those who have sought asylum. Tolerance ultimately retreats to its high ground. The active ingredient now needed to shake the tolerant out of their torpor is an invitation to embrace, to meet midway, to take by the hand, to sit face to face.

The exponents of American culture who make brave attempts to understand "the other" in their midst succeed to a degree through the simple, ubiquitous device of "acceptance"—that all-American gesture and nod to the stranger arriving on their shores. They welcome, make room, and delight in the strangeness of the creature they have adopted. It is evidence of the dash of pragmatism in the American recipe for survival. But deeper understanding eludes these exponents, particularly as the stranger resists easy labeling and categorization, defies familiar models of behavior and norms of conduct.

The Asian and other foreign representative will always remain elusive to some degree; his or her heart and soul will always seem inscrutable. In day-to-day dealings, this mystery will often pose barriers, give rise to minor annoyances and misinterpretations. Such simple issues as permissible eye contact, physical proximity, and touching can raise unanswerable questions. Inevitably, these are tied up with differences in professed values and styles of communication.

The Easterner lives comfortably with ambiguity of personality as well as language, without hankering after absolutist or categorical statements of position at all times. He is at home with contradictions, even unresolvable ones, since they are part of life's unsolvable problems back home or part of the larger mysteries of the universe. The indeterminate is a very real, fascinating, even venerated category of experience. This other world sits on a stalk and sways between the *yes, no,* and the *maybe;* it is poised between the this and the *not this.* The language of paradox is that native's natural medium. The state of uncertainty is not threatening; it is fertile, a state that entertains possibility.

This is clearly misunderstood, dismissed, and proves to be a source of provocation to a culture that insists on clear-cut definitions, scientific accuracy, statistical data, and the belief that inquiry must yield firm results, evidence must lead to truth. It is not so much the methodology that is inadequate but the underlying dogmas that make the process flawed.

Surely the challenge and exhilaration lies in the coming together of complementary viewpoints of the familiar and the strange, the mysterious and the intimately known, the distant and the close-at-hand. The question we must ask ourselves is: Can we hear the hum of the universal in the heartbeat of the particular? Despite the burning focus on undeniable particularities of difference—histories, heritages, communities, voices—we need to salvage the possibility of universal connection. This is our stage, our arena, our field of vitality. This is where we must meet to recover our faith, to find ourselves renewed.

Given the conditions of displacement, expatriation, and exile (in more than the geographical sense), what speaks to me is a statement by Novalis that I have rephrased: Poetry, travel, anthropology, is for me an endless homesickness; it is the urge to be at home everywhere.

Study Questions

1. What are the basic differences between American and Indian concepts of hospitality?
2. Compare Indian and American codes of privacy and personal space.
3. How does Professor Peeradina describe the concepts of the suburban American neighborhood?
4. What are the author's main criticisms about teacher-student relationships in higher education? What does he find to be the basic problem with the value system indicated by students' attitudes?
5. Do Americans have, as the author has suggested, an "urge to be at home everywhere"? Why or why not?

19

The Hidden Gaze and the Self that Is Seen
Reflections of a Japanese Anthropologist

CHIKAKO OZAWA-DE SILVA

EMORY UNIVERSITY

For decades now, anthropologists have been describing the Japanese self as "dependent, harmonious, group-oriented, and less individualistic" and the American or Western self as "independent, individualistic, concrete, and less situation-oriented." Selfhood is undoubtedly a cultural construction and varies across cultures; thus, the specific manner in which it is constructed will differ according to values, practices, and modes of interaction. However, this does not mean that selfhood is fundamentally different in Japan than it is in the US. In both, the self that is seen by others plays a vital role, but the specific ways it manifests and the cultural discourse around it differs, because being defined by others is taken for granted in Japan, whereas being a self-made individual is valorized in the US.

Chikako Ozawa-de Silva was born and grew up in Japan, moving to the United Kingdom in the mid 1990s for graduate work in Social and Cultural Anthropology at the University of Oxford. In 2000 she moved to the United States and has lived in Boston, Chicago, and Atlanta. She is an Associate Professor in the Department of Anthropology at Emory University.

As an anthropologist who grew up in Japan, left for graduate school in the United Kingdom in my early 20s, and then came to the US to work at the age of 30, my cultural lenses have naturally come to attend to modes of behavior and thought that appear rather distinctive in each place. Among these, one has increasingly interested me. Despite differences of culture, it seems that people are in certain ways not as different as they may appear on the surface. Wherever they may be, people care about how they are seen by others. Human beings are social animals, and they are constantly aware of other people's presence and of being observed and evaluated by others. But how this manifests itself across cultures can be quite different indeed.

In order to highlight differences and similarities, I would like to start with an episode in Japan that may appear strange to some Americans.

The Hidden Gaze

I suddenly caught myself feeling not quite comfortable at the International Center office of Keio University in Tokyo. It felt as if people were watching me closely and examining my every move. Yet when I looked around the office, no one was looking at me. Still, I couldn't help feeling that there was something wrong. My attention turned to my clothes and appearance, and I had a certain sense that I was not dressed properly.

I had just flown in from Atlanta with my husband and was about to begin my sabbatical in Tokyo, during which I would be conducting research on suicide and the "worth of living" (*ikigai*) among young Japanese. We had come straight from Narita Airport to the Keio University campus after a 16-hour flight, and I was rather casually dressed in jeans and a plain black winter jacket with a hood, bought from The Gap. It was not a new jacket, and not particularly stylish, but it was in reasonably good condition and didn't have any obvious marks or tears on it.

Sure, I probably wouldn't have dressed in that way on a typical teaching day at my home university, Emory. But what could people expect after such a long international flight, and while carrying several heavy suitcases? There was nothing rude, I felt, in being dressed in that way when all one was there to do was to pick up one's room key and sign a room contract. At least, I thought, that's how it would be in the US, would it not? Nevertheless, I simply felt awkward, and this was only exacerbated when I spoke with a young woman at the front desk and asked for Mr. Kurata. I had the sense that she couldn't quite place me or who I was.

Mr. Kurata, with whom I had been corresponding via email prior to arriving in Japan, appeared with a young woman, whom I took to be his assistant. Just like everyone else in the office, Mr. Kurata was dressed in a suit with polished shoes that looked brand new.

We sat on the couch, facing each other, and he presented me the contract form and explained how to pay the telephone bills, use the card key to enter my room, and other such information, all in great detail, thoroughness, and seriousness of tone. In his impeccably polite manner, I sensed a certain uneasiness, however, as if he was wondering whether I was really a professor. His assistant sat beside him and didn't say a word, but she studiously made notes on a pad as if she was taking down everything he was saying. I found the whole process rather amusing as he patiently but laboriously went through each nitty-gritty detail with such formality and gravity.

As my mind drifted from the tedium of what I was hearing, I couldn't help analyzing this situation. What was it that made Mr. Kurata seem so uneasy? What was it that was making me feel uneasy? Was it how I spoke Japanese? Although I regularly spoke with my parents and friends in Japan over the phone, I hadn't really conducted a business conversation in Japanese for close to ten years. The last time I spent more than a few weeks in Japan was in 1998, when I was doing fieldwork for my doctoral dissertation.

As a language, Japanese is rather complex in terms of the numerous levels of politeness one must use depending on the social situation. In a case like this, I had decided it was best to stick to the most polite manner. This involves using terms that constantly put oneself down while putting the other person up. However, it was a bit of a struggle to keep up with this in a constant manner without letting a more informal tone slip in, especially as I was unaccustomed to using this kind of speech on a regular basis. Conversations with family and friends are of course informal and casual, and we never worry about putting ourselves down and raising others up. Perhaps my business Japanese language skills had become rusty. But still, I wondered, how could my Japanese be so strange? After all, I was a native Japanese, who had been born in Japan and who grew up there. I hadn't even left Japan until I was 21. Perhaps it was my attire after all . . .

Looking back on that first day in Tokyo, I can see how it really took me by surprise to find how unsmoothly my first interactions in Japan proceeded. As I went about campus, I noticed how even the Keio college students were all much more formally dressed than I was—and not just formally, but also fashionably. Of course, many American college students can be quite fashionable, but I rarely saw them dressed formally unless there was a special occasion. At Keio, the students were always so impeccably dressed that for the first few days I couldn't help but feel a bit shabby. The feeling of not being dressed properly, an old and almost forgotten feeling, was gradually coming back to me. I asked my husband, who is a Bostonian, whether he felt anything like what I experienced. I was hoping that I was just feeling this way for no reason. Unfortunately, my American-born husband did notice some "awkwardness" in our interaction and thought I stood out, as if I were a foreigner. That confirmed that I wasn't being paranoid.

* * *

When I think about it, one can easily feel uncomfortable in a crowd if one is not dressed "properly," depending on the occasions. During weekdays in Tokyo, most people on the trains and subway are dressed in suits, and it is very rare to see anyone dressed in jeans or sneakers. Even the college students at Keio did not dress in jeans during the weekdays. But on weekends, the city has very different feel to it. People are dressed casually in jeans and sneakers, and there is a difference even in the way they walk and hold themselves. You can easily tell whether it is a weekday or a weekend just by looking at the people on the street and seeing how they are dressed, but it almost feels as if you could just tell it from the general atmosphere.

A few days after I arrived in Tokyo, knowing that a conference was taking place that week at Keio, I had to make a trip to the department store the next day, a task that was at the top of my "to do" list. I had realized with dismay that none of my formal attire from the US was going to look appropriate for the conference. My outfits were all too casual and too colorful in comparison to what I witnessed on the Keio campus.

I therefore made a visit to the Takashimaya Department Store, one of the well-known and highly regarded department stores in Japan. I checked the floor guide and noticed that the "Career Characters" floor seemed right for business attire. On the "Career Characters" floor, I was quite lost for a long time, overwhelmed by the number of stalls. Eventually I came across a store I recognized, *INDIVI*, and it was full of jackets and office skirts. I have never shopped at that store, but I recalled the name from conversations with my younger sister who was more aware of fashion in Japan, compared with me. I thought I was safe shopping at this store.

As a representative of both Emory University and Keio University, and as a professional academic, I knew I had to dress properly, as during the course of my research I would be having interviews with psychiatrists, academics, and government officials. But when I started selecting items in the store, I had no confidence in my judgment, and I eventually asked for advice. A young assistant listened politely as I explained that I needed formal clothing that would be good for business occasions. She immediately told me that the dresses I was holding were wonderful for weekend dinner parties, but perhaps not for business occasions. She quickly chose a grey dress and jacket, and I tried them on. I appeared very formal, even to myself, and I almost felt slightly uncomfortable with my own appearance. The assistant was pleased, however, and suggested that I might be interested in a matched skirt to the jacket, so that I would have a suit that would be useful. "A suit?" I thought. When would I ever need to wear a suit? Having a jacket and respectable "grey" dress seemed more than satisfactory. I politely declined her offer and bought the items. On the day of the conference, however, I entered the lecture hall only to find that 80 percent of the female scholars were in suits, not to mention all the men. I would not have been over-dressed if I showed up in suit; I would have merged even better in the crowd.

What is funny is how people often comment about how nicely dressed I am while I am in the US. But each time my parents visit me from Japan, my mother laments about how untidy I appear. For her, I do not properly dress up as a professional academic. One day when I came back from work, my mother sighed and said, "Is that really what you dress in for work?" She looked almost sad. All these years, I had simply ignored her advice, but coming back to Japan this time, her suggestions suddenly made so much sense. To dress in that way would simply be inappropriate, and it would reflect badly on my home institution. Even without people staring at me, I knew they were judging me based on how I dressed.

* * *

Of course it is true that even in the US, one is certainly judged by one's appearance, and both women and men go to great lengths to appear well-dressed and respectable. When it comes to appearance, however, Japanese women seem to be even more keenly obsessed with appearance, and they follow fashion closely and in a particular way. What I realized during my most recent visit to Japan was that Japanese women's sense of being "fashionable" consists of (a) looking appropriate for the occasion; (b) looking appropriate for their age; and (c) looking appropriate for their status. I believe both American and Japanese women like to appear youthful in general, but it is much more important for Japanese women to dress in an age-appropriate way.

What is considered age-appropriate is of course conventional in Japan, but it is also clearly laid out in fashion magazines, which are themselves rigidly categorized by age in a much stricter way than in the US. Certain magazines are only for women in their late teens to early 20s; others for women in their 30s who are unmarried; others for married women in their 30s; and so on. The appropriate age range is often even on the magazine cover or binding, much as one would see on the packaging for toys for young children. These magazines then contain very clear and explicit instructions on what it is acceptable to wear: women in their 20s can wear skirts that show their knees, but women in their 30s should opt for a skirt that at least partially covers the knees.

Despite occasionally having read fashion magazines in the US, I was unprepared for this level of segmentation. At the beginning, I realized that the magazines I knew from my college days were no longer appropriate reading for someone of my age. I also learned from my younger sister that *INDIVI*, the shop where I had bought my conference jacket and skirt, was indeed a shop in which she had bought clothing a long time ago, but now it was too young even for her. It had never occurred to me before leaving for Japan that I would have research which stores to shop at, and which magazines I would need to study in order to learn how to dress appropriately.

Fashion magazines are about much more than glamour in Japan. They are also "manual books" with many special issues ranging from what to wear if you visit your fiancé's house to how to dress for a funeral in the summer, as opposed to one in the fall. All of the instructions relate not only to appearing attractive but also to appearing proper on different occasions. I could not think of any equivalent among popular American fashion magazines. In the US most magazines seem to be roughly divided between teenagers and adults. In *InStyle*, one American fashion magazine for women, there is a page each month devoted to a "how to dress" manual for women. It is divided into three columns: one for women in their 20s and 30s; one for women in their 30s and 40s; and one for women in their 40s and 50s. That one magazine could include all those age categories, and also that the categories themselves could overlap with each other so broadly, would be unthinkable in Japan. In the US, I could probably pick up almost any fashion magazine at a bookstore without looking strange. In Japan, I had to be quite courageous to pick up even *AneCan*, a magazine targeting post-college women in their 20s and early 30s, and bring it to the cash register. Magazines for college-age women were too adventurous for me to actually buy.

* * *

Later, I wondered what could account for the "hidden gaze" I experienced so forcefully upon first returning to Japan, that feeling of being observed and evaluated. In hindsight, I think there are probably a few factors that contributed to it. Anthropologists have long argued that culture affects the way people perceive the world, but recently psychologists have noted that cultural differences may influence perception even on a very literal level. When presented with visual scenes, studies suggest that non-Asian Americans seem to focus on a central, foregrounded object and pay less attention to background objects and context than East Asians. Americans are therefore better able to report on foreground objects when later asked about them, whereas East Asians are better than Americans at recalling context and background objects (Boland et al. 2008). When you combine this with the insight, taken from phenomenology, that we can attend to things with our mind in our peripheral vision without actually moving our eye from a focal object, this suggests some interesting things. It may be that Japanese are better able to observe someone through their peripheral vision without actually looking at the person. Thus, whereas in America one might realize that one is being observed because people are staring, in Japan one feels the gaze of others but without others' eyes being directed on oneself. People are watching you, and you feel that, but they are not looking directly at you—they don't have to. The instant I thought of this, I realized this is a skill my sister has in abundance, but one I never had. I wonder if that is a subtle part of the reason why I feel, in certain ways at least, more comfortable in America than in Japan.

A second factor I think is relevant is a distinction between what we might call appearance and presentation. It seems to me that while both Americans and Japanese are concerned with how they look and are seen by others, Americans may tend to focus more on physical appearance, which is primarily the body and only secondarily its accoutrements; whereas Japanese are more concerned with presentation, which is the proper way appearance is presented and therefore puts more emphasis on accoutrements such as clothing, jewelry, and other similar signifiers. This would correspond to some of the differences noted by the cultural psychologists who compared East Asian and American modes of perception. It also connects with another idea I developed while in Japan, that of the self that is seen and the self that is not seen, an idea to which I will return later.

Appearance and Performance

What do these incidents tell us about America? Indirectly, quite a bit. Without knowing it, living for ten years outside Japan had caused American culture to slowly become more native to me. Japan, in turn, had become foreign. But being in Japan again also helped me to see in a new light aspects of American culture that seem foreign to Japanese.

Is it true, for example, that Americans do not judge people by appearances as much as Japanese do? Is the Japanese way of paying attention to performance somehow more superficial than American sentiment? Is there no "gaze" in American culture?

When I shared the above episodes of my first days in Tokyo with a friend who was born in Taiwan and moved to the US 30 years ago, she told me, "Japan sounds tough! Asian culture is good in many ways, but it is also an old culture, and it can be stifling and a bit suffocating. In America, we are more free to wear whatever we would like to." Others have reacted in a more or less similar way. But I think there are other factors at play here as well.

While being ever-conscious of how one appears to other people and conforming to the norms of cultural expectations certainly does not *seem* to match the idea in American culture of individuality and freedom, I am not sure that Americans are somehow lacking in self-consciousness a great deal more than Japanese. For decades now, anthropologists have been describing the Japanese self as "dependent, harmonious, group-oriented, and less-individualistic," while the American or Western self is "independent, individualistic, concrete, and less situation-oriented." However, despite the culturally sanctioned ideal of individual freedom, my experience in the US has led me to believe that Americans do care a great deal about how they are seen by others. It just manifests itself differently. Let me illustrate this with a few examples.

* * *

In comparison to Japanese, Americans might not seem to care as much about dressing appropriately for their age or for each "time, place, and occasion" ("TPO" as it is colloquially called in Japan, from the English words). But that does not mean Americans do not care about appearances. In the circles I have moved in since coming to the US, it has struck me that Americans are indeed very concerned about appearing "productive." Being a productive individual holds much positive value in the US, and there are so many ways this collectively held value manifests itself in American cultural behaviors.

One evening at a house party, I witnessed a conversation between two men in their early 60s. "Bob," one of them said, "I'm turning 61 soon. Two-thirds of our life is over. I really need to think about what to do with the rest of my career. Should I consider a new direction?" To which his interlocutor replied, "Two-thirds? Why be so pessimistic? Half, I'd say!"

I'm not particularly good at math, but 61 hardly seems like half-way in one's lifetime. I am from a country with the world's longest average lifespan for women—86—and where the average man's life expectancy is 79. Even by the Japanese standard, 61 would not be considered half-way through one's life. To think of a change of career direction at that age would likewise seem very strange indeed.

Of course, Bob's interlocutor might well have been joking, or just saying that to make Bob feel better about himself. But that only supports the point I am trying to make. People in America are concerned about their age, and that is in part because they are concerned with productivity as a measure of one's worth in society, and productivity, it seems, develops inversely to age after a certain point.

Initially upon coming to the US, I was relieved that I did not have to append the honorary suffixes "-kun" or "-san" to everyone's name, as we do in Japan. It is a sign of politeness, but can also create distance, like saying "Mr." before someone's name. This seemed like a nice sign of egalitarianism. Years later, however, I realized that not asserting their authority via seniority does not at all mean that people are not age conscious. Many people I have met would rather pay full price for a ticket than choose the senior rate and call to attention their age. Many people I know do not seem to wish to retire, and those who do retire, often because they are forced to, do not seem to take it well and are at pains to show that they are still engaged in productive work. Underneath the youthful attitude many Americans have, there seems to be a strong fear of aging. This fear of aging, it seems to me, shows that Americans are just as age-conscious as Japanese, but whereas Japanese take pains to dress in an age-appropriate way, many Americans take pains to hide the signs of their age. These might appear to be opposite attitudes toward aging, but they clearly share a commonality in that they reflect a social sense of self-consciousness.

In sharp contrast to Japan, it is hard to see what benefits one gains in social interactions in America from being senior. It is not that seniority is always connected with high social status in Japan, as some might think, but seniority clearly plays a major role in many Japanese social interactions. When I was in Japan as a college student, there was one thing I used to find rather annoying whenever I was talking to men who were senior to me. Even men who were just 30 would often say things like, "When you get to be my age, you'll understand how it is." Or, "Young people like yourself don't understand, but . . ."

One of the first things Japanese often try to figure out in their initial interaction with strangers is how old the other person is, as that will play a role in how they interact—even a one-or two-year age difference matters. In the US, the ideal seems to be "young and successful," and it is considered rude to ask a woman her age.

Similarly, a great deal of importance seems to be placed on appearing busy and "good" all the time, and these two attributes are even combined in the concept of "good busy," or "busy but good." Thus, the appropriate response to the question "How are you?" seems to be "Good" or "Great." Everyone is always supposed to be good all the time. It took me a while to realize this is a formality that must be maintained on most occasions for the sake of appearances. Once, while I was at Harvard, a friend asked me, "How are you doing, Chikako?" I was in the middle of finishing up my dissertation, and it was a rather stressful time. "Okay," I said, "not that great at the moment, maybe." It wasn't a response that I felt would have surprised any of my friends at Oxford in the UK. But my American friend suddenly looked very concerned. "Chikako, I'm so sorry. Are you all right? I know a very good counselor and I'd be happy to give you her contact information."

I was quite taken aback by this response. Did feeling not particularly "good" on a given day constitute the need for seeing a therapist? I still remember that particular conversation very vividly, and since then I've learned to answer, "I'm fine, thank you," pretty much regardless of how I actually feel. This episode also reminded me of an American student at Oxford who had acquired a reputation of being a bit strange, as every time he was asked, "How do you do?" he replied with a strongly affirmative answer such as "I'm extremely fine!" or "I'm great!"

The positive tone in Americans' talk about themselves and life in general is quite different from the way people tend to talk in Japan and in England— with none of the black humor, none of the self-deprecation. In Japan, a neutral tone (e.g., "not so bad") in expressing oneself in casual greetings is the norm and considered polite. In the UK, self-denigration or self-mocking is not uncommon. In both countries, saying things that are openly positive about oneself is typically considered superficial or arrogant. Indeed, this was the aspect that took the longest time for me to adjust to when I came to the US. For a while I felt strange, as if I always had to be faking my actual feelings in social interactions. Everything, it seemed to me, had to be fine and good. I'm fine, my job is good, my life is good, and even when people are extremely busy, they are somehow "good busy." For the first few years, I sometimes literally took people at their word, and assumed that they were extremely fortunate people who had wonderful families, friends, and jobs. Eventually I began to pick up a nervous tone if they were talking about anything in less than a positive light, followed by a quick disclaimer, ". . . but I think it's all good."

This is not to say that people do not complain about things in the US, as obviously they do. But when it comes to maintaining appearances of the self, a positive evaluation seems very important, and any kind of negative statements appear magnified and worrisome.

Let me return to the idea of being "good busy," as this is something that struck me as particularly strange, but is very common in my social circles, particularly that of academia. Many people complain about how busy they are in casual conversations in the US. The question "How are you? Busy?" almost always guarantees an eager response in the affirmative. It seems that people feel comforted through the acknowledgment of how busy they are. At the same time, being busy is seen as something good, and even people who are extremely busy may say that it is a "good kind of busy" and may feel happy about being occupied with so many things. Of course, Max Weber has written of the Protestant work ethic, and this seems to pervade much of American life. At the university, almost everyone is busy, and people appear very stressed. When my retired mother-in-law told me how busy she is and how little time she has to do things like read, it struck me that "being busy" is more than a fact of American life; it is also connected with the need to maintain a positive social appearance as a productive and important individual.

During my several months in Tokyo this year, that contrast became very clear: people who are obviously very busy in Tokyo do not frequently talk about how busy they are, and certainly not in the manner of it being a "good busy." However, a psychiatrist I interviewed in Japan did tell me that in some cases there were people who spoke about how busy they were and even showed him their schedule books. He said, "I find it quite off-putting and sad, because it seems these people find their self-worth in making themselves busy."

It is internationally acknowledged that Japanese businesspeople work extremely long hours and dedicate their lives to their workplaces. The importance of work in the identity of both Japanese and Americans is no doubt similar, but the idea of "good busy" plays the role of an important indicator of a cultural value more broadly in American society than in Japanese society. In Japan, "being busy" is a state associated with "company men" (called *salary-men* in Japanese), and not with housewives or college students, for whom being busy confers little respectability. In reality, housewives might be very busy, but "being busy" is a cultural discourse related to the company men, and not housewives. In the US, being busy seems to have expanded to become a positive moral value for everyone, regardless of age, gender, and status. Even among young children, it seems that there is a strong pressure to fill their lives with all sorts of activities and programs so that their lives and productivity will be enriched to the maximum degree.

But why, one might ask, is being busy associated automatically with being productive? I do not think that in Japan being busy necessarily has the connotation of being productive. Rather, there is a dominant view that being busy is a state of "being consumed (for no good reason)," as if one is merely a cog in a big machine. It may be that if one lives in a society where the ideal of independence and autonomy is cherished, and selfhood is thereby understood in that way, being busy implies a productivity of self that is to be valued. Whereas if one lives in a society in which the self is understood as part of a network of relationships and interdependencies, such as in Japan, being busy does not correspond to an ideal of self-actualization or greater productivity. In other words, in a network of interrelated parts, one part becoming more busy and active does not necessarily make the entire entity more productive. In a stand-alone model, however, where each unit is separate, each unit becoming more active would make that single unit more productive, and the desired goal might be for all the units to become more active so that they all produce more.

The Japanese word "busy" (忙しい) literally means "losing one's heart (or mind)." Many Japanese even express that they do not like to say "I am busy," because it is a feeling that does not produce positive emotions. Of course, it should be noted that being busy and feeling busy are not the same thing: a subjective perception of being busy does not necessarily correlate to some objective measure of being more busy than someone else. I have noticed many people who are extremely busy but who never speak about how busy they are, as well as others who constantly complain about how busy they are but actually have very little to do. In these cases, the perception of being busy seems to hamper productivity, so this makes the cultural rhetoric even more interesting.

One little example may serve to illustrate this difference that I see in the cultural value of appearing to be busy. His Holiness the Dalai Lama, the spiritual and temporal leader of the Tibetan people, came to Emory University in 2007 to be inaugurated as Presidential Distinguished Professor, the only university appointment he has ever accepted outside India. During his stay, a minute-by-minute schedule was prepared for him, jam-packed with meetings, events, speeches, and conferences from 8:00 A.M. until 6:00 P.M. each day (he goes to sleep at 9:00 P.M. and rises at 3:00 A.M.). I learned that his schedule is always like this when he travels abroad. After observing him for a few years, I can certainly say that he is one of the busiest persons on the planet, not just in terms of his schedule, but also in terms of his responsibilities for the Tibetan people, the Tibetan Buddhist religion, and the countless organizations he is involved in. Yet I read in Howard Cutler's book, *The Art of Happiness at Work*, that when Dr. Cutler asked His Holiness what kind of work he did, that is, what his job was, His Holiness replied, "Nothing. I do nothing." For me, this response exemplifies a difference in the importance of appearing busy between American and traditional Asian cultures.

* * *

The cultural importance of productivity manifests itself even in the way we eat in America. One evening at a restaurant in Boston, right after I moved to the US, my husband and I were enjoying a dinner out. I was barely halfway through my entrée when a waitress came to our table, took away my husband's plate immediately after he finished his meal, and asked me. "Are you still working on that?" I was taken aback by this comment. What did she mean by asking me if I was still working? It took me quite a while to realize that she was asking me if I was still eating my meal. How could having a leisurely dinner on a Friday evening be conceptualized as working, I wondered.

On another occasion, at a different restaurant, the waitress came and literally took away my plate while I was still eating. This, too, left me in a bit of a shock. My knife and fork were not in my hand, as I was taking a momentary pause, but I hadn't placed them in any way to indicate that I had finished eating.

Since then I have heard this phrase innumerable times. "Are you still working?" I've also learned to keep my knife and fork in hand and poised if a waiter or waitress appears at the table. I came to miss my experiences of dining out in England and Japan.

I've tried to figure out in my mind why using the word "working" to refer to eating seems so wrong to me. For many cultures in the world, including that of Japan, eating is a form of leisure and pleasure, and stands in a certain opposition to the concept of work. A few years ago, I dined with a colleague of mine who is a neuroscientist from Italy, and who, amazingly, was an even slower eater than I am. While he was taking a pause from his plate and engaging with me in conversation, a waitress came and asked him if he was still working on his meal. "I am still eating," he said pointedly, and turned back to me. We spoke about the phrase, and I realized he shared my bafflement at conceptualizing a dinner experience as some kind of work.

Of course, "working on one's meal" is just an expression, and some might think it means little and is just a harmless idiomatic expression. But there is certainly an emphasis on quick service in US restaurants, and I don't think it is a coincidence that the US is the country that invented and popularized "fast food." Fast service is proper service in restaurants in the US, and I realized that my waiters and waitresses were not being rude but were merely serving in a culturally sanctioned and expected way.

In France, by contrast, my husband and I once nearly missed our train in Lyon when the waiters refused to take our order or bring us our bill until we had spent an appropriate amount of time sitting there. The entire meal took three hours, and they blithely ignored our signs of agitation. But neither the waitress in the US who asked me if I was "still working" nor the waiters in that French restaurant were being rude, in my opinion. Dining service is a manifestation of a culture's value and idea about what "eating" means as human activity. Eating activity in the US often feels like fueling gas into one's car so that the car can run. In such situations, fast service is crucial and a good thing since it helps customers move on to more productive pursuits—other forms of "working." I think using the expression "working" for "eating" is another sign of how productivity is linked even to the act of dining.

Conclusion: The Self that Is Seen

A few years back, the video rental chain Blockbuster came out with an ad that struck me as preeminently American in its sensibility: "More is Better." My feeling is that there is a close link between a concern for productivity, on the one hand, and a strong cultural impulse to consume more and to link greater consumption with happiness, on the other hand. But to merely produce more so that one (and others) can consume more seems an endless race that is unlikely to lead to genuine fulfillment.

Even more insidiously, when productivity is linked so directly and narrowly to self-image and self-worth, the negative consequences of the elderly feeling useless and the ageing process being seen as a loss of productive worth, rather than a gain of wisdom and experience, inevitably follow. Being busy comes to attain a moral status, and not being busy leads one to feel like a less worthwhile human being.

Underlying this, however, is something that is not unique to American culture, in my opinion. Whether we are consciously aware of it or not, as human beings we are social animals and we are concerned deeply with how we appear in the eyes of others. As Goffman (1959) noted so well, we go to great lengths to project images that we think are positive in our society. In Japan, this manifests itself in a strong concern with looking appropriate for one's age, for the occasion, and for one's status. In the US—and again, let me qualify this by restricting this to the circles I have been in—this manifests itself in a wish to appear productive.

This points, I believe, to a universal aspect of selfhood that lies beneath the independent vs. interdependent construals often used to distinguish American society from East Asian societies like Japan. My colleague at Emory, the developmental psychologist Philippe Rochat, has argued from his work with small children and infants that there is a fundamental fear of rejection that he calls "the mother of all fears" and that drives social cognition (Rochat, 2009a). As a result of this fear of rejection and isolation, we all share a basic affiliative need, "the basic drive to be acknowledged in one's own existence through the eyes of others" (2009b: 314). In other words, we all feel a strong need for mutual recognition and acknowledgement, and this need is basic because, "we essentially live through the eyes of others. To be human . . . is primarily to care about how much empathy, hence acknowledgement and recognition of our own person, we generate in others—the fact that we care about our reputation as no other animal species does" (Rochat 2009b: 306).

How do we tease out the differences between cultures while acknowledging shared aspects of our existence? For a long time, anthropologists have been contrasting American and Japanese construals of selfhood. Selfhood is a cultural construction, and thus there is no question that it will vary across cultures. Thus, while it is everywhere constructed, the specific manners in which it is constructed will differ according to values, practices, and modes of interaction. However, I do not believe that selfhood is fundamentally different in Japan than it is in the US. In both, the "self that is seen" plays a vital role— but the specific ways in which the self that is seen manifests itself differ, and the cultural discourse around selfhood differs, because being defined by others is taken for granted in Japan, whereas being a self-made individual is valorized in the US (Ozawa-de Silva, forthcoming).

At the level of dominant cultural discourse, Americans are supposed to be individualistic and to stick to their values, not yielding to others, or even to the collective. Americans are taught they should have a solid sense of self that cannot be easily shaken or swayed by the influence of others or social pressure. The self-made person is an unspoken ideal in American culture. Yet, when we see how human beings as social animals exist, the reality is much more complex, as I hope these episodes have helped to show. In my humble opinion as a nonexpert, Americans are very much conscious about how they are seen and judged by others, just as Japanese are.

As a native anthropologist of Japan, I often notice a great deal of differentiation within one so-called culture. At the same time, I also notice that people across cultures are not as different as they might appear initially. Recognizing cultural differences without effacing common aspects of our humanity across cultures is one of the great challenges that face cultural anthropologists in this new century. Driving motivations are often manifestations of the social values individuals are accustomed to, and from this, I agree with Rochat that we are all extremely conscious of our "self that is seen" by others. We even share this concern, it seems, with many nonhuman animals. This is a humble essay from a Japanese scholar who has spent almost ten years in the US and five years in the UK after leaving her mother country Japan in her early 20s. I am not an anthropologist of the US, merely a nonexpert observer and participant in American life, a way of life I have come to appreciate and value greatly. All my biases no doubt appear in how I see the world, but these observations are only possible after having lived in three different countries for a long period of time, while being trained as a cultural anthropologist.

Study Questions

1. Why do Japanese care so much about their appearance according to this chapter?

2. Does this chapter argue that selfhood is fundamentally different across different cultures or not?

3. How does the author view the commonly shared notion that the Japanese have "relational and interdependent selfhood" as opposed to Americans having "individualistic and independent selfhood"?

References

Boland, J. E., H. F. Chua, and R. Nisbett. 2008. How We See It: Culturally Different Eye Movement Patterns over Visual Scenes. In K. Rayner, D. Shen, X. Bai, and G. Yan G (eds.), *Cognitive and Cultural Influences on Eye Movements*. Tianjin, China: Tianjin People's Press/Psychology Press. Pp. 363–378.

Goffman, Erving. 1959. *The Presentation of Self in Everyday Life*. New York: Doubleday.

Ozawa-de Silva, Chikako. 2010. Shared Death: Self, Sociality and Internet Group Suicide in Japan. *Transcultural Psychiatry* 47(3): 392–418.

Rochat, Philippe. (2009a). *Others in Mind: Social Origins of Self-consciousness*. Cambridge: Cambridge University Press.

Rochat, Philippe. (2009b). Commentary: Mutual Recognition as a Foundation of Sociality and Social Comfort. In T. Striano and V. Reid (eds.), *Social Cognition. Development, Neuroscience, and Autism*. Maiden, MA: Blackwell.

20

País de mis Sueños
Reflections on Ethnic Labels, Dichotomies, and Ritual Interactions

GISELA ERNST-SLAVIT
WASHINGTON STATE UNIVERSITY VANCOUVER

Ethnic categorization and labeling are questioned as abstractions of either reality or accurate features of the persons or groups to which these labels are attached. The author explores the polarizing and negative applications of English language qualifiers relating to "race" and ethnicity, viewing them as system-maintaining devices in service to the hierarchical structure of American society. The essay concludes with some of Ernst-Slavit's impressions of American friendliness viewed as ritual.

Gisela Ernst-Slavit grew up in Lima, Peru, coming to the United States in the 1980s to study sociolinguistics and anthropology at the University of Florida. She is Associate Dean for Diversity and International Programs and Professor in the College of Education, at Washington State University Vancouver.

> Some of the most interesting questions are raised by the study of words whose job it is to make things fuzzier or less fuzzy. (Lakoff 1972: 195)

Like Saint Paul, I have seen the light. It happened while I was finishing my master's degree, when I was introduced to sociolinguistics; what I learned about language, language use, and culture literally changed the direction of my career. I had found an area of study that allowed me to grapple with the interplay of linguistic, social, and cultural factors in human communication. During my doctoral program at the University of Florida, I had the opportunity to think more deeply about why people use language the way they use it and why language can be clear and precise. At the same time, language often can be characterized by vagueness, ambiguity, and imprecision.

Perhaps nowhere is the interplay of language and culture more "fuzzy" (to use Lakoff's term) than in the labels we use to define ourselves and others. In this chapter I will share some of my experiences, and my subsequent reflections upon those experiences, with the use of labels and terms used to refer to a person's ethnic, cultural, and racial background. Within this context I will share my feelings about, and explore the connotations of, the made-in-the-U.S.A. label "Hispanic." Then I will explore the use of dichotomies and negative constructions in English. These structures will be better understood by contrasting them to Spanish. This comparison will illustrate that the existence in English of extreme dichotomies can often influence how native English speakers voice and manage their relations with others. Finally, I would like to illustrate how some of us "foreigners" can often be taken in by the friendliness of people in the United States.

Ethnic Labels: "I Came as a Peruvian and Immediately Became a Hispanic"

I was a fortunate child who grew up in Lima, Peru. I was brought up in an upper-middle-class environment, attended private schools, lived in a handsome neighborhood, and was surrounded by a protected haven of mostly well-educated friends and acquaintances. Like many others in Peru, I was a *mestiza,* the daughter of an Austrian father and a Peruvian mother, the product of an encounter of two continents, of two races. Like many others, I had European names and Peruvian looks, spoke more than one language, and was proud to be a Peruvian who also had knowledge about and appreciation for her father's homeland.

In spite of my good fortune, I also encountered my share of problems, sorrow, and broken dreams. This is why, like many others who leave their familiar lands in search of better lives, I too left mine in search of *el país de mis sueños* (the land of my dreams). I had little money but lots of hope, confidence, and a clear sense of national identity as a Peruvian woman. Therefore I set off happily, in June of 1985, unaware of the need for "clear" labels to identify my ethnicity, race, and culture. Soon after my arrival in Florida, I did what many other foreign students have to do if they want to get into graduate school in the United States: fill out multiple forms. Throughout this process I discovered two things: first, the momentousness of the written word in this society, and second, the importance of race and ethnicity as forms of social classification in the United States. It quickly dawned on me that my avowed national identity was of little relevance to the society at large. I realized that I was seldom considered a Peruvian but was most often either "Hispanic," "legal alien," "Latino," "Spanish-speaking," "South American," "Spanish," or, what is worse, "Other"! Within the context of official forms, institutionalized inquiries, and government requirements, I was faced with having to find the appropriate label to describe my nationality, culture, and background. The following question about ethnic origin will help illustrate my feeling of dubiousness, doubtfulness, and diffidence as I attempted to answer what, for some, might be just another question on a form.

Ethnic Origin (mark one)
____ White (not Hispanic origin)
____ Asian or Pacific Islanders
____ Black (not Hispanic origin)
____ American Indian or Alaskan Native
____ Hispanic
____ Other

Not only did I find the emphasis on racial categorizations in the United States perplexing, but I felt that the selection offered was limited and problematic. I felt that I had to summarize my nationality, ethnicity, upbringing, language, culture—in sum, my whole existence—in one fixed and unappealing label. I was not only appalled but also confused. For example, given the categories mentioned above, I could have marked the first option since I appeared "white" in both of my passports (Peruvian and Austrian). Yet, at the same time, that option would be incorrect since I am also what could be called "Hispanic."

I thought about marking "American Indian" or "Alaskan Native" since, in fact, I was born in (South) America and there is some Indian blood in my mother's ancestry (even though she might not want to admit to it). But these labels did not reflect all my other influences: my mother's descent from Spain, my father's Austrian and German blood, and the fact that I do not speak the languages nor share the cultures of Peruvian Indians. Because I had to use my European passport, on which I appeared as "white" (it included my visa and my "alien" number), I felt that no available categories encompassed my national and cultural identity.

My confusion grew as the smorgasbord of categories changed—from form to form and from institution to institution, and I often found myself spending considerable time trying to select the most appropriate label. After several months and many more forms, I opted to leave the question unmarked (when possible) or to mark "Other" (if there was such an option). On some occasions, depending on my mood, when the question asked for "race," I would write "Cocker Spaniel," "German Shepherd," or "unknown" on the blank line next to "Other." Because there often was an indication that this information was optional, I did not feel any remorse for perhaps skewing some demographic data. On the contrary, this simple act provided me with an opportunity to show my dissent toward questions that limited my individuality to a generic label.

Do the classifications recognized by the U.S. Census Bureau offer us a useful way of understanding our national and cultural experiences? Do terms such as *black, Asian American,* and *Hispanic* have any real substance to them, or are they the creation of media czars and political impresarios? Let's examine the official definition of Hispanic (according to the 1990 U.S. census):

> A person is of Spanish/Hispanic origin if the person's origin (ancestry) is Mexican, Mexican-American, Chicano, Puerto Rican, Dominican, Ecuadorian, Guatemalan, Honduran, Nicaraguan, Peruvian, Salvadoran; from other Spanish-speaking countries of the Caribbean or Central or South America; or from Spain.

The ethnic label "Hispanic" began to be used heavily by state agencies in the early 1970s to refer to all people in this country whose ancestry is predominantly from one or more Spanish-speaking countries. As a result, millions of people of a variety of national and cultural backgrounds are put into a single arbitrary category.[1] No allowances are made for our varied racial, linguistic, and national experiences, nor for whether we are recent immigrants, long-time residents, or belong to an associated territory. Furthermore, using "Hispanic" to refer to those who are of Spanish-speaking origin can be problematic in that it excludes a considerable sector of the population in Latin America for whom Spanish is not a first language. Many "Hispanic" immigrants come from regions that are not necessarily predominantly Spanish. This is the case of those who speak Nahuatl and Tiwa in Indian villages in Mexico; Kanjobal and Jacaltec in the southern part of Guatemala; Quechua and Aymara in the highlands of Peru and Bolivia; Guarani, Chulupi, and Mascoi in the Chaco region of Paraguay; Tukano and Tuyukaf in the swamps of Venezuela and Colombia; and others from predominantly non-Spanish-speaking regions. Thus, given that their native language may not be Spanish, it is inaccurate to call these people of "Spanish-speaking origin."

Furthermore, as Berkeley social scientist Carlos Muñoz writes, the term Hispanic is derived from *Hispania*, which was the name the Romans gave to the Iberian peninsula, most of which became Spain, and "implicitly emphasizes the white European culture of Spain at the expense of the nonwhite cultures that have profoundly shaped the experience of all Latin Americans" through its refusal to acknowledge "the nonwhite indigenous cultures of the Americas, Africa, and Asia, which historically have produced multicultural and multiracial peoples in Latin America and the United States" (1989: 11). It is a term that ignores the complexities within and throughout these various groups.

Dichotomies and Negative Constructions: "I Didn't Realize I Was a Minority until I Came to the United States"

As mentioned earlier, I always felt special and different among my fellow Peruvians. However, it was only when I came to this country that a label for being different was assigned to me: I became a minority! I must say that being labeled as such has not always been that bad; on occasion I have received some special treatment just because I fit the category of minority. However, the term minority has heavy connotations, especially when we realize that it signifies differences from those who make up the majority in this county. In other words, my status was assigned to me because I am not part of the majority, so therefore I should be part of the minority. The term minority, like other terms used to identify people's racial, ethnic, and cultural backgrounds, is defined in opposition to another term.

The same can be said about the term Hispanic. In contemporary discourse the term Hispanic has come to be used as a nonwhite racial designation. It is not unusual to read or hear people use the terms *whites, blacks,* and *Hispanics* as if they were mutually exclusive when, in fact, the 1990 census states that 52 percent of Hispanics identify themselves as white, 3 percent as black, and 43 percent as "other race."

The English language is constructed as a system of differences organized as extreme dichotomies—white/black, majority/minority, good/bad, dark/fair, and so on. The existence of this polarization influences how English speakers manage their relations with others. Consider the case of qualifiers or adjectives. The heavy emphasis on opposites often compels speakers of English to use one of two opposite adjectives when formulating questions. As a result, people in the United States commonly use evaluative terms in questions and descriptions, and find it easier to be critical rather than positive or neutral. For example, let's compare pairs of adjectives in English and in Spanish:

English		Spanish	
old	young	viejo	joven
long	short	largo	corto
far	near	cerca	lejos

At first, it may seem as if both the English and Spanish pairs contain words that are opposite in meaning but equal in their power to describe a point on a continuum. However, this is not the case. Consider how the English adjectives are used in asking questions: "How old is he?" "How long is that ruler?" and "How far do we have to go?" Questions are not phrased using the secondary term, as in "How young is he?" (unless in reference to a baby or small child), "How short is that ruler?" and "How near do we have to go?" In all of these questions one of the terms is designated as the defining term—for age, *old;* for size, *long;* and for distance, *far.*

To the Spanish speaker, these same dichotomies do not have the same dependent hierarchy; rather, these pairs enjoy symmetry. This weaker polarization of Spanish pairs is evident in the way questions are phrased. In Spanish, "How old is he?" becomes "*¿Qué edad tiene él?*" which can be literally translated as "What is his age?" The question "How long is that ruler?" becomes "*¿Cuánto mide esa regla?*"—that is, "What's the measurement of that ruler?"—and so on. In Spanish, the emphasis is placed on the middle ground of the continuum rather than on one of its ends.

Thus, one important aspect of opposing adjectives in English is that the primary term appears as the defining term or the norm of cultural meaning, while the secondary term is much more specific or derives its meaning from its relation to the first one. Examples of the "good–bad" dichotomy help to illustrate this point. If you ask a friend to help you with a new software program, you will probably say, "How good are you with MacMisha 5.1?" rather than "How bad are you with MacMisha 5.1?" That is, the use of the term *good* reflects a more general qualifier, while the use of the term *bad* already suggests that something is not good; thus this latter term is more specific (in a negative sense).

This same polarity can be applied to some of the qualifiers used in discussing issues of race and ethnicity. For example, in the case of pairs of labels, as in white/black, majority/minority, resident/nonresident, white/colored, and American/other, the defining term of the norm is given by the primary term; the secondary term represents what is different, alien, or abnormal.

The negative precision of English qualifiers yields a linguistic base for qualifying as negative whatever appears to be different. Thus, the labels and distinctions made among different ethnic and racial groups perpetuate a hierarchical system where some groups are the norm while the others, by default, do not fit the norm.

Ritual Interactions: "People Are Incredibly Friendly!"

My brother, who recently visited me from Peru, shared with me his thoughts about American friendliness after spending two days wandering around a large northwestern city. He was taken aback by the Pacific Northwest because he found people to be "incredibly friendly." He went on to say that during his three-week stay in this part of the country, a number of people on the street, on the road, and in the parks had smiled or said "hello" to him. He found it "kind of strange because you just don't see that in Lima, New York, Vienna, or Paris." I was a bit taken aback myself when I heard the story, thinking to myself, "Is the difference tangible?" After pondering a moment, I answered my own questions, "Absolutely!" There's a unique, friendly spirit you find throughout the Pacific Northwest. I think we sometimes lose sight of that fact. When you live something every day, there's a chance you'll start taking it for granted. My brother's comments were somewhat of a wake-up call for me and reminded me of my first months in the United States.

Although at that time I was in northern Florida, I can recall having similar feelings about this unusual kind of friendliness. I clearly remember feeling incredibly special when someone would welcome me to the town, ask me how I was feeling, and wish me a pleasant day. Furthermore, I still remember how shocked I was when an auto mechanic spent almost two hours trying to install a tiny plastic hook in the door of my 1966 VW bug and charged me only $1.50 for the part. And, in perhaps the most startling demonstration of American "friendliness," I vividly recall how, just two months after my arrival in this country, a smiling police officer said, 'Welcome to America" after she gave me two (undeserved, I must add) traffic tickets.

Instances like these remind me of an incident recounted by British-born journalist Henry Fairlie in an article entitled "Why I Love America":

> One spring day, shortly after my arrival, I was walking down the long,
> broad street of a suburb, with its sweeping front lawns (all that
> space), its tall trees (all that sky), and its clumps of azaleas (all that

color). The only other person on the street was a small boy on a tricycle. As I passed him, he said "Hi" just like that. No four-year-old boy had ever addressed me without an introduction before. Yet here was this one, with his cheerful "Hi!" Recovering from the culture shock, I tried to look down stonily at his flaxen head, but instead, involuntarily, I found myself saying in return: "Well—hi!" He pedaled off, apparently satisfied. He had begun my Americanization. (1983: 12)

For Fairlie the word "Hi!" had an important meaning:

(I come from a country where one can tell someone's class by how they say "Hallo!" or "Hello!" or "Hullo," or whether they say it at all.) But [in America] anyone can say "Hi!" Anyone does.

Like my brother and Henry Fairlie, I was also very impressed with the friendliness of people in this part of the globe, in particular the friendliness and concern of store clerks and waiters, who would often introduce themselves by their first names and treat me in a casual, friendly manner, even asking how I was feeling today. I was really taken by this caring manner. I remember thinking, How can you not feel special in this great nation if everyone is always trying to see if you are okay? In Lima, where everyone is in a hurry (and sometimes trying to take advantage of others), store clerks and waiters barely say "thank you," if they speak to you at all. And of course, as a customer, you would not spend time chatting or exchanging greetings with those who are in such unsuccessful positions.

One day, however, I was struck by a somewhat sad discovery: What I thought was true concern and friendliness was just a ritual interaction. On that day, I had just learned that Max, my roommate's Golden Retriever, was at a veterinary hospital; he had been run over by a car. On my way home, I stopped by the grocery store to get some milk. As on other days, a friendly clerk checked my groceries, and when she asked me, "How are you?" I responded, "A bit sad." To my surprise, the friendly clerk said, "Great! Have a nice day" After a few seconds of puzzlement, I grabbed my paper sack and left the store. Later, my roommate, a native Floridian, explained that this type of greeting was routine and that stores often require their employees to display "extreme friendliness" with customers. It was only after this explanation that I realized that the caring tone used by clerks and others working with the public was routine chat, part of a ritual exchange.

Ritual exchanges such as "How are you?" "I'm fine, thank you," "Nice meeting you," "Hope you have a nice day," and other similar phrases are, like any ritual exchange, more about form than substance. In other words, questions and answers are (or should be) the same, regardless of the participants in the interactions and their feelings. In the above incident, even though I responded candidly with an unscripted answer to the customary "How are you" questions, I got a conventional short and scripted answer.

The brevity and formulaic aspects of these ritual exchanges, I believe, have little to do with whether people are friendly or not. Rather, this behavior might be related to an informal, egalitarian approach to other characteristics of American culture. It might also have to do with the brevity, informality, and practicality that characterizes the American style of communication (which, by the way, reminds me of the typical monosyllabic answers that I receive from my students when I ask even complex questions: "Sure," "OK," or "Nope").

Ritual interactions, like many other aspects of language and communication, vary from culture to culture and from country to country. This becomes evident when contrasting the little and often impersonal ritual exchanges of Americans with the long and personal ritual interactions of Peruvians. In Peru, ritual exchanges like those mentioned above are not as common as in the United States. When they do occur, however, one generally asks about family members' health. On these occasions, one needs to be accurate in one's questioning and attentive in one's listening, not only in terms of asking about the appropriate family members (for instance, not asking a widow about her husband's health), but also in relation to the substance of the answer (for example, showing some empathy when someone mentions an illness in the family).

Final Thoughts

The study of communication and miscommunication across cultures is a relatively new area of research and one that holds much promise in terms of what it can teach us about language and intercultural communication. In this piece I have shared my experiences and reflections about the powerful role played by some terms and ethnic labels in the construction of people's social identity. In addition, I have also discussed some aspects of face-to-face interaction that vary from culture to culture and, as in the case of ritual interactions, provide fertile ground for miscommunication. My intent has been not only to illustrate how individual misunderstandings emerge but also to signal how these interactional processes reproduce and reinforce larger patterns within a society.

All in all, my years in the United States have for the most part unfolded like a dream. Sure, I encountered some problems, misunderstandings, and barriers, and often I had to adjust my expectations and appeal to my flexibility in order to keep going. But then, that is life. I am still learning about how to survive in this, my new home, and in the process I am trying to figure out why we use language the way we use it and why language can make things fuzzier and or less fuzzy.

Study Questions

1. Why are there problems with the designation "Hispanic"?
2. What is the original derivation of the word *Hispanic*, and why is the contemporary use of the word incorrect?
3. How do the English and Spanish languages differ in relation to the primacy of defining terms? Which language is more culturally accurate, positive in content, or sensitive?
4. What did Professor Ernst-Slavit eventually learn about the true cultural meaning of "extreme friendliness" in America?

Acknowledgments

I am grateful to Professors Cynthia Wallat at Florida State and Ginger Weade and Allan Burns at the University of Florida, who introduced me to the study of sociolinguistics. Appreciation is also due to Kerni Richard, David Slavit, and Elsa Statzner for feedback on drafts of this essay.

Note

[1] Ethnic labels, like all names, are constructs, abstractions of a reality. In this respect, social scientist Suzanne Oboler (1995) argues that perhaps the inevitable use of ethnic labels includes singling out particular socially constructed attributes, whether related to race, gender, class, or language. The attributes are assigned to be common to the group's members and used to homogenize the group—regardless of whether this designation corresponds to the reality of the group to whom the label is attached.

References

Fairlie, H. 1983, July 4. Why I Love America. *The New Republic*, p. 12.

Lakoff, G. 1972. Hedges: A Study in Meaning Criteria and the Logic of Fuzzy Concepts. *Chicago* Linguistic *Society Papers*. Chicago: Chicago Linguistic Society.

Muñoz, C. 1989. *Youth, Identity, Power*. London: Verso.

Oboler, S. 1995. Ethnic *Labels, Latino Lives: Identity and the Politics of (Re)presentation in the United States*. Minneapolis: University of Minnesota Press.

21

The Obligation to Give, Receive, and Make a Return
Comparing the Meanings of Reciprocity in America and Japan

YOHKO TSUJI
CORNELL UNIVERSITY

Reciprocity is a universal rule of human life. People everywhere are bound by the obligation to give, receive, and make a return. However, cultural differences exist in what motivates people to enter reciprocal relationships and why making a return is essential. This article compares ethnographic cases in two cultures—mutual support among older Americans and Japanese exchange of funerary gifts—to highlight the significance of independence, individualism, and egalitarianism in American culture.

Yohko Tsuji is Adjunct Associate Professor of Anthropology at Cornell University. Raised in Japan, she came to the United States as a student in the mid-1970s. She received her PhD from Cornell University in 1991 after conducting dissertation research at a senior center in a small city in upstate New York.

Introduction

When I moved to America nearly four decades ago, differences in supposedly universal motherhood gave me a culture shock. One American mother said she found her infant son's total dependency on her disconcerting. Another mother of a preschool girl claimed she did not want to be responsible for her child 24 hours a day seven days a week and regularly hired a babysitter. These mothers' seemingly self-centered words puzzled me, partly because their maternal love was apparent in their interactions with their children, and partly because their idea of mothering was notably different from that of Japanese women. In Japan, where young children's dependency on mothers was taken for granted, mothers were expected to devote themselves to their children and give them total care. In other words, mother and child constituted one inseparable unit, and motherhood was regarded not only highly but also as a core attribute of Japanese women's identity. Not surprisingly, hiring a babysitter was not culturally approved (Fujita 1989).

I chose to study anthropology as a result of repeated exposures to this kind of cultural difference between America and Japan. I was eager to know what caused the cultural differences and why certain social phenomena in America that made sense to Americans bewildered me. To put it another way, a major goal of my anthropological journey was to open my eyes to other ways of looking at the world. I expected to learn, for example, why a baby's total dependency frustrated an American mother and why hiring a babysitter was so widespread in America.

The topic of this article is not motherhood, however. It is reciprocity, another social phenomenon that is as pan-human as motherhood (Mauss 1967). I discuss two ethnographic cases: mutual support among older Americans and exchange of *kôden*, or the funerary cash gifts among Japanese. In both cases, making a return has utmost significance. Therefore, to conform to the rule of reciprocity, both older Americans and Japanese mourners behave in a way that may perplex outsiders. Japanese may wonder why feeble elderly Americans refuse to accept assistance, which Japanese think is an entitlement of old age. Similarly, Americans may question why Japanese spend a large amount of money when they attend a funeral, often that of someone they have never met.

To acquire an insider's logic in these cases, I examine them in relation to the dominant cultural values in each society, in particular, independence in America and interdependence in Japan. I explore two primary questions: What are the similarities and differences in the meaning of reciprocity in these cases? What roles do dominant cultural values play in shaping individual actions in them? The data for this article come from my two longitudinal research projects: on older Americans at a senior center in upstate New York since 1987 and on mortuary rituals in the Osaka-Kyoto region of Japan since 1992.

Two Ethnographic Cases

Mutual Support among Older Americans

Like motherhood, aging is a universal phenomenon. Therefore, when I moved to America, I was not prepared for the disappearance of older people from my daily life and Americans' strongly negative attitude toward old age. While I was in Japan, older people were an integral part of my life. Like many Japanese of my generation, I grew up in a three-generation household. Although my grandfather died long before I was born, my grandmother played an important role in raising my sister and me. My neighborhood was full of old folks who were the grandparents of my playmates. Children were taught to be kind and respectful to them. Imagine my shock when I heard my roommates' comments on my octogenarian friend from Indiana after he had visited me in San Diego: "I would rather die before I become like him."; "He has outlived his usefulness. He would be happier dead." How could they say such cruel things about a sweet old man? Didn't they know they, too, would be old someday? Didn't they think it wonderful that this octogenarian was healthy enough to spend several days on the bus to cross half a continent? My shock and puzzlement was one of the reasons why I chose to conduct my dissertation research on older Americans.

I vividly remember my first visit to a senior center in 1987. It gave me a feeling that I had entered a different world. It was a shock to see such concentration of old folks after they had ceased to be a part of my life for more than a decade. The flood of gray hair, which was in striking contrast to their brightly colored clothing, only accentuated this feeling. Moreover, many of them had disabilities. Some used a cane to walk, and others limped. Those who showed no obvious signs of impairment moved slowly.

The scene was an antithesis of the American ideal of youth, strength, and physical beauty. This disparity between the ideal and the real, I learned, was the major cause of strongly negative views of old age in America. I thought the senior center offered a strategic setting where I could not only learn about actual experiences of older Americans vis-à-vis negative stereotypes but also explore how they negotiated the gap between the cultural ideals (e.g., independence and productivity) and the realities of old age (e.g., infirmity and retirement).

Initially, I was surprised that despite their diminishing abilities people at the senior center frequently and adamantly declined offers of help. Even though I had learned by then how important being independent was for Americans, I found it disturbing to see feeble older people slowly walking to the kitchen and pouring coffee with shaking hands. Eventually, my research disclosed elderly Americans' ingenuity to receive help without violating the cultural taboo of dependency. Reciprocity played an important role in preventing them from becoming supplicants. But how did they manage to reciprocate with their shrinking resources and functional abilities? I will address this question in the section, "Meanings of Reciprocity in Two Ethnographic Cases."

Exchange of Kôden or Funerary Cash Gifts in Japan

Death in Japan is expensive. Japanese funerals are costly not only for the bereaved family[1] but also for mourners who are required to bring a cash gift called *kôden*. The expense of *kôden* is inescapable for the Japanese because attending funerals is a major social duty that binds relatives, neighbors, colleagues, and business associates, as well as those who have social ties to the deceased or his or her family.

The *kôden* custom involves numerous cumbersome rules, such as how to present money, what kind of envelope to put money in, and what kind of bills to use. It is not easy to determine the appropriate amount to give, either, because it depends on the relationship between the giver and the receiver. For example, when people of different status are involved, the amount of *kôden* must reflect the hierarchical relationship among them. Thus, when a death occurs in a coworker's family, his or her superior is expected to give a larger amount of *kôden* than those who are equal or subordinate in status. When someone in the superior's family subsequently dies, the subordinate should reciprocate with a smaller amount of *kôden* than his family received from the superior. Among many rules, the most important is reciprocity. To ensure unfailing repayment, the *kôden* records are carefully kept in a register, which the funeral service company brings with other paraphernalia of the funeral. It is not unusual that *kôden* received by one generation is reciprocated by another.

The custom thus serves as a kind of social insurance, but its premium is high. The *kôden* records from the 1992 funeral for Mr. Yamada, the head of a middle-class family, show that 457 mourners gave a total of over $35,000.[2]

While the average amount of *kôden* per donor was $107, six gave as much as $1,000, five $500, and thirteen $300 (Tsuji 2006: 396–397).

Although one of the functions of *kôden* is to help defray the cost of a funeral, its monetary value is drastically reduced by *kôden gaeshi*, or the return gift. Before the 49th-day memorial service,[3] the bereaved family must send all the *kôden* donors a gift with a value of half the amount of their respective *kôden*. To follow this custom, the Yamadas spent at least $17,500. Because the funeral ceremony itself cost well over $20,000, the *kôden* they received did not cover all the expenses of the funeral. Furthermore, the bereaved family had the tedious and time-consuming task of dividing 457 donors according to the size of their contributions, making separate lists of their names and addresses, and selecting appropriate gifts for each group of donors.

It is not surprising that Japanese often complain about the cost and inconvenience of these mortuary customs. Nevertheless, they dutifully attend funerals. Why do they continue this practice? This question will be considered in the following section.

Meanings of Reciprocity in Two Ethnographic Cases

Mutual Support among Older Americans

"Senior citizens help themselves to help each other," a popular slogan at the senior center in the 1960s, aptly indicates how crucial mutual support is for older Americans to maintain an independent life in the face of declining self-sufficiency. Although mutual support is an integral part of human life everywhere, how support relationships are established and how they are maintained vary cross-culturally. In many societies, participation in these relationships is mandatory because their formation is based on membership in kin, communal, and occupational groups. In addition, well-established protocols govern people's actions. *Kôden* exchange in Japan fits this pattern, as discussed in the next section.

In striking contrast, the senior center participants form their support relationships out of volition and individual choice. This leads to the diversities in these relationships. Some support partners see each other almost every day while others communicate primarily on the phone and seldom see each other.[4] Older Americans also find their partners in various categories of people, such as former colleagues, neighbors, or those who share interests (e.g., hobbies) or experiences (e.g., preretirement occupation or grandparenthood). Furthermore, older Americans have the freedom to continue, modify, or cease their support relationships. This is a choice Japanese do not have with regard to their funeral attendance.

Despite such notable differences, older Americans follow one paramount rule just like Japanese funeral attendees do: a rule of reciprocity. When they receive something from their friends, they need to reciprocate. How do they comply with this rule with their shrinking resources and abilities?

They adopt several strategies. Complementing each other's missing resources is one of them as the case of two octogenarians, Diane and Helen, illustrates. Both are retired teachers and go to the senior center regularly. They live on the same block and belong to the same church. Neither has been married nor has close relatives living nearby. So, they spend a lot of time together and regard their partnership indispensable. Among other things, they frequently share a ride because Helen does not drive while Diane still does.[5] But this is not one-way but mutual dependency. Although Helen depends on Diane for a ride, Diane, hard of hearing and lame, relies on Helen's good ears and legs. While Diane drives, Helen draws her attention to the significant sounds that sometimes occur when driving, such as the siren from a fire engine or the car's turn signal that did not stop automatically. After they reach their destination, Helen does errands for Diane while Diane waits in the parked car. Helen also navigates for Diane when they go to an unfamiliar place.

Minimizing the cost of reciprocity is another strategy. Some of the exchange "currencies" at the senior center entail no monetary cost and enable those with meager resources to reciprocate and maintain a balanced exchange with their peers. Most highly appreciated and most frequently reciprocated among them are gestures of affection (hugging and patting on the shoulder), kind words, and compliments, as well as useful information, such as about a new type of hearing aid and how to deal with Medicare statements. What people wear, for example, triggers the following comments: "I like the color of your sweater. It brightens a dreary day like today."; "What a beautiful brooch you wear!" They are also generous in praising and encouraging their peers' class performance: "I like the way you draw this blue flower."; "How quickly you learn to knit! You started just last week and finished this much." As this kind of exchange requires no monetary or material resources, it allows everyone's participation. It also brings emotional satisfaction by making both the giver and the receiver feel good.

In addition, group-based exchange reduces the cost of reciprocity. It is common at the senior center to send greeting cards collectively. When someone becomes ill or has lost a loved one, center participants circulate a get-well or sympathy card for signatures and notes and send it to their peer. When the occasion arises, people are reciprocated by a card from a group of friends rather than by multiple cards. Savings from this practice add up considerably because illness and death are frequent enough in old age to make one center participant exclaim, "Gee, we sign a card every week!" A dish-to-pass meal also has the advantage of group-based exchange. It is a less expensive alternative to hosting a dinner party or inviting friends to a restaurant. It also releases people from "the obligation to make a return" (Mauss 1967: 37) because giving and receiving take place simultaneously. It is no wonder that a dish-to-pass meal is popular at the senior center.[6]

These strategies—complementing missing resources and cutting costs—make reciprocity affordable for those with limited resources. In addition to reciprocating, their support relationships are characterized by their endeavor to minimize dependency and increase self-help. This explains why feeble older Americans decline the offer of help and try to do things on their own despite some difficulty and the need for more time to finish the task. Furthermore, to avoid total dependency on any one source of assistance, older Americans participate in multiple support networks, including those with kin, friends, and facilities and services for older people. Again, Diane and Helen's case illustrates the point.

Although Diane and Helen depend on each other and maintain a close relationship, both have other networks of supporters. Diane says that there are three friends she could not do without. One is Helen, of course. The second is Louise with whom she spends holidays and exchanges books to read. The third, Marcia, is the daughter of Diane's deceased cousin. She is one of the few people Diane, the last survivor of her generation of relatives, can share family memories with. Marcia and her husband also help Diane with some paperwork and heavy domestic chores, such as moving furniture. Helen has friends of similar importance including those she spends holidays with. She also has networks of friends with whom she exchanges hospitality. When Helen hosts a dinner party at her home, Diane drives Helen for grocery shopping. But Diane is invited only on those occasions when she and other guests belong to the same social circle.

Diane and Helen also try to increase self-help and decrease dependency on each other. Thus, Diane is not the only provider of Helen's rides. Helen sometimes uses the bus or the local transportation service for the elderly. Similarly, Diane occasionally does errands by herself, walking slowly with a cane. She also hires some helpers to manage her life alone in a big, old house.

Three major efforts older Americans make in their support relationships—to reciprocate, to decrease dependency, and to increase self-help—indicate their wish to avoid "unreciprocated dependence on others [that] bring[s] debasement of status in American culture" (Murphy 1987: 201). In other words, getting help is not demeaning as long as it is reciprocated. By reciprocating the help they receive and by being an equal partner in support exchange, older Americans conciliate their dependency on others and the cultural ideal of independence. By contrast, not reciprocating puts them in a position to comply with their help provider's wishes. Since such compliance is costly to self-esteem and thereby is not acceptable as social currency for exchange, the inability to reciprocate often compels older Americans to withdraw from social relationships (Dowd 1975; Matthews 1979). In short, older Americans' conformity to the rule of reciprocity strongly reflects their quest for *independence*. As we will see in the next section, this is strikingly different from Japanese *kôden* exchange in which reciprocity, prompted by *giri* or obligation, serves as a culturally established means of bringing people into *interdependent* relationships.

Exchange of Kôden or Funerary Cash Gifts in Japan

Japanese frequently explain their conformity to funerary tradition in terms of external pressure. They say *giri* or obligation leaves them no other choice but to attend the funeral and give *kôden*. As noted earlier, this *giri* derives from belonging to social groups, most importantly, kin, neighborhood, and workplace, and binds people in a web of reciprocal obligations with its iron rule of reciprocity. In other words, Japanese entry into *kôden* exchange is involuntary.[7]

Powerful though *giri* may be, external pressure alone is not sufficient to account for human behavior. What other factors motivate Japanese to attend the funeral and fulfill *giri*? There are some pragmatic gains in honoring mortuary tradition. The most obvious is its function as social insurance. Giving *kôden* promises repayment when a death occurs in one's own family and helps defray the cost of the funeral even if the amount collected may not cover the entire expense.

Following tradition also provides "a [culturally] strategic way of acting" (Bell 1992: 8). The case of the Yamadas' contractor demonstrates how tradition legitimizes an individual's actions that are advantageous for him. When the contractor's family moved to the Yamadas' neighborhood in the 1970s, he took advantage of the customary gift-giving to establish his business at a new location. First, he sent biannual seasonal gifts to his customers, which, strictly business-based, required no reciprocity. With the passage of time, his gift-giving expanded to include ceremonial gifts, such as *kôden* and wedding gifts. Since tradition demands such gifts be reciprocated, his customers gave *kôden* when his mother died and a wedding gift when his son married.[8] Thus, *giri* and the ensuing cycle of reciprocity came to bind the customers to the contractor. Such enduring relationships benefit his business because most of his customers would find it embarrassing to hire another contractor.

In addition to external pressure and pragmatic gains, the Japanese sense of self also plays an important role in compelling people to attend a funeral, though, unlike the first two, they may not consciously recognize this third instigator of their action. One major characteristic of the Japanese conception of self is being other-oriented rather than ego-centered. Dorinne Kondo argues, "Persons seemed to be constituted in and through social relations and obligations to others" (1990: 22). Likewise, Margaret Lock maintains, "In Japan, individuals . . . are conceptualized as residing at the center of a network of obligations, so that personhood is constructed . . . in the space of ongoing human relationships" (1995: 22). In other words, social embeddedness— one's affiliation with groups and one's positions and roles within them—is the most essential building block of Japanese identity rather than each individual's attributes.[9] Therefore, being unaffiliated and being isolated indicate social anonymity and personal failure (Lebra 1992: 110). Attending a funeral provides a powerful cultural mechanism to secure and confirm this sociocentric identity, because it anchors oneself in "a network of obligations" and "ongoing human relationships" (Lock 1995: 22) and, as the contractor's case demonstrates, creates them.

The importance of group membership for Japanese identity is manifested in that *giri* often falls on a group rather than on an individual. In cases of *kôden* exchange among relatives and neighbors, it is the family who has *giri* to repay *kôden*. This rule creates an apparent anomaly in which some of next of kin are not obligated to give *kôden*.

For example, at Mr. Yamada's funeral, of the two children of his elder brother, the daughter gave *kôden*, but the son did not. The custom did not require Mr. Yamada's nephew to give because he and his family lived with his parents. With the family as a unit of obligation, it was his father, the head of the family, who had *giri* to attend his brother's funeral and give *kôden*. However, unlike her brother, Mr. Yamada's niece was required to give *kôden* because her marriage created the *giri* relationship between her uncle's family and her husband's family. The family-based *kôden* exchange is also apparent in that her *kôden* was given in the name of her husband, the family head, even though she was the close relative of the deceased. The difference in the amount of *kôden* these two families gave ($1,000 from Mr. Yamada's older brother and $100 from the husband of his niece) also indicates the status differences between them. Based on age, gender, and descent line,[10] the family of Mr. Yamada's older brother had a higher status and the heavier obligation than the family of his niece within the kin networks of the Yamadas. Odd though these customary rules may seem, they identify the individual's position in the hierarchy of his or her kin group (Tsuji 2006).

Kôden among work-related people is not family-based but individually given because their *giri* to attend the funeral derives from the individual's occupational relationships.[11] Yet, the family still plays a significant role in generating *giri* because the death of the family member of a coworker or a business associate requires Japanese workers to attend his or her funeral. This is why Japanese attend funerals of those they have never met, such as the boss' mother and the spouse of a business associate. One funeral specialist says normally only 30 percent of mourners at a Japanese funeral personally know the deceased (Himonya 2003).

To understand the sociocentric Japanese sense of self, it is also essential to note that conformity has positive meanings in Japan. Japanese say they attend the funeral out of *giri* instead of individual choice. Such an act of compliance is regarded as a sign of maturity rather than weakness of succumbing to pressure. Underlying this view are two Japanese understandings. First, Japanese are keenly aware of the heavy burden of social demands imposed upon them and often experience them in conflict with their personal wishes. They conceptualize *giri,* a powerful normative force for compliance, in juxtaposition with *ninjô* or human feelings. They know that people fulfill *giri* at the cost of sacrificing personal feelings and desires (Befu 1971).

Second, the positive meanings of conformity are closely tied to the belief that each individual is incomplete by him- or herself, and thereby interdependence is imperative (Edwards 1989). To promote interdependent relationships, Japanese culture encourages sensitivity to others' needs, as well as accommodation to social and cultural demands. Consequently, Japanese equate the assertion of individual desire with selfishness or arrogance and conformity with "a virtue" (Smith 1983: 98). In short, fulfilling *giri* is vital for "a social and moral being" in Japan (Befu 1971: 169). Being called *giri gatai hito* or a person who dutifully fulfills *giri* enhances one's reputation and self-esteem. By contrast, the label of *fugiri na hito* or a person who neglects to fulfill *giri*, marks social disapproval and personal failure. The Japanese funeral publicly displays whether one lives up to the cultural ideal of *giri gatai hito* through his or her presence at it.[12]

In summary, the most significant meaning of reciprocity in *kôden* exchange in Japan is to incorporate people in sustaining interdependent relationships. *Giri*, a Japanese normative concept, not only serves as a strong motivational force—both external and internal—for reciprocity, but it also locks people into a cycle of obligations.

New Challenge: Discoveries of Follow-Up Research

My longitudinal research on both older Americans and Japanese funerals enabled me to witness changes over time. The following examples will illustrate how older Americans and Japanese mourners continue to fulfill their "obligation to make a return" (Mauss 1967: 37) under the circumstances in which reciprocating has become more challenging.

Older Americans: Disability and Equal Exchange Partnership

Since my initial fieldwork in 1987, I have observed many changes in older Americans' lives on both personal and societal levels. For one thing, many of my informants became frail or ill and eventually died. A good number of them moved to a nursing home, where they received assistance for their basic needs, such as eating, getting dressed, bathing, and toileting. Because the care they received was paid for, they were, in principle, engaged in balanced exchange with their caregivers. However, when one depends on others for his or her very existence, the possibility of becoming a supplicant is high. The case of Diane illustrates how she managed to make a return under these circumstances.

Diane acquired respect, admiration, and affection from the nursing home staff despite her total dependence on them. One important factor behind this is her ability to maintain balanced exchange with her caregivers. Although "just about anything under the sun . . . can all serve as resources for exchange" (Befu 1977: 270), these resources must have some value for exchange partners. Did Diane have such resources to reciprocate for the care she received in addition to the fee she paid?

Expressing gratitude is one of them. Kathy, a nursing home nurse, remarked that Diane always said "Thank you," even for a little routine task she performed for her (e.g., giving pills, bringing water). She very much appreciated Diane's courtesy because some residents took her and other staff for granted and those with dementia did not respond or their responses created troubles. Moreover, there were days when grumpy residents yelled at her and demanded she attend to their needs right away because they paid her salary.

A positive attitude toward life also generates respect and admiration. Diane's disability did not deter her from living her life. When she moved to a nursing home in 1996, she said, "Most people came here to die, but I came here to live." True to her words, she attended many activities in the home though she was wheelchair bound and almost blind and deaf. As one of the senior center staff said, Diane had no self-pity in a situation that may have made other people feel sorry for themselves.

Her advanced age (she died at age 101) also contributed to the staff's admiration of her. At age-homogeneous communities (e.g., senior centers and nursing homes), advanced age loses its negative connotations (Ward 1984), and those who have lived an unusually long life are viewed as an asset. Diane became such an asset for the nursing home community due not only to her age but also to her other remarkable qualities.

Diane also had regular visitors, "highly visible resources" (Gubrium 1975: 98) that may affect the staff's treatment of the residents. Among her regular visitors was Marcia, the daughter of her late cousin who visited her once a week, often more.

Diane's case shows that older people with physical infirmity are still able to engage in balanced exchange with their caregivers. Her case also indicates that disability in old age is not necessarily a synonym for unsuccessful aging.[13]

Japanese Funerals: Changes in Kôden Practices

In 2013, I studied the funeral of Mrs. Yamada, the widow of Mr. Yamada whose funeral in 1992 was mentioned earlier. One of the notable changes at her funeral concerns kôden practices. The family received kôden only from relatives and declined it from other mourners, even though kôden donors at her husband's funeral included not only relatives but also neighbors, work-related people, and those who had some relationships with the family.[14]

In recent years, declining kôden has become more common. Why did Japanese give up the opportunity to receive money that would help them pay for the funeral? Does this new trend indicate the diminishing value of interdependence and obligation in contemporary Japan?

Answering these questions is complex because myriad factors are involved. However, one important catalyst of this change in mortuary tradition is an adaptation to rapid social change. Limiting the size of the *giri* circle (i.e., networks of people who are tied with obligation) is practical or even necessary in today's highly industrialized Japan, where mobility is high and people have more expanded social networks than in the past when they mainly consisted of kin and neighbors.[15]

Imagine, for instance, how tedious and time-consuming it would be to prepare the return gift for a large number of mourners. For Mr. Yamada's funeral in 1992, the family sent return gifts to 457 mourners, choosing a variety of items that were worth one half of the amount of *kôden* received. Limiting *kôden* donors to relatives for Mrs. Yamada's funeral in 2013 is a compromise, which enabled the family to maintain the *giri* circle for mutual assistance—albeit smaller in size—and to continue funerary tradition in a modified form. It is also important to remember that even though they did not give *kôden*, neighbors and work-related people attended Mrs. Yamada's funeral just as they did her husband's funeral in 1992. Relieving all the mourners except for relatives from the obligatory *kôden* exchange contributes to the continuation of the funerary tradition because it helps to reduce the cost of attending the funeral, one of the important social duties for the Japanese.

Conclusion

In this article, I have examined two kinds of exchange: peer support among older Americans and exchange of *kôden* or funerary gifts among Japanese. These two cases show some notable differences. For example, older Americans voluntarily enter support relationships with their peers whereas Japanese participation in *kôden* exchange is mandatory. The relationship of exchange partners is egalitarian, at least ideally, among older Americans but normally hierarchical in Japan. The unit of exchange also differs. Although a group, such as the family, neighborhood, and workplace, is the basis of *kôden* exchange in Japan, mutual support among older Americans is always between individuals. The duration of such individual-based relationships tends to be shorter than that of *giri*-bound, group-based relationships in *kôden* exchange, which may extend over generations.[16]

Different though these two cases may be, reciprocity is tremendously important in both of them. Americans and Japanese alike reciprocate at the cost of personal inconvenience or sacrifice, not only because the rule requires they do so, but also because honoring this rule is the mainstay of their personhood. However, what is required to be a socially and personally worthy person and how reciprocity helps to create such a person differ in these two cultures. For older Americans, reciprocity enables them not only to maintain an equal partnership with their peers but also to receive necessary assistance for prolonging independence without violating the cultural taboo of dependency. On the other hand, by reciprocating, Japanese become a highly regarded *giri gatai hito,* or a person who dutifully fulfills *giri,* and secure a position in the interdependent and hierarchical relationships that are bound by mutual obligations. Thus, reciprocity helps both Americans and Japanese to conform to cultural ideals.

Nonetheless, what reciprocity "express[es] or embod[ies] or exemplif[ies]" (D'Andrade 2008: 24) differs. It is independence, individualism, and egalitarianism in older Americans' support relationships. It is interdependence, group-orientedness, and hierarchy in Japanese *kôden* exchange. In short, the same act of making a return has distinctively different cultural meanings.

Using Japanese culture as a distant mirror that reflects American culture, I have come to understand how vital independence, individualism, and egalitarianism are for Americans. Furthermore, knowing the differences in cultural values between America and Japan helped me unravel my original puzzlement over American motherhood. A strong emphasis on independence explained why the aforementioned American mother felt frustrated by her infant son's total dependence on her. The cherished American value of individualism also opened my eyes to see the mother and the child, not as an inseparable unit but as a pair of individuals, and helped me to understand why hiring a babysitter, a practice that is uncommon and frowned upon in Japan, is well accepted in America.

Study Questions

1. As their resources diminish, how do older Americans manage to reciprocate the assistance they received?

2. Attending a Japanese funeral requires a cash gift called *kôden.* It also involves the time to travel to the funeral site and adjust one's schedule. Many Japanese complain about the cost and the inconvenience of this custom. Why do they not stop it?

3. What is the most important rule that governs both older Americans' support relationships and Japanese exchange of *kôden*? What is the dominant cultural value in each case that makes people conform to this rule?

4. What are the most important American values mentioned in this article? How do they guide or constrain Americans' behavior and thought? Consider the same questions for the Japanese case as well.

5. What are the similarities and the differences between reciprocity in the two ethnographic cases you read in this article?

6. Cross-cultural comparisons allow us to see what we take for granted about our own culture. What did you learn about American culture by looking at its reflection in the "distant mirror" of Japanese culture?

References

Asahi Shimbun (Asahi newspaper). 1997. Sôshiki ni Mizukara no Jinsei Utsusô (Let's have our lives reflected in our funerals). *Asahi Shimbun*, January 21.

Befu, Harumi. 1971. *Japan: Anthropological Introduction*. San Francisco: Chandler.

———. 1977. Social Exchange. *Annual Review of Anthropology* 6: 255–281.

Bell, Catherine. 1992. *Ritual Theory, Ritual Practice*. New York: Oxford University Press.

D'Andrade, Roy. 2008. *A Study of Personal and Cultural Values: American, Japanese, and Vietnamese*. New York: Palgrave Macmillan.

Dowd, James P. 1975. Aging as Exchange: A Preface to Theory. *Journal of Gerontology* 30(5): 584–594.

Edwards, Walter. 1989. *Modern Japan through Its Weddings: Gender, Person, and Society in Ritual Portrayal*. Stanford: Stanford University Press.

Himonya, Hajime. 2003. *Shinikata o Wasureta Nihonjin* (The Japanese have forgotten how to die). Tokyo: Daitô Shuppansha.

Fujita, Mariko. 1989. "It's All Mother's Fault": Childcare and the Socialization of Working Mothers in Japan. *Journal of Japanese Studies* 15(1): 67–91.

Gubrium, Jaber F. 1975. *Time, Roles and Self in Old Age*. New York: Human Sciences Press.

Kondo, Dorinne. 1990. *Crafting Selves: Power, Gender, and Discourses of Identity in a Japanese Workplace*. Chicago: University of Chicago Press.

Lamb, Sarah. 2014. Permanent Personhood or Meaningful Decline?: Toward a Critical Anthropology of Successful Aging. *Journal of Aging Studies* 29:1–52.

Lebra, Takie Sugiyama. 1992. Self in Japanese Culture. In Nancy Rosenberger (ed.), *Japanese Sense of Self* (pp.105–120). Cambridge: Cambridge University Press.

Lock, Margaret. 1995. Contesting the Natural in Japan: Moral Dilemmas and Technologies of Dying. *Culture, Medicine and Psychiatry* 19: 1–38.

Matthews. Sarah H. 1979. *The Social World of Old Women: Management of Self-Identity*. Thousand Oaks, CA: Sage.

Mauss, Marcel. 1967. *The Gift: Forms and Functions of Exchange in Archaic Societies*. Trans. Ian Cunnison. New York: W.W. Norton.

Murphy, Robert F. 1987. *The Body Silent*. New York: Henry Holt.

Smith, Robert J. 1983. *Japanese Society: Tradition, Self and the Social Order*. Cambridge: Cambridge University Press.

Tsuji, Yohko. 2006. Mortuary Rituals in Japan: The Hegemony of Tradition and the Motivations of Individuals. *Ethos* 34(3): 391–431.

Ward, Russel A. 1984. The Marginality and Salience of Being Old: When is Age Relevant? *Gerontologist* 24(3): 227–232.

Notes

[1] The average cost of the Japanese funeral is $30,000 in comparison with $4,500 in America (Asahi Shimbun 1997).

[2] All the dollar values in this article are based on the exchange rate of one dollar for 100 yen.

[3] After the funeral, memorial rituals continue every seven days until the 49th day and again on the 100th day. They are followed by the 1st year death anniversary, 3rd, 7th, 13th, 17th, 23rd, 27th, 33rd, and 50th. Some changes have occurred, however. For instance, it is now a common practice in urban areas to combine the funeral and the first 7th-day memorial service.

[4] Some older Americans in support relationships call each other every day, often at a previously agreed-upon time. Such daily calls offer an opportunity not only to chat, but also to check if their partner is doing all right. See note #5.

[5] They also call every day at the designated time to check on each other. Each has a key to the other's house. When Diane fell in the bathtub and was unable to move, she said she was not panicked because she knew Helen would eventually come and call for help. Help did come as Diane had anticipated.

[6] Bringing a bag lunch to eat together is also common among the senior center participants.

[7] Japanese may give *kôden* voluntarily. However, such cases are in small minority. In addition, *kôden* voluntarily given still obligates the receiver to make a return, creating a new *giri* cycle.

[8] Although the contractor was obliged to give *kôden* as the Yamadas' neighbor, the amount of his *kôden*, $300, was ten to fifteen times as much as that of other newcomers to the community and as large as that given by 30 percent of relatives. This indicates that the "business" binding him to the Yamadas was much heavier than the *giri* neighbors ordinarily owed to each other.

[9] Hence, to the question "what is your occupation?" Japanese tend to answer by the company they work for (e.g., "I work for Toyota") instead of the kind of work they do (e.g., "I am an engineer").

[10] Relatives are divided into two categories: *chokkei* and *bôkei*. *Chokkei* means the direct line of descent and refers to those who stay and assume designated posts in the family, such as the family head and heir. *Bôkei* means the collateral line of descent and includes married-out members of the family and their descendants. *Chokkei* outrank *bôkei* relatives.

[11] Some work-related mourners, normally junior members of the workplace, collectively give *kôden* to minimize the cost. However, their *kôden* envelopes list all the names of individual donors.

[12] The same is applicable when Japanese have a funeral of their family member. A large crowd of mourners and a substantial amount of *kôden* exhibit they have dutifully fulfilled *giri* and are firmly embedded in expansive social networks. In contrast, too small a number of mourners and too small a sum of *kôden* indicate their social marginality and poor past performance in *giri* obligations.

[13] During the three decades of my research, Americans' negative attitudes toward old age have not changed, nor has their denial or reluctance of accepting the facts of aging and death (Lamb 2014). However, with the rapid aging of society, the number of programs and facilities for senior citizens (e.g., discounts, housing, and transportation service) has dramatically increased. Older Americans' initial avoidance or rejection of them has been replaced by their acceptance over time.

[14] Among them were the deceased's World War II army buddies, the people who took the flower-arrangement lessons with his daughter, the family doctor, the contractor, and Mrs. Yamada's beautician.

[15] Today, work-related people may include foreigners who receive or give *kôden*. This may create an anomaly because if their stay in Japan is temporary, it is most likely that they will not have an opportunity to reciprocate or to be reciprocated. An English professor who taught at a Japanese university for one year found a good solution. When his father died in England, he received *kôden* from his Japanese colleagues. He donated the same amount of cash he received as *kôden* to a Japanese charity.

[16] Some of the support relationships among senior center participants consist of more than two people. There are also some long-lasting relationships among older Americans. One of them extends over three decades. Yet, all of them are based on participating individuals' choice and decisions.